CANADIAN ART

STORMY WEATHER: GEORGIAN BAY

F. HORSMAN VARLEY

CANADIAN ART *its origin & development*

BY WILLIAM COLGATE

with a foreword by C. W. Jefferys, R.C.A., LL.D.

McGRAW-HILL RYERSON LIMITED

TORONTO · MONTREAL · NEW YORK · LONDON · SYDNEY
JOHANNESBURG · MEXICO · PANAMA · DÜSSELDORF · SINGAPORE
SAO PAULO · KUALA LUMPUR · NEW DELHI

First Edition, November 5, 1943.
Designed by Thoreau MacDonald.

First Paperback Edition, 1967

3 4 5 6 7　MP-74 9 8 7 6 5 4

PRINTED AND BOUND IN CANADA

IN MEMORIAM

W.F.C., 1859-1939
M.R.L.C., 1919-1942

FOREWORD

A KNOWLEDGE of the environment and background, a persistent recognition of the chronological sequence, and an objective attitude are essential to any permanent and penetrating estimate of human activities. Much of what passes for art history, here and elsewhere, is lacking in these qualifications, and attains only the ephemeral status of "current criticism." I know of no work dealing with Canadian art which so nearly approaches the requirements of an authoritative record as this book. The late Albert H. Robson's *Landscape Painting in Canada,* is the only one which, to my mind, shows much of the same character of historic detachment, and its field is necessarily more limited. It is a hopeful sign that Canadian art is now receiving the scholarly and critical examination which it has so long and so sorely needed.

The time is ripe for a book of this kind. It serves no propaganda, it supports no theory, it is not morbidly anxious to be "in the movement." Its purpose is expressed by its title, Canadian Art: Its Origin and Development, and it seems to me to adequately fulfil its intention.

The book contains much matter that hitherto could be found only in scattered papers, or reports, or archival records, especially with regard to the early artists and topographical draughtsmen. This material has been collected and made accessible for the general reader and at the same time has been fitted into the general history of Canadian Art in a better way than has hitherto been done. In Canada, as elsewhere, the earlier pictorial productions were informative "views" of localities, "scenes" of aboriginal or pioneer life, etc.; the work of topographical recorders reproduced by engraving or lithography. Such works generally are now regarded more as historical documents than as works of art, and their importance in the development of native Canadian painting has been unperceived or under-estimated. Original paintings, either by old masters or by contemporary artists, were very few in Canada. Engravings of such works, however, were available, and doubtless it was from these and from the early topographical pictures that our native artists and our public alike, especially during the nineteenth century, derived their ideals. The author has given considerable attention to them, and has shown how these literal representations gradually gave place to works revealing interpretative vision and more personal expression, but which at the same time retained a definite statement of truth to natural appearance. He properly calls attention to the technical excellence and truthful observation of these early topographical drawings, and shows that their aesthetic qualities helped to create a healthy and sincere appreciation of art and nature, and to establish standards of craftsmanship for the more creative art which in time developed.

The concluding chapter is an excellent summary of the Canadian art situation, with many suggestive and thoughtful comments. It links Canadian art development with its environment, its physical background, its social life, its racial traditions and its present and future needs. Moderately and reasonably stated, it presents Canadian art development as an integral part of Canadian life, and supplies ample evidence to its claims to this position.

CHARLES W. JEFFERYS.

York Mills,
Ontario.

PREFACE

MY purpose in writing this book has been to depict as well as printed record and oral testimony might allow the major influences at work in the early days of the arts in Canada which were eventually at a much later date to flower in a school of painting far beyond anything of the kind originally contemplated.

Now since the Ontario Society of Artists, the Royal Canadian Academy, the Toronto Art Students League and the Graphic Arts Club had much to do with the shaping of the new movement, both by precept and active association when it crystallized first as the Group of Seven, it is but natural and indeed inevitable that attention should be directed to their activities during the long period antecedent to the formation of the new school.

Of the rise and development of the Ontario Society of Artists and the Royal Canadian Academy we are pretty well informed. Of the Toronto Art Students League, a comparatively minor but important body, curiously enough, very little is known. I trust I have done something to lighten the darkness, and make its achievement clear.

The Toronto Art Students League, or, as it was later called, the Toronto Art League, as an organized group devoted to the study of pictorial art, was active from about 1886 to 1905, a period of, say, twenty years. Many, if not all, of the members employed black and white as their chief medium of expression; that is to say, they were engaged as illustrators or commercial designers, often both. It may be asked therefore what possible relation could subsist between them and their successors of the new movement who worked in colour, and what was for Canada, at any rate, revolutionary colour? Well, as I have tried to show in the following pages the relationship consisted not so much in the means of expression as in the possession of a common ideal which in time resolved itself into the recognition of the·need of reproducing the Canadian scene, not in terms of foreign schools and foreign climes, but rather in the light of conditions as they knew them. And that the earlier painters supplied the impulse and gave direction to the revolutionary trend subsequent changes were to confirm. That the artists of the 'seventies, 'eighties and 'nineties, no less than many of their predecessors, were among the first to feel the need of translating the landscape of the country in an idiom peculiar to the country is, I think, equally self-evident.

If therefore we have today a Canadian art virile, self-reliant and indigenous to the soil, it is mainly because of the pioneer work, often done under depressing and discouraging conditions by this earnest and hopeful band of students and painters of a former generation. It is part of a pleasant task here to record their works as best I can, and to acknowledge an obligation long past due. We already have the story of the Group of Seven as told in *A Canadian Art Movement.* It is my hope that the present volume will fulfil its avowed purpose, in part, of relating what went before.

For practical assistance in the preparation of this essay, I wish to acknowledge my debt to previous writers whose researches have added greatly to the sum of accurate and detailed knowledge concerning the progress of the arts in Canada. These men and others less well known have laid all Canadians, including not least myself, under a great obligation; how great the full-length bibliography appended to this volume is fairly indicative. Not only have I profited by the labours of my predecessors, but I have used manuscript material as well as information privately communicated wherever available.

To Frederick H. Brigden, R.C.A., O.S.A., I am indebted for facts and records concerning the Toronto Art Students League; to Mr. W. W. Alexander for information about our etchers, past and present; to Mr. T. W. McLean for details of the formation and subsequent history of the Graphic Arts Society and the Mahlstick Club; to Mr. F. S. Haines, R.C.A., for particulars of the Little Billee Club as well as for other relevant material; to

Preface

Dr. G. R. Lomer, Librarian of McGill University, for knowledge of Beaucourt's painting; and to Dr. J. F. Kenney of the Public Archives of Canada for facts about our early painters and topographers. Mr. H. O. McCurry, curator of the National Gallery, and Mr. Martin Baldwin, curator, the Art Gallery of Toronto, have generously assisted me; and Dr. James MacCallum and Mr. Thoreau MacDonald have furnished me with much original information about Tom Thomson and the Group of Seven for which I heartily thank them. My thanks are also due to Mr. Joseph Lister Rutledge, former editor of *The Canadian Magazine*, for granting me free access to the fyles of that periodical, as well as to all others who have in any way assisted me with material or advice. More specifically, I wish to express my gratitude to Sir Joseph Chisholm, of Halifax, Miss Elizabeth Styring Nutt, A.R.C.A., Principal of the Nova Scotia College of Art, and Miss Annie F. Donohoe, Librarian of the Legislative Library, Halifax, for information on the painters of Nova Scotia, and, similarly, to Mr. John Bruce Cowan, of Vancouver, for details concerning the artists of British Columbia.

My obligation to Dr. Charles W. Jefferys is of a very special kind. To him I am grateful for a description of the early life of the Toronto Art Students League in which he took an active and prominent part, for the loan of much valuable material, and for his unwearying generosity and kindness upon which I need not here dilate since it is well known to all interested in Canadian art or who have had occasion to write about it. Dr. Lorne Pierce read the entire manuscript with a care and vigilance for which I cannot thank him sufficiently. In so far as it is free from errors and ambiguities I owe it largely to his precise knowledge and patient toil. Lastly, I wish to thank my son, Dr. Forbes Colgate, for having typed the script.

William Colgate

THE OLD RECTORY,
WESTON,
June, 1943

xi

CONTENTS

ILLUSTRATIONS

Illustrations

Illustrations

CANADIAN ART

*"The days of journeying are not generally days of harvest; but
the seeds which fall in those pleasant times are apt to sink deep."*

—BARRETT WENDELL

1

IT IS customary for us to confuse the birth of a national art
movement in Canada with the emerging of the Group of Seven in
1919. The fact is, that Canadian art, as we know it today,
had its inception at a much earlier time. It really began with the
arrival in Canada of Paul Kane and Cornelius Krieghoff, the one
born in Mallow, County Cork, Ireland, and the other a native of
Dusseldorf in Rhenish Prussia. Both Krieghoff and Kane were
the first recorded painters to explore the Canadian landscape for
subjects. Both were to suggest to native-born painters the
pictorial possibilities inherent in their own country. Paul Kane,
son of an Irish liquor dealer living in Toronto, was to spend many
of his early years sketching and painting among the nomadic tribes
of the great north-west; and the fruits of his labours there are to
be seen in the Kane Collection at the Royal Ontario Museum,
Toronto, the National Gallery at Ottawa, and in the Speaker's
Chambers, House of Commons, Ottawa. Krieghoff, on the other
hand, was to devote his skill with the brush and pencil to the
depiction of scenes and incidents of Lower Canada in which the
Indian encampments of Lorette, the inns and inn-life of the post-
roads and the soldiers of the garrison at Quebec add interest and
spice to his gay and colourful canvases. Neither Kane nor
Krieghoff, it may be noted, was a painter of more than ordinary
competence. Of the two, Krieghoff perhaps surpassed Kane in
actual skill and technical resource. Although it may be conceded,

1

and I proffer this view with some diffidence, that Paul Kane possibly owed less than his successor to European influence for his individual style and workmanship. However true this assumption, it may be admitted at once that both painters are notable chiefly for their considerable, and historically valuable, contributions to the sum of available knowledge concerning the early life of Canada—the life as it was lived in those fascinating days of the forties, fifties, sixties, and even later.

Other contributors there were, of course, both literary and pictorial. Of these Mrs. John Graves Simcoe and Anna Jameson in landscape and Agnes Fitzgibbon in botanical drawing and painting are among the most notable. Mrs. Simcoe, who was the wife of the Lieutenant-Governor of Upper Canada, Colonel John Graves Simcoe, spent much of her leisure in the years from 1792 to 1796, when she and her family returned to England, in sketching various points of interest in the new country. These she recorded with a fairly nimble hand, a shrewd, seeing eye, and an assurance that implied some previous training. Many of her sketches had for subject material picturesque bits, often interesting historically, in and around Niagara, Queen's Town, and the town of York, now Toronto, as her husband in the round of his official duties went from one place to another. Among her more important drawings are: the QUEEN'S RANGERS HUTS, Queen's Town (Queenston), U.C., 1792; QUEEN'S TOWN, LOWER LANDING, 1792; NIAGARA FALLS FROM THE CANADIAN SIDE, 1793; THE GARRISON, YORK (Toronto), 1796, showing the first houses in the fort and the magazine on the shore; YORK (TORONTO) HARBOUR, 1793, near the old fort; CREDIT RIVER, NEAR YORK, 1796; NEAR THE THOUSAND ISLANDS, 1792; and POINT AU BODET, QUEBEC, 1792. These early sketches, done over a period of about five years, during the brief periods of relaxation from the cares of a household and a young family, now form part of the collection of paintings and drawings in the King's Library of the British Museum. Their undeniable value as historic documents of eighteenth-century life in Canada really entitles them to a place in the department of national archives at Ottawa, where they would be the more readily accessible to the student and research worker in Canadian history.

Agnes Fitzgibbon, a water-colourist of taste and skill, is remembered chiefly for her drawings of Canadian wild flowers.

Her work is distinguished by its accuracy, faithful colouring and attention to detail. A collection of her paintings and lithographs was reproduced and published in Montreal, in 1868, under the title of *Canadian Wild Flowers*, with botanical descriptions by C. P. Traill. "The graceful grouping of the flowers makes these hand-coloured plates among the most desirable of their kind." This was probably one of the first books in colour to appear in Canada,

John H. Price, Esq., Quebec.

AN EARLY CANADIAN SETTLER

Cornelius Krieghoff

and although its appeal is chiefly to the naturalist, it contains much of interest and instruction for the general reader as well.

Anna Jameson, an Englishwoman of gentle breeding, visited Toronto and Western Ontario in 1836. In 1838 appeared her *Winter Studies and Summer Rambles in Canada*. The wife of Robert Jameson, Vice-Chancellor of Upper Canada, afterwards Speaker of the House of Assembly, she had been able to acquire more than a superficial acquaintance with conditions here. In

3

her *Studies and Rambles*, she gives us the best word pictures available of Ontario, or Upper Canada as it then was, in the thirties—momentous years as they proved to be in the life of the two Canadas. Artistic by nature and training, Mrs. Jameson's approach to the contemporary scene is as much that of the painter as the writer; which may account in part for the lively, vivid and graphic quality of her recorded impressions, both written and pictorial. Later, as a natural consequence of her increasing concern with the visual arts, she became distinguished in the field of art criticism and is now remembered for her *Sacred and Legendary Art*. Valuable as it is to Canadians, "the writing of her one Canadian book was a small episode in her life," her real interests lay elsewhere. Even so, "she wrote so well of her travels here that it is not improbable her Canadian sketches may yet be her lasting memorial. Her critical work is becoming out of date; but good pictures of early Canadian life—either in print, or pencil, or brush—are rare and of permanent value." Again, such books as Mrs. Susanna Moodie's *Roughing It in the Bush*, Catherine Parr Traill's *The Backwoods of Canada*, have all the vividness and spontaneity of first impressions, "and their pictures are essentially true." It is well to bear in mind, moreover, since this essay deals mainly with a discussion of the visual arts, that a number of these pioneer writers were also skilful water-colourists, and supplemented their written impressions of the country with those of the brush and pencil. Thus what in the Old Country was deemed a polite or fashionable accomplishment became in process of time and change a thing of solid worth and desirable utility. A Canadian art was in the making.

It was not, however, until the late thirties that the publishing house of George Virtue, of London, England, commissioned William Henry Bartlett to gather material in Canada for an illustrated book on Canadian scenery. Drawings were to be made on the spot from which plates were later to be engraved and suitable descriptive letterpress written. In 1842 the book was issued under the title of *Canadian Scenery*, the drawings by Bartlett and the text by N. P. Willis, a popular American author of the time. The plates, of course, were steel engravings, and while well enough done, somewhat after the manner of Turner's *Liber Studiorum*, the volumes, now a collector's item, are today chiefly valued for their historic interest and antiquarian charm.

4

At this period in Toronto there were a number of workers in the arts whose names survive in the records of the time. Among them was Richard Coates, whose name is associated with the early dawn of the fine arts in York. Largely, if not altogether self-taught, he executed, not unsuccessfully we are told, portraits in oil of a number of prominent men of the time. Among subjects of a general or historical character, he painted also for David Willson, the founder of the "Children of Peace," the symbolical decorations of the interior of the Temple at Sharon, Ontario. Coates, like so many of his confrères, both English and American, was adept at many things. He cultivated music, both vocal and instrumental. "He built an organ of some pretensions, in his own house, on which he performed. He built another for David Willson at Sharon." Besides, in the yard of his house, he constructed "an elegantly-finished little pleasure yacht of about nine tons burden."

Mention of early art in York recalls the name of John Craig, who had much to do with the interior decoration of the many successive churches of St. James. In the fire of 1839, which ended in the destruction of St. James' Church, was destroyed a very large triplet window of stained glass over the altar containing three life-size figures by Craig, who as a local "historical and ornamental painter" was not well skilled in the ecclesiastical style. As home-productions, however, these objects were tenderly eyed; but Mrs. Jameson in her work on Canada denounced them as being "in vile tawdry taste," which of course they may well have been, measured by English and Continental standards. "Conceive, in the presence of these three Craigs," observes Dr. Scadding, "the critical authoress of the *History of Sacred and Legendary Art*, accustomed in the sublime Cathedrals of Europe, to

> See the great windows like the jewelled gates
> Of Paradise, burning with harmless fire.

Although Craig did not profess to go beyond his sphere as a decorative and heraldic painter, the spirit that animated him did really tend to foster in the young community a taste for art in a wider sense.

A skilful teacher of drawing in water-colours and the "introducer of superior specimens" was Charles Daly, who did much to promote an interest in the arts at this time. In 1834 we find him concerning himself with an exhibition of paintings by the "York Artists and Amateur Association," and acting as Honorary Secretary, when the exhibition for the year took place. James Hamilton, a teller in the bank, produced in oils several noteworthy landscapes of York and its environs.

For the first thirty years of the nineteenth century artists in York were few. When Upper Canada College was opened, in 1830, a Mr. Drewry or Drury was the drawing master; but three years later an open competition was held to determine who should receive the appointment permanently. Six men submitted drawings. The choice fell upon John G. Howard, who was thereupon appointed to the staff of the College in April, 1833, at an annual salary of 100 pounds. He was to remain for thirty-three years. Howard was an Englishman, lately arrived in Canada, who had served an apprenticeship in the office of Ford & Gagen, architects, of London. Subsequent to his arrival in York, he was able to induce the junior partner of the firm to follow him. The son of that junior partner, Robert Ford Gagen, was for many years secretary of the Ontario Society of Artists and a marine painter of note.

Of any concerted movement in Canadian art during the forties, fifties and sixties, there was noticeably little. The English artist, Daniel Fowler, farmed for many years on Amherst Island, while Cresswell, assisted by remittances from home, lived the life of an English squire in Huron County. It was no day for painters, unless we except George Theodore Berthon from France, whose fame as a portraitist earned him many commissions among the wealthy and professional classes. More fortunate than his contemporaries who painted landscapes, Berthon, as a portraitist, had the field almost entirely to himself; his brush was seldom idle. The old-established families, the eminent Georgians and Victorians of Upper Canada, such as the Robinson's and Boulton's, the Macaulays and Powells, as well as the judiciary and politicians, furnished him with a steady succession of sitters from the time of his arrival in 1844, all anxious to have their more or less distinguished features limned for a reverent posterity to savour and admire.

It is not surprising that, in a country like Canada, the progress of the fine arts should be punctuated with the formation at intervals

The W. H. Coverdale Collection, Manoir Richelieu, Quebec.

A VIEW OF TORONTO IN 1837

James Hamilton

of art societies, organized for the purpose of bringing those of common tastes and common aspirations into close relationship for the advancement of their common interest—which was painting.

The first organization of artists in Upper Canada of which we have record is that of the Toronto Society of Artists, begun in 1834, of which the architect, J. G. Howard of Colborne Lodge, High Park, was the founder. It was not strictly a society of professional painters, for it included among its membership a number of amateurs. Its first exhibition was held, in the same year the society came into existence, in the Parliament Buildings, Toronto. Among its members were Charles Fothergill, the naturalist, Paul Kane and Captain R. H. Bonnycastle, R.E. Unfortunately, the organization was short lived and not until 1847 was it succeeded by the Toronto Society of Arts, which held exhibitions in the City Hall, near the St. Lawrence Market. Little is known of its activities save that the Society during its life held three exhibitions; and among the exhibitors were Paul Kane, G. T. Berthon, Cornelius Krieghoff, and J. G. Howard, one of its founders.

It will be recalled that J. G. Howard was one of the organizers of the first art society in Toronto. In the Reference Library, Toronto, is the printed catalogue of the first *Exhibition of the Society of Artists and Amateurs of Toronto*, held in the Parliament Buildings in 1834, the same year in which Toronto set out as a city. Admission was 1s. 3d.; Catalogue, 7½d. The catalogue was made up of a list of one hundred and ninety-six pictures of all sorts, contributed by thirteen associated artists and eleven honorary exhibitors. We may presume the latter to have been non-professional. The thirteen associates consisted of: Captain (later Sir Richard) Bonnycastle, R.E., Henry J. Castle, Charles Daly, Charles Fothergill (better known as King's Printer and naturalist), G. S. Gilbert, James Hamilton (one of whose water-colours is here reproduced), John G. Howard, Paul Kane, John Laing, John Linnen, John Pottlewell, S. O. Tazewell and Samuel B. Waugh.

The chief officers of the newly organized Society were Captain R. H. Bonnycastle, president, with Charles Daly, honorary secretary. Its successor, the Toronto Society of Arts, held three exhibitions, the last in May, 1848, in the old City Hall, before it too dissolved. A prominent member of this Society was Hoppner

Meyer, who was a painter of the early days of Toronto, and did many small, but excellent, portrait studies in water-colour, among them, it is said, were several of the Chief Justices, as well as those of Dr. Henry Scadding and his wife. Some of these subsequently were engraved by himself; others by his friend, Lowe, of Toronto. Meyer also painted miniatures. He was the son of Henry Meyer, a German painter and engraver who settled in London, England, and who is remembered for his fine portrait of Charles Lamb. The father's friendship for John Hoppner, the portrait painter, caused him to name his son after him. Hoppner Meyer returned to London, where he died. At the time there were seventeen portrait and miniature painters in Toronto[1]. It was, we may observe, prior to the period when the camera was to compete with the portrait painter in perpetuating the features of contemporary men and women. Daguerre and his invention were yet a few years off.

A portrait painter in Toronto, in the thirties, was Nelson Cook whose chief claim to fame is that he had as sitters Sir John Beverley Robinson and Sir Francis Bond Head. Robinson he painted as an officer of militia—the year was 1837—and Bond Head he painted as Lieutenant-Governor of Upper Canada, complete with star. Neither canvas bears traces of anything more than ordinarily competent workmanship; though the skill shown is beyond what was customary at the time. In fairness it should be admitted that the Robinson painting appears to have been damaged and then repainted in part. A mezzotint of the Bond Head portrait bears the inscription "Painted by Nelson Cook, Esq. Engraved by C. Turner, A.R.A., London. Published Sept. 1, 1837, by Fred C. Capreol, Upper Canada, and in London, for the Proprietor, by Messrs. Dominic Colnaghi & Co., Printsellers, 14 Pall Mall East." An effort was made by the publisher to get permission to dedicate the engraving to Queen Victoria, but this was refused. It is more than probable that the Queen was not amused by the strange antics of her eccentric representative overseas. Where the original painting is we do not know.

In the Public Archives of Canada there is one example of the work of Nelson Cook. This is a portrait, dated on the reverse side 1835, of Alicia Fenton Russell, who died a widow at Aylmer,

[1]Toronto then had a population of about 20,000.

P.Q., in August, 1878, after having lived many years in Belleville, Ont. She was a relative of Sir John Harvey, Commander of the Forces at the Battle of Stoney Creek in 1813, and subsequently Lieutenant-Governor or Governor of New Brunswick, Newfoundland and Nova Scotia. Little is known of the artist beyond the statement in Walton's 1837 *Directory of Toronto* (p. 11) which lists Mr. and Mrs. Cook as portrait painters living at 106 King Street.

An article in the *Courier* of Toronto, dated April 1, 1837, devoted to the Bond Head portrait, says in part: "It is a source of pride and gratification to us, as public men, to observe the state to which the arts have attained in Upper Canada." On the same topic the Toronto *Patriot*, of April 21, 1837, says: "We are glad that a work of Toronto's respectable artist is about to be subjected to the criticism of London Connoisseurs from which we predict it will lose nothing of the value set upon it here." From these excerpts it would seem reasonable to infer that Nelson Cook was a citizen of Upper Canada, and, at least at the date of the picture, of Toronto. In the following years of 1841-1844 we find him plying his trade at Saratoga Springs, a favorite watering place of the period of Southern planters and their families, attracted thence by its gay and glittering social life. The fashion of the day probably kept the services of the portrait painter in demand. In 1852, he exhibited a painting of Alexander Mann, editor of *The Rochester American*, at the National Academy of Design. Cook is recorded as having lived until the late fifties at Saratoga; after that all trace of him is lost.

Captain Bonnycastle, who seems to have been a man of varied gifts, was also the author of *The Canadas in 1841*. The title-page credits the work to Sir Richard H. Bonnycastle, Lieutenant-Colonel, Royal Engineers, and Lieutenant-Colonel in the Militia of Upper Canada. The publisher's imprint reads "London: Henry Colburn: 1842."

One of the first of the artists and topographers to explore the Canadian West was Henry James Warre, of Durham, England, a lieutenant in the 14th Buckinghamshire Regiment. In 1844 President Polk of the United States had been elected largely on the slogan of "Fifty-four forty or fight." In 1845 the British Government, through Sir Charles Metcalfe, Governor-General of Canada, gave instructions that two officers were to be sent on a secret mission across the continent from Montreal to the Oregon country to make a report on matters of military interest. They were to accompany Sir George Simpson, Governor of the Hudson's Bay Company, from Montreal. Sir Richard Jackson, Commander of the Forces in Canada, chose for this mission Lieutenant Warre and Lieutenant M. Vavasour, of the Royal Engineers. On May 5, 1845, they left Montreal. On July 31 they reached the Columbia River, west of the Rocky Mountains, and there began their

Royal Ontario Museum, Toronto.

THE BUFFALO POUND

PAUL KANE

investigations of the Oregon country. They were back in Montreal about the end of July, 1846. Warre had meanwhile made sketches of the territory through which they had travelled, and twenty of these were published as lithographs in London by Dickinson and Co., in a folio volume entitled *Sketches in North America and the Oregon Territory. By Captain H. Warre (A.D.C. to the Late Commander of the Forces.)* The Public Archives at Ottawa has nineteen of the original wash drawings from which the lithographs were made. The twentieth is in a private collection in Ottawa. The

11

Archives has also one other drawing belonging to the same trip; and two small rough sketches made by Warre in Lower Canada in 1844. All of these drawings appear to present a clear and interesting and faithful impression of the West at the time they were taken; and have a pictorial as well as documentary value.

Although born in Ireland, Paul Kane came to this country young enough to receive his early education here. He attended the Old Grammar School on Church Street, in York, where he was instructed in drawing by Thomas Drury or Drewry, later of Upper Canada College. Young Kane was not especially studious; instead, he preferred the company of Indians and voyageurs, whose tales of life outside the bustling town aroused his interest and excited his curiosity, so much so that before long he betook himself to the road. For four years, in circumstances often of extreme difficulty, he travelled through Europe, studying its peoples and visiting their art galleries. Upon his return to Canada, in 1846, he wandered by canoe, boat and packhorse throughout the then scarcely known West. There he devoted himself to the painting of scenes of savage life and recording likewise his impressions on paper. The pictorial records of his trip throughout the Canadian West are to be seen in the Sir Edmund Osler Collection at the Royal Ontario Museum of Toronto. Paul Kane's way was made easy, insofar as a life such as his could be, by the liberal patronage of the Honourable George W. Allan, of Moss Park, Toronto, and the friendship of Sir George Simpson, governor of the Hudson's Bay Company, who because of his intimate knowledge of the West was able to assist the young artist in his travels by canoe and trail and on foot, from Montreal through the Rocky Mountains, Puget Sound and Vancouver Island to the Pacific. Many commissions were executed by Kane for the Hudson's Bay Company and the Legislature of Upper Canada. In his recorded impressions, published by Longman's of London in 1859, as the *Wanderings of an Artist Among the Indians of North America*, Kane narrates the story of his travels in the West, "from Canada to Vancouver's Island and Oregon through the Hudson's Bay Company's territory." Some interesting sidelights on his life and character are also contained in the published essays of Nicholas Flood Davin, former Canadian statesman, and among the writings of Sir Daniel Wilson, sometime President of the University of Toronto, who was himself an artist of more than ordinary aptitude.

2

In the early days of the country's settlement, when commissions were few, the field of portraiture was largely left to visiting Europeans and the occasional Yankee itinerant. One of the first to investigate the opportunities offered by the new country was George Theodore Berthon. Born in Vienna, Austria, of French parents in 1806, Berthon came to Canada in 1844. Berthon came by his painter's talent honestly. His father, René Theodore, was a painter at the court of the first Napoleon. Berthon had studied portraiture under David. The association may be considered a doubtful honour, for David is said to have passed more than three hundred pupils through his studio. Be that as it may, Berthon *père* bestowed on his promising son a careful training in the rudiments of painting, supplemented by study in the galleries and museums of the various European capitals. Upon attaining his majority, Berthon quitted his father's household and went to England, where he lived for a short time with the family of Sir Robert Peel, to whose daughters he taught painting. After fourteen years in England he came to Canada. In Toronto he opened a studio, where, although his services at first were not in great demand, he acquired a reputation as a portrait painter of ability. A canvas of his sent to the Philadelphia Exposition of 1876 by the Ontario Government, took the Centennial gold medal. Berthon then applied himself wholly to portraiture, using as mediums both oil and pastel with equal facility. A portion of his time he gave to teaching.

Of the numerous portraits executed by Berthon, he always considered that of Chief Justice, the Honourable John Beverley Robinson, his masterpiece. This canvas, portraying him in his ermined robes of office, is now in the library of Osgoode Hall, Toronto. Another, a copy, done by Sir Wyly Grier, now hangs in Strachan Hall, Trinity College, Toronto. Through the influence of his friend, Colonel Forlong, who had been formerly attached to the 43rd Regiment and was present at Waterloo, he was entrusted with commissions by several notable military officers living in Toronto, among them Colonel E. W. Thomson for the Board of Agriculture of Upper Canada, of which Colonel Thomson was chairman, and Lieutenant-Colonels R. L. Denison and George T. Denison. Conspicuous among his canvases is his dignified and impressive portrait of the Honourable and Right Reverend John Strachan, D.D., Lord Bishop of Toronto, which now hangs in the dining-hall of Hart House in the University of Toronto. This work was presumably done shortly after Berthon's arrival in Canada. Mezzotint engravings by W. Warner of this portrait are still extant, and occasionally at long intervals are to be seen in the auction room and the second-hand book shop. In Upper Canada College hang the portraits of former principals McCaul, Barron and Stennet, who also sat to Berthon; but probably the finest and most representative paintings by Berthon are to be found in the collection of Chief Justices, Chancellors and Judges in the corridors and chambers of Osgoode Hall, Toronto. Here, as already mentioned, is the large presentment of Chief Justice Robinson, in oils, in which, as Scadding justly observes, "his finely-cut Reginald Heber features are well delineated."

To have had at that early date a painter such as Berthon was fortunate, for there is much that is admirable in his work. His drawing was sound, his colouring often rich and subdued, and his compositions were obviously directed by a thoughtful and trained intelligence. All the portraits of former judges on the walls of Osgoode Hall, to the time of his death, were from his brush. Similarly, portraits of Ontario's successive lieutenant-governors formerly in Government House, Toronto, were by him. It has been asserted by some that Berthon worked under a long-term contract with the Provincial Government; and also that he painted a number of Speakers of the Senate at Ottawa. Credible evidence, however, disposes of both statements as nothing more than gossip. Berthon had no formal agreement with the Ontario Government, and there are no portraits of his in the Senate Chamber at Ottawa. A painting of Queen Victoria which hangs in the City Hall, Toronto, was copied by him from an original by John Partridge, R.A. (1790-1872). Berthon made his copy for the Honourable George W. Allan, of Moss Park, Toronto, who later presented it to the city of Toronto, following his term as mayor in 1855. Other portraits by Berthon include that of the Reverend Dr. Henry Scadding, D.D., author of *Toronto of Old;* and that of Sir Isaac Brock, probably copied from a miniature in possession of relatives in Guernsey; and THE THREE MISS ROBIN-

J. Beverley Robinson, Esq., Toronto.

THE THREE MISS ROBINSONS

GEORGE THEODORE BERTHON

SONS, presumably inspired by Reynold's THE LADIES WALDEGRAVE. Apart from the Osgoode Hall collection, probably the largest and certainly the most diversified assemblage of Berthon portraits ever gathered together were seen at the Toronto Centennial Historical Exhibition held at the Art Gallery of Toronto, in 1934, when both private families and public institutions generously lent their pictures to mark the event. Among the paintings on view during the exhibition were those of: William Henry Boulton, mayor of Toronto, 1845-1847 and again in 1858; Mrs. Goldwin Smith of the Grange, wife of the celebrated publicist; Bishop Strachan; the Honourable Robert Baldwin, C.B., Attorney-General of Upper Canada, 1829-1862; the Honourable Edward Blake, sometime Premier of the Province of Ontario; and THE THREE ROBINSON SISTERS already mentioned.

Berthon's portrait of Sir John Beverley Robinson is a showy piece of work done in the rather pretentious manner of the time. His study of the three Robinson sisters, a charming group of girls in ringlets and early Victorian costumes, on the other hand, is demurely reminiscent of the fashion plates of Godey's *Lady's Magazine*. Although to us his painting now appears tight, literal and hard in finish, measured by the pictorial standards of his day it is something more than merely competent. His portraits of men are marked by a certain air of repose and quiet dignity; and those of his women and children often have grace and beauty and simplicity. It is well to remember, moreover, that his pictures in general possess a degree of merit which renders them superior to mere portraits; they assume in fact the importance and value of historic documents. If Berthon did nothing more, he brought, at least insofar as Canada is concerned, dignity and taste to portraiture. His style was sound if undistinguished; the painting highly skilful, if not brilliant. The probability is that it did not aspire to anything more, for George Berthon was essentially a modest man and, like men of his kind, thought more of his work than of popular acclaim. His final canvas was of Chief Justice Sir T. W. Taylor, of Winnipeg. He died in Toronto on January 18, 1892, at the advanced age of eighty-six. At his death he was an honorary life member of the Ontario Society of Artists. In 1880 he had been nominated a founder-member of the Royal Canadian Academy, but failed to qualify. He was buried in St. Michael's cemetery, Toronto. From the Canadian historian of the arts

George Theodore Berthon has yet to receive the recognition to which his merits entitle him.

In ill-health and discouraged, Daniel Fowler came to Canada in 1843 and bought a farm on Amherst Island, near Kingston. Fowler had received his early training under J. D. Harding, an English water-colourist and lithographer by whose style he seems to have been influenced. Following a year of travel on the Continent, he established himself in England as a drawing master. His first Canadian venture was not successful. After fourteen years of struggle with the hardships of farming, a fire destroyed all he had built up. By 1857, however, he was able to revisit England for a short time. Turner, his idol, was gone, but art circles were stirred by the theories of the Pre-Raphaelite School, and Fowler was moved to begin painting again. At first his sketches were small, tentative, experimental and, as he says, were "worried into existence." Soon his power developed and he began to specialize in still-life subjects—flower studies and dead game—paying special attention to background. His pictures of dead game are vigorous and strong in colour. At a period when patronage in Canada was slight, his work was soon contended for by rival dealers, and he was made in 1880 a founder-member of the Royal Canadian Academy. The crowning point of his career came in 1876 when, at the Philadelphia Centennial Exhibition, in competition with artists from all over the world, he was awarded one of the twelve medals given for water-colour for his now-famous drawing of HOLLYHOCKS. In 1886, he received a diploma medal at the Colonial and Indian Exhibition. In the National Gallery, Ottawa, he is represented by several studies of game, and a self-portrait in charcoal, presented by himself.

In the story of Canadian painting, Daniel Fowler has a place among those who came to this country and painted the landscape and its details as sustaining material for those who were also immigrants from older lands. His colour, his draughtsmanship and his vigorous handling bear out his own statement that he worked on one principle only: that of "producing as closely as possible, the appearance of reality. That is," he said, "the one effect I always strove to accomplish, the one quality I sought to gain."

One of the first, if not indeed the very first, of our native painters to visit the West was Frederick Arthur Verner, who spent many years in the foothills of the Rockies reproducing in water-colour scenes of Western life, introducing the buffalo, the Indian encampment and the pioneer settler. So prolific was he that rare is the picture gallery or antique shop that cannot show one or more examples of his work. In almost all his drawings he seems to have striven for an effect of light and atmospheric depth, with the result that many of his pictures are inclined toward sensitive, subtle values rather than to show strong contrasts of sunshine and shadow. Indeed the misty atmosphere which envelops many of his water-colour drawings is more peculiar to the Scottish Highlands than the bright clear sunlit distances of the prairie land-scape. Born in 1836, in Sheridan, Ontario, the son of a principal and superintendent of grammar schools, Verner went to England at the age of twenty, and studied at Heatherly's in London and at the British Museum. Wearying of the close application which formal training involved, and eager for adventure, he enlisted in the 3rd Yorkshire Regiment and served for three years. Later he joined the British Legion and fought with Garibaldi in 1860-1861 in the struggle for Italian liberation. At the close of the war, Verner quit the army and returned to Canada in 1862, where he was to spend the remainder of his days recording the life of the West. Ten years later he was elected a member of the Ontario Society of Artists, in 1893 an associate of the Royal Canadian Academy, and in 1905 of the Royal British Artists, by whom he was awarded a diploma in 1910. Verner was also awarded medals and diplomas at the Pan-American Exposition, Buffalo, in 1901, at the Philadelphia Centenary Exposition, at the International Exhibition of Fine Arts, Buenos Aires, 1910, and at the Centennial Exhibition, Santiago, Chile, held in the same year. He is repre-sented at the National Gallery of Canada by an oil portrait—one of his very few—of Sir John A. Macdonald; and by three water-colour drawings: A STREET SCENE, TURNED OUT OF THE HERD, and A MISTY MORNING. He died in 1928, at the extreme age of ninety-two.

A pupil of W. E. Cook, R.A., and of Clarkson Stanfield, R.A., William Nichol Cresswell came to Canada in 1855 and settled on a farm in Huron County, near Seaforth. He was then in his thirties, having been born in Devonshire, England, in 1822. Robust and thickset, rough in his dress and with a voice like a sea-captain's, Cresswell lived the life of a country squire, dividing his time

FISHING SHACKS ON THE ST. LAWRENCE

WILLIAM NICHOL CRESSWELL

William Colgate, Weston, Ont.

between sketching and fishing. Examples of his work now extant show him to have been a landscape and marine artist with a fine sense of colour. Happily escaping or avoiding the often finical and intensely literal style of his contemporaries, his painting reveals imagination, vigour and manipulative skill. Remittances which he regularly received from the homeland tended to put a brake on greater achievement. However, he lived to become in 1880 a charter member of the Royal Canadian Academy and one of the early instructors of Robert F. Gagen to whom he taught water-colour drawing. He died in 1888, aged sixty-six.

With the exception of Paul Kane, observes Gagen in *Early Days in Canadian Art*, Upper Canada had not produced a native artist. [Kane was Irish-born, but for the purpose of the argument, the point is immaterial.] The residing artists were all from Europe

19

—England mostly—and they worked in the manner of the schools they had been trained in. With the exception of the portrait painters, few painted in oil, and the landscapes, marines, etc. [The catalogue of the 1883 R.C.A. Exhibition held in Toronto listed 148 oils as compared with 177 water-colours.] were nearly all water-colours of the English school—at this time at its best: but although the style was suitable to the conditions of the old land, it was not, when rigidly adhered to, adequate to convey the breath and light and other qualities of this country. The critics and art lovers, having been brought up under English influence, failed to detect or point out the lacking qualities. So advancement had to come from without, and did in this way.

In 1867 William Notman, of Montreal, opened a photographic studio in Toronto and sent, as manager and junior partner, John Arthur Fraser, a young man of Scottish and Danish descent, who had studied art in the Royal Academy School with George du Maurier as a classmate, and also in the studio of F. H. Topham, supporting himself, while doing so, by painting portraits. His father, Alexander Fraser, was a London tailor of advanced liberal ideas, and a strenuous supporter of the moral force of the Chartists. His principles did not render him popular, with the result that he failed in business and emigrated with his family (including John and his young wife) to Canada, where they settled in Stanstead, Eastern Townships.

Fraser became known as a painter of promise, with the result that William Notman, already famed as a photographer, invited him to come to Montreal and try his hand at painting photographs. This invitation he accepted and he revolutionized the doubtful art. With his dexterity in handling water-colours, he painted over light prints on drawing-paper, succeeding so well that it was difficult for even artists to detect the photographic base, and in the case of his miniatures they resembled in every way the real thing done on ivory, with rich backgrounds, broad draperies and clean flesh colours. They were a pleasure to behold, and ultimately became one of the principal features of Notman's business. The artist's room was the academy from which several of our leading artists (e.g. Henry Sandham, W. Lewis Fraser, John Hammond) were graduated.

The same success followed Fraser when he came to Toronto, where he was assisted by Eugene Nice, Horatio Walker, R. F. Gagen

THE FOAMING SEA

ROBERT F. GAGEN

and afterwards F. McGillivray Knowles. Nor were his gifts confined to the painter's art. Blessed with a fine tenor voice, he sang
"My Queen," "Ruby," "The Message," "My Pretty Jane" and
other songs of the period so well that the great Brignoli deigned to
sing with him at concerts and complimented him highly. Without
doubt Fraser assessed his talents at their full worth. Once, when
greatly elated, he exclaimed, "A man that can paint like that
should wear a gold hat!" In consequence of his florid self-
appreciation he was disliked by many, but all, says Gagen,
appreciated his art.

Later still, in 1867, the year of Confederation, Fraser assisted
in forming the Society of Canadian Artists, which had but a brief
career. With John Bell-Smith, father of F. M. Bell-Smith, as its
president, it marked the first recorded attempt to bring under the
ægis of one organization the artists of the new Dominion. The
society had as founder-members W. L. Fraser, Otto R. Jacobi,
Henry Sandham and A. Vogt. A book of poems by John Fraser,
entitled *Cousin Sandy* (published by Dawson Bros., Montreal,
1870), contains illustrations by all four artists. Evidently the
organization was still in existence at that date, for the title page
carries the line "of the Society of Canadian Artists." It was at all
events the forerunner of the Royal Canadian Academy, the formation of which was to take place twelve years later. The country
meanwhile was progressing. Confederation had become an accomplished fact, and a federal government, concerned with the welfare
of the Dominion as a whole, was at length established. With the
increase of immigration, the building of railroads and the expansion
of commerce and industry, the newer Canada was entering upon a
period of material prosperity. But as yet, because the people of
the country were absorbed for the most part in quest of material
things, there were attempts, and these few, feeble and sporadic, to
satisfy the hunger of the mind and the spirit. Thus, about the only
outlets available to the artist of the time for placing before the
public the products of his skill were the facilities afforded by the
few dealers of the principal centres of population, as in London,
Toronto and Montreal, and the annual Provincial exhibitions where
he was forced to compete for public interest on terms of something
less than equality with the products of the farm and the forge.

At this time most of the artists working in Canada were either of British or foreign birth. Notable exceptions were Dickson Patterson, Lucius O'Brien and Homer Watson.

It was in some such formative state of society that the Ontario Society of Artists, in 1872, came into being, to be followed eight years later by the Royal Canadian Academy of Arts.

W. D. Blatchly, R. F. Gagen, Hamilton MacCarthy, T. M. Martin, W. A. Sherwood, J. W. L. Forster, M. Hannaford.
M. Matthews, Hon.-Sec., Hon. G. W. Allan, President, Wm. Revell, Vice-President and Treasurer.

GROUP OF THE ONTARIO SOCIETY OF ARTISTS—1889

Living in Montreal, W. L. Fraser, who had been an active member of the now defunct Society of Canadian Artists, occasionally exhibited his pictures in New York. One of these, THE RIGHT OF THE ROAD, caused him to be elected a member of the American Society of Water Colours. In Toronto he missed the excitement of the politics, the exhibitions and the meetings of an art society, and soon took steps to fill this void. He consulted with Daniel Fowler, who was one of the few men he really admired, and also

23

with Marmaduke Matthews, whose work he did not admire, about the formation of a society. At first he met with very little encouragement as the local artists were very jealous of the rapid popularity his work had obtained; but in time these lesser lights were led to a proper frame of mind, largely by the persuasive talks of James Spooner and George Gilbert, the so-called art critics of the day. Spooner, it may be added, kept a combined tobacco shop, picture gallery and dog kennel on King Street in Toronto.

Having succeeded in enlisting the support of his fellow artists for the undertaking he had in mind, Fraser called a meeting at his house, 28 Gould Street. This was on the evening of June 25, 1872, and those invited were Charles S. Millard, T. M. Martin, James Hoch, Marmaduke Matthews, J. W. Bridgeman and R. F. Gagen. Fraser laid before them a plan to form a society of artists similar to the Canadian Society of Artists of Montreal, and he was requested to draw up a constitution and rules and submit them at a meeting to be held at the residence of Charles S. Millard, Wood Street, on July 2nd. To this meeting, in addition to the artists above mentioned, came H. Hancock, an architect and painter, who acted as secretary, with Fraser in the chair. Fraser read the draft of the constitution which, after some alterations, was adopted. Fraser was then appointed vice-president, H. Hancock, secretary, and H. J. Morse (a coal merchant), treasurer. William Holmes Howland was appointed president of the Society. The first business was to provide for an Art Union similar to those conducted in London and Glasgow. This was successfully done, and thus the first Annual Exhibition was held in a new art gallery built by Notman and Fraser on part of the site now occupied by the King Edward Hotel. It opened with a private view on Easter Monday, April 14, 1873. A contemporary engraving of the event still exists. Pictures, chiefly water-colours, covered the walls from floor to ceiling without apparently an inch between them. It is clear there was no regard shown for size, spacing or natural propinquity as there is today. Women in bustles and men in top hats viewed the exhibits with affected grace. The drawing of the event was so meticulously done, that virtually all the pictures are recognizable.

After a lapse of fifty years (comments Robert Gagen) it would be difficult to give any reliable criticism, or even description, of the pictures, but as the gallery was only 50 feet by 30 feet, and it contained

252 works, the majority must have been small. In the matter of titles our predecessors were more poetic and romantic, for instance—STORM AT DAYBREAK, FLASHES OF LIGHT IN THE DARKNESS, GLINT AS FROM FLINT AND STEEL, WINONA'S HOME—also with poetry; DESPAIR OF MEDEA, VIRGINIUS AND VIRGINIA. L. R. O'Brien and G. Harlow White were introduced to the public at this exhibition, and the total sales made $3,935, a large sum in those days.

Let us remember this achievement to the credit of our immediate ancestors whose claims to culture were not so great as ours, nor yet, perhaps, so audible.

Sixty years later, the proceeds were exactly nil. Nor as a rule do current exhibitions, apart from those of the commercial art dealers, fare better. The public may come to look; seldom does it remain to pay. One factor that may have influenced the sale of pictures at this time was a body of honorary members attached to the new society and presumably taking an active interest in its development. More than that, many of these lay members were wealthy and influential, had a taste for pictures and homes to accommodate them. Among the more than one hundred names listed were those of the Honourable George W. Allan, the Honourable Edward Blake, the Reverend Vincent Clementi, botanist, water-colourist and teacher of Mrs. C. P. Traill, Sandford Fleming, Sir John Macdonald, Goldwin Smith, James Spooner, John Payne, amateur and dealer and friend to Homer Watson, Dr. Daniel Wilson, President of the University of Toronto, and Quetton St. George, an early merchant of Toronto.

Through numerous difficulties that beset its course, the Ontario Society of Artists progressed until, in 1876, it established the Ontario School of Art, in a hall sixty by thirty feet in area, situated over a store at 14 King Street West, Toronto. Six years later the institution was removed to the Normal School, where it remained for a number of years. Later in the nineties, the opening of the galleries of the Ontario Society of Artists over the Princess Theatre on King Street West (since demolished to make way for the extension of University Avenue), made possible the removal of the School to larger and more permanent quarters. The School now assumed the new title of the Ontario School of Art and Design, and maintained classes in primary drawing, drawing from the antique, a life class and in later days drawing from the nude. A competent teaching staff was engaged made up of Robert Holmes, C. M. Manly, William Cruikshank, George A. Reid, Frederick S. Challener and J. W. Beatty. Finally, in 1910, the establishment of the Art Gallery of Toronto made the erection of a suitable building possible ten years later.

3

The newly-founded Ontario Society of Artists had no warmer or more faithful friend than the Earl of Dufferin, who fraternized with its members and often came to sketch in its gallery. At a farewell luncheon held in his honour by the members in 1879, His Excellency hinted at the establishment of a Canadian Academy. His successor, the Marquis of Lorne, fortunately lost no time after his arrival in acting upon the suggestion.

In the month of February, 1879, the vice-president of the Ontario Society of Artists, L. R. O'Brien, waited upon His Excellency with a request that he and H.R.H. the Princess Louise would become patrons of the society as the late Governor-General Lord Dufferin had previously been. The Marquis of Lorne expressed the hope that it might not be long before a Royal Canadian Academy of artists should be instituted, to be composed of and managed by Canadian artists. On May 26th, when the new building of the Arts Association of Montreal was opened by the Governor-General and the Princess Louise, he again alluded to the project of forming such an academy in these words:

To pass to our present prospects: I think we have good promise; not only of having an excellent local exhibition, but that we may, in course of time, look forward to the day when there may be a general art union in the country, and when I or some more fortunate successor may be called upon to open the first exhibition of a Royal Canadian Academy to be held each year in one of the capitals of our several Provinces; an academy which may, like that of the Old Country, be able to insist that each of its members or associates should on their election paint for it a diploma picture; an academy which shall be strong and wealthy enough to offer as a prize to the most successful students of the year money sufficient to enable them to pass more time in those European capitals where the masterpieces of ancient art can be seen and studied. Even now in principal centres of the population you have shown that it is perfectly possible to have a beautiful and instructive exhibition; for besides the pictures bequeathed to any city, it may always be attainable that an exhibition of pictures be had on loan, and that these be shown beside the productions, both in oil and water-colour, of the artists of the year. It may be said that in a country whose population is yet incommensurate with its extent, people are too busy to toy with art; but without alluding to the influence of art on the mind, in regard to its elevating and refining power, it would surely be folly to ignore the value of beauty and design in manufactures; and in other countries blessed with fewer resources than ours, and in times which comparatively certainly were barbarous, the work of artists have not only gained for them a livelihood, but have pleased and occupied some of the busiest men of the time, the artists finding in such men the encouragement and support that is necessary.

The Governor-General then went on to speak of the subject material that the Canadian landscape offered to the native painter, and in doing so forecast the desire that was to be subsequently aroused for a school of painting distinctively Canadian:

If you leave the realm of imagination and go to that of the Nature you see living and moving around you, what a choice is still presented. The features of brave, able and distinguished men of your own land, of its fair women, in the scenery of your country, and the magnificent wealth of water of its great streams, in the foaming rush of their cascades, overhung by the mighty pines or branching maples, and skirted with the scented cedar copses; in the fertility of your farms, not only here, but throughout Ontario also, or in the sterile and savage rock scenery of the Saugenay. In such subjects there is ample material; and I doubt not that our artists will in due time benefit this country by making her natural resources and the beauty of her landscapes as well known as are those of the picturesque districts of Europe; and that we shall have a school here worthy of our dearly loved Dominion.

In a communication to the vice-president of the Ontario Society of Artists, of June 8th, bearing on the subject, the Governor-General outlined his plans for the formation of the proposed academy. Among other items he suggests "that it be a standing rule that each capital city of each Province be visited in turn by the Dominion exhibition, leaving of course the local societies to have an exhibition of their own each year as they like." The plan was to bring the academy exhibition to Ottawa only after Halifax, Fredericton, Quebec and Toronto had been visited, namely, every fifth year. This regulation seemed necessary because "the jealousy between our widely-scattered cities is great." It was the intention to except Winnipeg and Victoria until they were united by rail; and, for the want of good communication, Prince Edward Island was also to be left out so far as an exhibition there was concerned.

At the same time it was proposed to have the new academy consist, besides the usual classifications, of honorary members, "to include all men willing to assist, everywhere, if approved, by the members who are not honorary." The scheme of organization as then laid down by the Governor-General was adopted almost *in toto* and has continued in practice to this day. That is, all but the admission of honorary members who no longer form part of the Academy membership, as they no longer do in the Ontario Society of Artists, which ceased about 1900 to admit laymen to membership.

In a letter to the *Montreal Herald*, presumably of June, 1879, though the date is not mentioned, L. R. O'Brien, president of the newly-formed Canadian Academy of Arts, expressed the bright hopes entertained of the beneficial results likely to accrue from holding the yearly academy exhibition at various centres throughout the Dominion. Since the matter is of general importance and the question is one which doubtless arises even today, we may quote that portion of his letter which deals directly with this phase of the subject:

Some exception has been taken, naturally, to leaving Montreal and Toronto, the chief cities of the Dominion, last upon the list of places selected for holding exhibitions. This has been done at the express desire of His Excellency, and has been cordially assented to by the artists, although their immediate personal interests would have been best served by holding the exhibitions in the largest and most wealthy places; but Montreal and Toronto have already efficient art organizations of their own, and I am confident that their liberal and public-spirited citizens will be glad to lend a helping hand, in the first place, to those who have no such advantages. We may reasonably hope that in Halifax, St. Johns, and Quebec, the visit of the Academy will lead to the formation of such local art societies as may be best suited to their circumstances and available material.

Any city which fails to form and support some such local association can scarcely be deemed sufficiently advanced in civilization to justify a second visit of the Academy. London, in the West, has much to offer as inducement to hold an Academy Exhibition there, and the generous appreciation of art which has induced so many artists to make their home in the Province of Ontario will no doubt soon make it advisable to add the Forest City to the list.

It is not on record that St. Johns, Quebec, or London were ever visited by the Academy, though Halifax was—once. However, the intention of the founders was good; the time alone was unpropitious. Interest in the arts was still confined to the relatively few.

A. T. Taylor, A.R.C.A., F. M. Bell, R.C.A., J. W. H. Watts, R.C.A., Robt. Harris, R.C.A., Forshaw Day, A.R.C.A., J. W. L. Forster, A.R.C.A., Hamilton MacCarthy, R.C.A.

Wm. Brymner, R.C.A., O. R. Jacobi, R.C.A., L. R. O'Brien, Prest. R.C.A., A. C. Hutchison, R.C.A., J. Smith, Sec. R.C.A., J. Forbes, R.C.A. (standing)

COUNCIL OF THE ROYAL CANADIAN ACADEMY—1889

At an organization meeting held in September, 1879, in the gallery of the Ontario Society of Artists, with His Excellency in the chair, the Royal Canadian Academy was founded, and Daniel Fowler, John A. Fraser, Napoléon Bourassa, A. Allan Edson, James Griffiths, Robert Harris, Eugene Hamel,[1] William Nichol Cresswell, William Raphael, Henri Perré, T. Mower Martin, Lucius O'Brien, Henry Sandham and Mrs. Charlotte M. B.

[1] A portrait of Edward Blake, by Eugene Hamel, hangs in the Great Hall, Hart House, Toronto.

29

Schreiber were named Academicians. The following architects were also elected: J. W. Hopkins, William George Storm, T. S. Scott, James Smith and H. Langley. A sculptor, F. C. Van Luppen, was nominated to represent his classification. L. R. O'Brien became first president and N. Bourassa, the vice-president, with James A. Smith as treasurer and Marmaduke Matthews as secretary.

Antagonism to the new body made itself vocal just as it some-times does today, and some scepticism was expressed as to its probable influence upon Canadian art. Thus Lord Lorne, in his opening address, replied with delicate irony to those critics who thought the enterprise would be more suitable in 1980 than in 1880:

> Art will no doubt be in vigorous life in Canada a century hence; but, on the other hand, we must remember that at that time these gentle critics may have disappeared from the scene, and they will themselves allow that it is for the benefit of the Academy that it should begin its existence while still subject to their own friendly supervision.

As so often happens, the *fait accompli* silenced criticism. The opening of the first Academy exhibition on Saturday, March 6, 1880, was a brilliant occasion. The Clarendon Hotel building had been loaned by the Canadian Government for the accommodation of the new society. The gracious and inspiring address by the Marquis of Lorne had evoked an equally tactful and gracious response from the Academy president, Lucius O'Brien, who by birth, breeding and education was admirably fitted for the task, as was also in Gallic eloquence Napoléon Bourassa, the vice-president.

The following is an account of the opening ceremonies as reported next day by *The Mail*, Toronto:

Ottawa, March 6, 1880.

To-night the first exhibition of the Canadian Academy of Arts was opened by His Excellency the Governor-General, in presence of a brilliant company. No more auspicious circumstances could have surrounded the initial public effort of the institution. Its patron is the Queen's representative. Among its warm supporters is H.R.H. the Princess Louise, from whom a welcome message was received to-night. The Dominion Government have manifested their desire to encourage art by placing the old Clarendon Hotel at the disposal of the Society, while its supporters already include leading men of all political opinions. The Academy has, moreover, been honoured by receiving an intimation from the Queen, through His Excellency, that Her Majesty will be a purchaser from the walls of the Exhibition. It has received the general support of Canadian artists in the respective Provinces, between whom no bond of union has hitherto existed. The contributions of loan pictures are large and valuable. His Excellency, Her Royal Highness and suite, sent a most interesting collection, and the galleries of private lovers of art, such as Mr. Allan Gilmour, of this city, have been freely placed under contribution. The Academy has been at length fairly launched. It is unnecessary to review the circumstances which brought about its establishment. The task of nominating the first Academicians devolved upon His Excellency as patron. The following are the first to fill that distinguished position:—Allan Edson, Montreal; W. N. Cresswell, Seaforth; D. Fowler, Amherst Island; J. A. Fraser, Toronto; James Griffiths, London; Eugene Hamel, Quebec; R. Harris, Toronto; J. Hopkins, Montreal; H. Langley, Toronto; L. R. O'Brien, Toronto; Wm. Raphael, Montreal; H. Sandham, Montreal; Mrs. Schreiber, Toronto; F. C. Van Luppen, Montreal; James Smith, Toronto; T. S. Scott, Ottawa; William Storm, Toronto; T. M. Martin, Toronto. The following have also been nominated Academicians, but have not yet complied with the condition of presenting a diploma picture:—G. T. Berthon, Toronto; Forshaw Day, Kingston; J. Forbes, Hamilton; O. R. Jacobi, Toronto; H. Perré, Toronto; Bell-Smith, Sr., Hamilton; W. S. Thomas, Montreal. The first business meeting of the Academy was held this afternoon, and according to constitution, the election of Academicians will subsequently devolve upon the Academicians and Associates.

Altogether it was a memorable event. A few wealthy Ottawa collectors of taste had enhanced the exhibition with loans from their private possessions. The later intimate relationship of Canadian art to industry was foreshadowed by an exhibit of industrial drawings. The foresight of the first Academicians has nowhere been more fully confirmed than by the subsequent opening of schools of art in Halifax, Montreal, Ottawa, Toronto, Hamilton, St. Catharines, Winnipeg, Vancouver and elsewhere. The alliance between industry and art became closer with the years. In alluding to industrial, or applied art, as then shown, Lord Lorne said:

English manufacture, as you know, has become famous for its durability, French manufacture for its beauty and workmanship; and here we have a people sprung from both races, we should be able to combine these excellences, so that Canadian manufacture may hold a high place in the markets of the world.

Henceforth painting in Canada was to have a new inspiration and a new purpose. But it was to be Canadian in subject only.

The scene was the Canadian scene, but the style was still the style of the European schools. The thraldom of foreign influence was too complete to permit any thought of emancipation. As yet, the system was not even suspect. Quite plainly there had to come a change in point of view before there could be a change of style. That day was yet somewhat distant.

In the meantime it might be well for us to examine the motives by which the founders of the Academy were actuated. These perhaps cannot better be explained than in the Governor-General's own words delivered upon the occasion of its opening:

It is impossible to agree with the remark that we have no material in Canada for our present purposes, when we see many excellent works on these walls; and if some do not come up to the standard we may set ourselves, what is this but an additional argument for the creation of some body which shall act as an educator in this matter? Now, gentlemen, what are the objects of your present effort? A glance at the constitution of the Society will show your objects are declared to be the encouragement of industrial art by the promotion of excellence of design, the support of schools of art throughout the country, and the formation of a national gallery of art at the seat of Government.

If one or two of the objectives, thus set forth, have failed of attainment in the succeeding years, much good has nevertheless been accomplished. Only in one department have the Academicians failed to realize the hopeful beginning of the society, and that is in the field of industrial design, which has been left to other organizations to explore.

Lucius O'Brien, president of the newly-formed Royal Canadian Academy, was born of Irish parents at Shanty Bay, Simcoe County, in 1832. He was educated first at Upper Canada College and later became a civil engineer. Dissatisfied with engineering somewhat late in life, he turned what had previously been a hobby into a profession and began to paint the scenery round about Ontario and Quebec. Later he journeyed through the then wilderness of the West, and was one of the first Canadian painters to depict the beauties of the Rockies and Selkirks. Essentially a watercolourist, he painted in a limpid, flowing style, and was technically an expert in his craft; but his pictures are often destitute of imagination and invention, since they are to a noticeable degree exact copies of nature, and subject as they were to his training as an engineer, valuable chiefly for their topographical interest. The Marquis of Lorne bought his paintings, as did Queen Victoria, who commissioned him to paint two views of Quebec. His SUNRISE OF THE SAGUENAY is in the National Gallery of Ottawa; and MIST IN THE MOUNTAIN in the Parliament Buildings, Toronto. What knowledge of painting he had, O'Brien taught himself and, even when old, showed a desire to learn more. He continued as presi-

The National Gallery.

KAKABEKA FALLS

LUCIUS R. O'BRIEN

dent of the Academy for ten years, when he was succeeded by Otto R. Jacobi.

Jacobi's term of office, 1890-1893, was in the main uneventful. He had now been in Canada for thirty years, having been invited to this country in 1860 to paint a picture of Shawinigan Falls, Quebec. The country appealed to him, and he had remained to paint landscapes noted for their delicacy of form, and for their shimmering, broken colour much after the manner of Monticelli, by whose technique he may have been influenced. Born in Konigsberg, Prussia, in 1812, in the same year as Krieghoff, he studied art in the Academy of Berlin, and in 1832 won a prize of $1,000, with the privilege of studying at Dusseldorf, Krieghoff's birthplace, for three years. There he painted many important water-colours and received commissions from the Duke of Westphalia, the Empress of Russia and the Grand Duke of Nassau; the latter appointed him court painter at Wiesbaden, which position he held for twenty years. One of his important works there was a fresco for a Greek memorial chapel. Jacobi numbered among his pupils Ludwig Knaus, and was fond of showing a sketch-book of that eminent painter. His pictures were appreciated outside his own country, some of them being taken to England and America. At one time an exhibition was held showing a full range of his paintings from the time he worked in Europe until his later years. Even today his paintings, and more especially his water-colours, are to be encountered in the auction rooms of Toronto and Montreal, where the demand for them is likely to be steady if not keen. For many years he lived in Toronto, but afterwards joined his son, a rancher in Travia, in the Western States, where he died in 1901.

Of the period of O'Brien and Jacobi was Henry Sandham, R.C.A., born in 1842. He continued active until his death in 1910. He is probably most familiar to Canadians through his drawings for *Picturesque Canada* and his illustrations during the seventies and eighties for the *Century*, *Scribner's*, *Harper's* and other American magazines of the period. His early tuition he gained in Notman's studio, Montreal, under Fraser, Vogt, Jacobi and C. J. Way, R.C.A. Later, as was the custom of the day, he went to Europe to complete his studies. In 1880 he settled in Boston, where besides drawing illustrations, he painted in oil and water-colours. He was an excellent draughtsman. Some of his figure groups in water-colours are most skilfully composed. However, his portrait of Sir John A. Macdonald, which hangs in the Parliament Buildings, Ottawa, shows clearly enough that he lacked the same mastery of oils. Other important canvases of his include THE DAWN OF LIBERTY, in the town hall of Lexington, Massachusetts, and THE MARCH OF TIME, in Washington. Late in life he returned to England and worked in London.

A name unknown to many Canadians, even to such as are interested in art, is that of Allan A. Edson, R.C.A., who was born in 1846 at Stanbridge, Quebec, of American parentage. When he was but a youth his family moved to Montreal; at the age of eighteen he crossed the Atlantic and studied art for two years. Again he visited Europe, and after a year returned with many sketches which were quickly sold. A third visit was spent in England and Scotland. Then he spent five years in France as a pupil of Pelouse at Cerney-La-Ville, and became a friend of that master. Edson had the honour of exhibiting at the Royal Academy

Lorne Pierce.

FOOTHILLS

HENRY SANDHAM

in London, the Salon in Paris and the Royal Canadian Academy of Arts of which he was a charter member. He also exhibited at the Ontario Society of Artists. Ever keen to express a practical interest in Canadian art, the Princess Louise, wife of the Marquis of Lorne, presented two of his pictures to Queen Victoria. Unhappily, a life of much promise was destined to be cut short at fruition when Edson died, in 1888, at the age of forty-two.

It will be seen that men like Fowler, Fraser, Sandham, Edson and O'Brien—unlike certain of their European contemporaries who came to Canada—were in the main water-colourists, whose aesthetic point of view had a certain influence at the time and since.

Through the establishment of the Royal Canadian Academy the National Gallery at Ottawa had its beginnings; though curiously enough for many years it gave small evidence of life. In 1907 an Order-in-Council was passed by the Dominion Government establishing an Advisory Council of Fine Arts, whose advice and assistance should be available to the Minister of Public Works in connection with the administration of the annual subsidies granted for the Gallery. The members of the Council, composed of men already known to possess sound judgment in matters of art, were Sir George Drummond, Montreal; Mr. Byron E. (later Sir Edmund) Walker, Toronto; and the Honourable Senator Boyer. Sir George died in 1909 and Dr. Francis J. Shepherd, a prominent Montreal physician, succeeded him. The chairman was Sir Edmund Walker. In 1913 the National Gallery was incorporated by Act of Parliament and placed under the management of a Board of Trustees appointed by the Governor-General in Council. Sir Edmund remained as chairman and, under his administration, the value and importance of the Gallery steadily increased. In 1916 the Trustees, realizing the remoteness of Ottawa to the rest of the country, adopted the policy of holding annual loan exhibitions in the various cities of the Dominion. In 1922 the Director, the late Eric Brown, undertook a lecture tour from Ottawa to the Pacific Coast, when he spoke on the development and strength of native Canadian art. The present members of the Board, 1942, are H. S. Southam, C.M.G., chairman; the Honourable Vincent Massey and Elwood B. Hosmer; with H. O. McCurry, director.

The relationship of Toronto to the work of the National Gallery has been very close, not only by reason of the activities of Sir Edmund Walker who, fortunately for Canadian art, possessed a breadth of culture that matched his business acumen, but because Toronto has been perhaps the most important centre of education in the arts. It is in fact noteworthy that among the artists represented in the National Gallery collection many received their earlier training at the Ontario School of Art and Design, now the Ontario College of Art. A complete list is not possible, but it would include William E. Atkinson, J. W. Beatty, Frederick H. Brigden, Frederick S. Challener, Thomas G. Greene, Frederick S. Haines, Principal of the Ontario College of Art and President (1942) of the Royal Canadian Academy, Francis H. Johnston, J. E. H.

MacDonald, T. W. Mitchell, Herbert S. Palmer, George A. Reid, Sidney Strickland Tully, A. J. Casson and Mary Evelyn Wrinch. The Gallery can now boast a collection of more than five thousand pieces, including prints. The collection is especially valuable to Canadians because almost every artist of importance in the Dominion, past and present, is represented there; though it also contains a growing number of paintings of great masters—both ancient and modern. The War Collection (1914-1918) alone has 974 items.

Hamilton Art Gallery.

THE BATHERS

BLAIR BRUCE

Apart from the organization of the Royal Academy of Arts (observes Newton MacTavish in *The Fine Arts in Canada*), the year 1880 has its further measures of significance. For it was in this year that Charles G. D. Roberts published his first volume of verse, *Orion*, and that Calixta LaVallée gave *O Canada* to the public. It might seem absurd to affirm, that the publication of the young poet's book meant as much for literature as the formation of the Academy meant for painting. But *Orion* served, nevertheless, as the clarion call of a renaissance in Canadian letters. Analogous to the Academy in effect, it was as well contemporaneous with it.

The fresh interest thus aroused probably had the effect also of bringing Canadian artists of the eighties to a realization of the rich material which lay subject to their hand. Their eyes were opened to the unexplored pictorial possibilities of the Canadian landscape—a vision which likely gained strength and impetus from the nature poetry of Charles G. D. Roberts, of Bliss Carman and of Archibald Lampman, who sang the songs of Nature and of Nature's lore with fresh, sweet voices. However that may be, following the stimulus given to Canadian art by the formation of the Ontario Society of Artists and the Royal Academy of Fine Arts, with their slow-maturing, nation-wide influence, there was set in motion the common desire, which had been crystallized by Confederation in 1867, to give Canadian art an authentic impress of its own. Canadian art students, it is true, still sought to augment the meagre and undeveloped instruction of the Canadian schools with courses in the famous ateliers of Paris and London and Antwerp; less often into those of New York and Philadelphia. Among our earlier painters who thus sought to sharpen their native talent in a foreign field were Charles Huot, Napoléon Bourassa, Blair Bruce, Paul Peel, Homer Watson, Curtis Williamson, William E. Atkinson, James Macdonald Barnsley and George Agnew Reid.

4

With improved instruction and the passage of time came change. The transition, though steady, was as yet scarcely perceptible. The dry manner of Kane and Krieghoff and their contemporaries was gradually being superseded by a style less tight, less literal and less subservient to an art convention now outworn. Instead there was to arrive, thanks to more enlightened influences from abroad, a freer technique and a broader vision more in accord with the spirit and the movement of the day. Art in Canada stood on the threshold of great and revolutionary changes. Painting was beginning to abandon the artificial atmosphere of the studio to seek the lessons that Nature herself had to teach out-of-doors. "And what became more and more apparent with each successive exhibition of paintings by Canadians was the fallacy of the contention that Canadian subjects were aesthetically unpaintable." Yet many years were to elapse before any considerable body of picture-buyers became possessed of sufficient courage and faith in their own judgment to venture upon collecting the work of Canadians. Meanwhile newspapers and periodicals, notably *The Canadian Magazine*, began to recognize and esteem such art as contributing to the highest national development. The art of individual painters was appraised and reproduced, while literary and art groups throughout the Dominion contrived to study not only the productions of "the pre-Raphaelites or the Lake Poets, but the work of the poets and painters of their own country."

Economic conditions, it must be admitted, as well as costly processes of reproduction, effectively checked any latent demand there might have been for Canadian colour prints. Neither was there any incentive to artists in pen-and-ink to produce anything apart from the exigent demands of magazine and newspaper illustration. True, *Grip*, a political and satirical weekly founded in the seventies by J. W. Bengough, opened its pages to aspiring talent. Apart, however, from Sam Hunter, a regular contributor, there were few working in black-and-white competent enough to profit by the opportunity. Nevertheless, thanks to the growing needs of an expanding commerce, lithographing and engraving-houses were providing technical schools for young draughtsmen. The appearance of the commercial engraving-house, indirectly subsidized by organized industry, was in the end to do more for Canadian painting than an art footloose and free from wholesome restrictions and a salutary discipline.

The year 1882 saw the publication of *Picturesque Canada*. Published in instalments and circulated in thousands of homes throughout Canada, its great achievement was the impression left on its readers of the rich and varied beauties of their native countryside, a feat analogous to that of the English nature poets of the late eighteenth century. Fortunately, in the reproduction of Canadian scenes the publishers were able to enlist the skill of such American artists as F. Fopkinson Smith, T. Hogan, Thomas Moran, W. T. Smedley and F. H. Schell, all men of ability who had previously been engaged on the production of *Picturesque America* and were now free to apply their talents to the production of the Canadian work, a collaboration, as it turned out, which operated to our mutual advantage; for without their aid little of a practical or permanent nature could have been accomplished. A point of particular interest is that a great number of the illustrations for

Picturesque Canada were engraved on wood from the original drawings, a process which the introduction of zinc-etching some years later was to render all but obsolete. One may venture the assertion that the publication and circulation of *Picturesque Canada* did more to kindle an interest and pride in Canadian scenery and Canadian pictorial art than any single agency up to that time. Moreover, it gave work to the Canadian painters Lucius O'Brien,

FAMILY PRAYER
GEORGE A. REID

Victoria University, Toronto.

Robert Harris, F. M. Bell-Smith, W. Raphael, Henry Sandham, J. A. Fraser and others. Altogether, more than a score of artists, American and Canadian, were employed in the illustrating of this work. Taken with the descriptive prose of Principal George Monro Grant of Queen's University, Kingston, and his editorial associates, it is hardly astonishing that there was awakened among Canadians a consciousness of the natural beauties of their own country, fresh, vernal and unspoiled. It was, we may observe, before the era of the ubiquitous billboard and the roadside gasoline station.

Opportunities for the public presentation of black-and-white work were still lamentably few. At this time, in the early eighties, the two major art bodies offered no inducement to the engraver and the artist in pen-and-ink, charcoal or crayon; consequently in September, 1886, an effort was made by A. H. Howard, designer and illuminator, in Toronto, to organize a sketch club having as one of its chief objects drawing from the living model. Organized schools of instruction at this time there were of course both in Toronto and in Hamilton; but since lessons consisted largely in drawing from the antique, that is, from the cast, under the supervision of instructors not always adequate in technical knowledge, a more advanced training was obviously needed. This education the proposed organization aimed to provide. Accordingly notices were sent out and prospective members were enjoined to bring a sketch-book. Later this somewhat informal group of earnest workers was to adopt the name of the Toronto Art Students' League.

"In beautiful accord with the traditions of Bohemia," remarks Robert Holmes in writing of the event, "no date for proposed meeting appeared in this cyclographed announcement. It seems, however, to have occurred to these people that it might be well for even them to pay some slight heed to the limitations of time and so a note reading, 'Friday next—3.30 p.m.' was afterwards appended in red ink." The meeting was held at 56 King Street East, opposite what is now the King Edward Hotel.

An authority on such matters [to quote Mr. Holmes again] has said that the rooms in which one works should not be decorated, and this was certainly above reproach in this respect. It had a little light, a little heat, a little furniture, but otherwise it was merely an enclosed space, and as guiltless of decorations as our first parents. It was up very near the sky, apparently within speaking distance of the beautiful place reserved for the final home of Art students; but the approach to it was through darkness and danger; and, as one made the ascent to it, groping his way up the tortuous and tottering stairs, with no voice to cheer and no hand to guide, it seemed as if the passage of the Styx, with Charon for pilot, would be a pleasure excursion in comparison.

Apparently the ascent on this occasion, however, was successfully negotiated not merely by Mr. Holmes himself, but also by Mr. Howard, whose name appeared on the circular. Other charter members present were J. D. Kelly, C. M. Manly, W. W. Alexander and O. R. Hughes. Although not a large meeting, it was made up of men prepared to do something, of men who recognized the value of added strength that comes from union, and saw in the union they proposed to form a better means for the pursuit of their studies than could be obtained by individual effort. The Club at once projected the formation of a life class and a composition sketch class. Meetings were held once a week. At the first gathering of each month members followed the plan of submitting their compositions for "friendly discussion and criticism." Afterwards the Club, imitating the custom of the English art club; spent the remainder of the evening in general relaxation and good cheer. For a time at least the Club got along very well with but two officers, A. H. Howard as treasurer and O. R. Hughes as secretary. The office of president seems to have been ignored or forgotten.[1] On All Fools' Day, 1887, the Club removed to a larger and better place in the Imperial Bank Chambers at the corner of Wellington Street and Leader Lane. Here the League "became healthier and slightly wealthier with each succeeding year." The new rooms were made comfortable and the surroundings more cheerful. This, the first home of the Toronto Art Students' League, afterwards became the studio of Sir Wyly Grier, R.C.A., D.C.L., and later the offices of the architects, Darling and Pearson.

Consequent upon the publicity given the League and its activities, new members were added, of whom David F. Thomson, Fred H. Brigden, W. D. Blatchly, C. W. Jefferys, W. J. Thomson and J. D. Kelly were among the most active. Soon after, women were admitted to membership, including Gertrude Spurr, later Mrs. W. Spurr Cutts, A.R.C.A., Henrietta Hancock, later Mrs. Harry Britton, and Mary Wrinch, A.R.C.A., later Mrs. G. A. Reid.

"It is inevitable," observes Charles W. Jefferys in one of his talks on Canadian art, "that a country with such strongly marked physical characteristics as Canada possesses should impress itself forcefully upon our artists. One can see in the work of our earliest painters, whether native born or adopted sons of the country, the fascination of Canadian landscape." To the influence of this

---

[1]Evidently the members later thought it well to conform to convention, for the catalogue of an exhibition held by the League at Roberts' Art Gallery, King Street West in 1896, records the "officers for the current year" as follows: President, R. Holmes; Vice-President, F. H. Brigden; Corresponding Secretary, Miss G. E. Spurr; Recording Secretary, J. Willson; and Treasurer, Miss H. Hancock.

fascination the members of the Toronto Art Students' League were extraordinarily susceptible.

As has been said, the Toronto Art Students' League, in 1886, was organized at a meeting called by A. H. Howard, "an accomplished designer and a man of wide culture." Many of the members have since won wide recognition in the arts. W. W. Alexander, still living, specialized in etching and, with W. J. Thomson, was to found, in 1916, the Society of Canadian Painter-Etchers. Indeed, on the score of personal achievement alone, Thomson deserves a chapter by himself. Whilst a student at the Toronto Art School he studied water-colour painting under John A. Fraser, R.C.A. In 1885, the year of the North West Rebellion, he was one of a group of Canadian artists to form the Toronto Etching Society, which included in its membership: W. J. Thomson, W. H. Howland, T. Mower Martin, William Cruikshank and Arthur Cox. In the following year the Society sponsored one of the finest international exhibitions of prints ever to be shown in Toronto. But with a small membership, it was not possible to fill the walls with the work of members alone and it was found necessary to make good the deficiency with a showing of prints by Rembrandt, Seymour Hayden, S. Parrish, Thomas Moran, and others. Opening on the day the local troops were mobilized to set out for the scene of the rebellion the gallery rooms were completely deserted. The deficit which faced the sponsors was so large as effectually to discourage for a time any similar venture, and eventually Thomson was the only one producing any plates of consequence. When, at the turn of the century the daily press began illustrating the news, Thomson joined the staff of the Toronto *Globe* as staff artist. It was not until many years later, or during the first World War, that another revival of etching led to the formation of the Society of Canadian Painter-Etchers, of which he became the first president.

Though probably not appreciated at his true worth by the casual collector, the more discerning connoisseur eagerly sought Thomson's work, and among the public collections which have been enriched by his characteristic prints are the National Gallery at Ottawa and the Art Gallery of Toronto. During the war of 1914-1918, when there was a shortage of metals for munitions, Thomson donated a large batch of his old etched copper plates to the melting-pot to be converted into cartridge and shell cases. In 1927, just

AT PORT UNION

Quebec—Along the Grand Battery

At Springfield

Fort George—Niagara

SUMMER SKETCHING.

SKETCHES BY MEMBERS OF THE TORONTO ART LEAGUE

[From *The Canadian Magazine*, December, 1894.]

before the opening of the spring exhibition of the Painter-Etchers, he died. During his lifetime his work had been shown in the United States and Canada, and at the Wembley Exhibition, England, in 1926. His work, notable chiefly for its great versatility and variety of subject, is treated with ease and grace and spontaneity; proving indubitably his mastery of his medium.

Manly was from the first the moving spirit in the composition class of the newly-formed Art Students' League, and the week-end sketching trips were largely under his direction. W. D. Blatchly, the lithographic artist, also a capable water-colour painter, was a regular student. His intense British prejudice, and his keen appreciation of English humour as displayed in the pages of *Punch*, made him an agreeable insurgent and entertaining companion. Edmund Morris, later co-founder of the Canadian Art Club, was for a time a member of the League, as were also T. G. Greene, a painter of life and scenery in rural Ontario and a bit of a recluse, Sam Jones, who designed stained glass windows at McCausland's, John Cotton, internationally known for his exquisite aquatints, R. Weir Crouch, designer, and D. A. McKellar, the poet-artist, who died in early manhood. When not teaching at the Ontario College of Art, William Cruikshank enlivened proceedings at the League with his dry Scot's wit, often more caustic than kind. Robert Holmes displayed unusual artistic skill and love of the outdoors, which has resulted in a collection of flower paintings as faithful in botanical accuracy as they are remarkable for their beauty of colour and design. Holmes had much to do with the prosperity of the League, and with the atmosphere of good-fellowship which accounted in part for its relatively long life.

Another outstanding member was Charles W. Jefferys,[1] who has since risen to a high place in Canadian art. The vitality of his drawings was an example to the younger members who strove to imitate his style. His intense Canadian spirit, "which sought to discover the real nature of our landscape," made him the first to preach the doctrine of the pine and the spruce as themes fit for the painter. If there is anything in the theory that Canada has developed an art expression peculiar to this country, we must consider Jefferys as one of the very first to initiate the movement. The publicity attending the anniversary of Confederation, as well

[1]See *Charles W. Jefferys*, *R.C.A.*, *LL.D.*, by William Colgate, in The Canadian Art Series, The Ryerson Press, Toronto.

as the more recent publication of his pictorial history of Canada, has drawn forcibly to the attention of Canadians the extraordinarily valuable and permanent contribution he has made to the history of their country through his richly documented drawings and paintings.

So far as is known, the Toronto Art Students' League was the first organization of its kind to work in the interests of the graphic arts by conducting life classes, by holding exhibitions periodically and by illustrating publications issued by its members. It was an important and ambitious undertaking, worthily supported. Consciously or unconsciously the League strove to realize a Canadian ideal in interpreting the life of the country around it. As their work clearly indicates, the members of the League believed wholeheartedly in the primary importance of drawing. They subscribed, apparently, to the tenet that a fine drawing is one in which an infinity of observation is expressed with perfect manual dexterity. Without omitting their duty to the present, they studied reverently the drawings of the old masters, no matter of what school, and aimed at fine draughtsmanship, in contradistinction to the modern school which seems to have abandoned all idea of fine draughtsmanship. One of the more important books closely studied by the members of the League was *Pen Drawing and Pen Draughtsman: Their Work and Their Methods: A Study of the Art of Today*, by Joseph Pennell. This volume, first issued in 1894, reproduced drawings from Durer to Howard Pyle, and contained "interesting, thoughtful criticism of the more important pen artists and illustrators." *Le dessin est la probité de l'art* is an axiom which present-day artists overlook to their peril. We may be sure that if the artist chooses to forget, the public will not: and no group of Canadian artists was ever more seized with the vital necessity of sound drawing than the members of the League, who did so much to preach and practise that gospel and to inspire with its wisdom those who followed them.

Impetus had previously been given to the development of black-and-white drawing when, in 1885, was organized the Toronto Etching Society, a group of ten Canadian artists, of whom William J. Thomson was the prime mover. About this time also George A. Reid and his wife, Mary Wrinch, opened a studio on the site of the present King Edward Hotel in Toronto. They had recently returned to Toronto from Philadelphia, where they had pursued studies in drawing and painting at the Pennsylvania Academy of Design, under Thomas Eakins. Here in their newly-opened quarters they kept open house for Toronto's young art students; and by furnishing them with a room and a model kept the youthful artistic flame alive. In a social way also they offered a cordial welcome, with gracious and informal hospitality and relaxation, and also the valuable discipline which regular and supervised study enforced. At this time Canadian art possessed a dual character: it safeguarded the past with an eye to the future. It was too much of its own time, perhaps, to cherish historical retrospection or an archæological outlook. Under the awakening and stimulating influence of the French impressionists, Manet, Monet, Sisley and Renoir, and the inspiration of the English and American line illustrators, George du Maurier, Randolph Caldecott, Edmund J. Sullivan, Claude Shepperson, Edwin Abbey, Howard Pyle, C.S. Reinhart, A. B. Frost, members of the Toronto Art Students' League gradually discarded the outworn conventions of an earlier day; they became free, natural and spontaneous. Canadian artists experienced a renaissance of good taste and good style. Their erudition and professional equipment were simple, almost meagre, but the exigencies of their work led to a profounder knowledge of themselves, and this knowledge inevitably pointed the way to a higher form of achievement. So it happened that the change, gradual as it was, may almost be said to have adumbrated the rise of a new school founded on similar principles thirty years later.

In the meantime the Toronto Art Students' League flourished. It grew in vision and stature. New members were added to the roster, among them William Bengough, a much more competent draughtsman than his brother, John W. Bengough, the cartoonist, and Arthur C. Goode, who with A. A. Martin left for London, England, at the turn of the century to found the Carlton Studio, a group of commercial illustrators founded upon the rapid rise of newspaper and magazine advertising. Norman Price, now prominent as an illustrator and magazine cover designer in the United States, and J. E. H. MacDonald, who became one of the original members of the Group of Seven, were to join the League later. The earlier cover designs for the League *Calendars* had been furnished by A. H. Howard; they were notable for their elegance, restraint and beauty of form, as were also those of R. Weir Crouch at a somewhat later date. The motto of the League, selected by

47

NULLA DIES SINE LINEA—NOTEBOOK SKETCHES

[From *The Canadian Magazine*, December, 1894]

MEMBERS OF THE TORONTO ART LEAGUE

Robert Holmes, the Latinist of the group, *Non Clamor Sed Amor*, was fairly indicative of the character of the members, who were more avid for good work than loud acclaim. Serious and ardent, they felt justly enough that if the work was sound, both approval and praise would naturally follow.

Much of the spare time of the members of the League was spent in the out-of-doors exploring the countryside for material for sketches, which when found would be translated to canvas or paper through the medium of pencil, pen-and-ink and colour. Saturday afternoons and Sundays would be devoted to such excursions since the members were precluded by the necessity of earning a livelihood from venturing out at other times. It was the day before the motor car, and the bicycle craze had not yet arrived, so that sketching was usually and necessarily confined to the near-by suburban areas, such as the valley of the Don, Rosedale Ravine, Richmond Hill, the valley of the Humber, Weston, Port Credit (with its fishing harbour), Cooksville, Unionville and Springfield (now Erindale) with their winding roads and flowering orchards, ploughed lands and cattle, all of which were fertile in subject matter, varied with occasional trips across Lake Ontario to Queenston and the Niagara Peninsula. When midsummer came around, members of the League would wander farther afield, where the changing beauties of Canadian hill and dale and stream took them as far east as Quebec and even to the ancient marshes of Nova Scotia. Much of the spoils thus acquired subsequently found a circulation far beyond club walls, when the sketches and drawings of the summer solstice appeared in the pages of the *Toronto Art League Calendar* issued yearly from 1893 to 1904.

Among the chief contributors to the Calendar were: Robert Holmes, noted for the beauty and fidelity of his floral studies; J. D. Kelly, landscape and historical painter; Duncan A. McKellar, who went to New York with Peter McArthur to engage in illustrating for magazines and there was to die, a comparatively young man; W. D. Blatchly, water-colourist; C. M. Manly, a pen-and-ink draughtsman and water-colourist and later instructor at the Ontario College of Art and Design; and Charles W. Jefferys, a young artist whose clever, even brilliant, work in pen-and-ink and wash was soon to make him widely known as a draughtsman of rare ability. At this time Jefferys was working as an apprentice with the Toronto Lithographing Company, engravers and lithographers, where he early evinced a natural bent toward linear design. This ability and training stood him in good stead when later he was sent to various points throughout Ontario to sketch bird's-eye views of cities, industrial plants and commercial buildings to adorn business stationery and the rather stereotyped and false-front advertising of the day.

Tiring of the local scene to which he was more than ordinarily habituated, and grown somewhat weary of a monotonous round of repetitive duties, young Jefferys, like so many other Canadians of his time, quitted Canada for the States to seek work as an illustrator. He wanted particularly to illustrate for magazines like *Harper's* and the *Century*, as Sandham had done before him and other Canadian artists were to do later. Soon he was engaged on the art staff of *The New York Herald*, haunting police courts and pursuing ambulances to the scene of accidents; for it was before the day of the press camera and rapid processes of engraving. In Chicago, where he was sent on an assignment for his newspaper, he had some exciting and amusing experiences and added appreciably to his capacity as a rapid sketch artist. The railway strike of 1893 was on, and he had plenty of opportunity to extend his skill and reputation. To C. W. Jefferys as much as anyone was due the long life and useful activities of the Toronto Art League, to whose *Calendars* he continued to contribute during his stay in New York; and to him is also largely due that independence of mind and outlook which gave impetus and direction to the movement, then gaining in strength, toward a Canadian art that was to discover Canada anew.

Another member of the League at that time, whose work was to become a pride and an example to others, was David F. Thomson, probably the finest pen-and-ink artist Canada has yet produced. A pioneer and a gifted painter in water-colours of the north country, his genius as a black-and-white draughtsman is clearly and charmingly manifest in the pages of successive Art League *Calendars* to which he was a regular and prolific contributor. But Thomson, like Jefferys, heard the siren call, and no consideration of local ties or patriotic sentiment was to prevent his going to the United States. He eventually joined the art staff of the Forbes Lithographing Company of Boston, where he has been steadily engaged for the past forty years. His departure was a loss which Canada could ill afford. Such men as these had much to do with shaping

Lorne Pierce.

THE SURVEYORS, 1793

[From the Toronto Art League Calendar, 1898]

DAVID F. THOMSON

a Canadian art movement as we were to know later, but were forced by economic reasons to forsake their native land to live and work elsewhere. Fortunately for this country, if not for himself, Jefferys returned to Canada to influence through the years the younger generation of creative artists by his knowledge, his teaching and, most of all, by his example.

5

Before leaving the subject of the Toronto Art League, we might give some attention to the series of *Calendars* it published each year from 1893 to 1904. Copies of these, incidentally, are now rare items in Canadiana, and a complete set is almost impossible to find. The idea of a yearly calendar took definite form in 1892; early in December of that year the first one of twenty-four pages was issued, with the inscription *Ninety-Three* on its lithographed cover of pale blue and gold. There were twelve pages of drawings and designs, illustrations of the Canadian seasons and the life of the Canadian people, contributed by members of the League; on opposite pages appeared appropriate selections of Canadian verse. *Ninety-Four* followed in due course, larger and more lavish of picture and poem; and *Ninety-Five* proved in every respect a worthy successor to its fellows of the previous years, striking the same chords and bringing out a like harmony. The cover design by A. H. Howard, R.C.A., is in a delicate and graceful scheme of red and yellow greys relieved with white and gold. These contained drawings depicting various phases of Canadian life and scenery. The issue of 1895, for example, was devoted in drawings and verse to a portrayal of the Canadian seasons. Excerpts from the writings of Charles G. D. Roberts, E. Pauline Johnson, Charles Sangster, Duncan Campbell Scott, Charles Heavysege, Bliss Carman and William Wilfred Campbell serve to complement the various illustrations done in wash as well as the customary pen-and-ink. *Ninety-Six* of the same decade contained "Wayside Notes of Wanderings over Canadian Roads by members of the Toronto Art Students' League," as well as verses by Roberts and Carman. The title-page set forth that it was "designed and published by the

Toronto Art Students' League, 75 Adelaide Street East, Toronto, Canada." The keynote of the number is struck by Bliss Carman's "The Deep-Hollow Road," and since it is one of his lesser-known lyrics, it is reprinted here:

> Cool in the summer mountain's heart,
>   It lies in dim mysterious shade,
> Left of the highway turning in
>   With grassy rut and easy grade.
>
> The marshes and the sea behind,
>   The solemn fir-blue hills before;
> Here is the inn for Heavy-heart,
>   And this is weary Free-foot's door.
>
> You hear? That's master thrush. He knows
>   The voluntaries fit for June,
> ' And when to falter on the flute
>   In the satiety of noon.
>
> A mile or two we follow in
>   This rosy streak through forest gloom,
> Then for the apple orchard slopes
>   And all the earth one snowy bloom.

A fine sympathetic pen-and-ink illustration by C. W. Jefferys seems to exhale the very fragrance of the poet's thoughts. Further unity is achieved by the hand-lettered text done with grace and freedom, without, as so often happens, sacrifice of legibility. Throughout the entire series of *Calendars* this illustrated poem remains a memorable contribution, fit, I think, to take its place with anything shown.

The *Ninety-Eight* calendar, printed in red and black, is illustrated with "some drawings suggestive of the everyday life of the past in Canada." A significant change may be noted here: "Students" is dropped from the title. It is now the Toronto Art League. An effective cover design, consisting of a formalized maple tree against a rising sun in red, is by R. Weir Crouch. One of the chief contributors to this issue is C. W. Jefferys, who decorates the calendar proper with diminutive drawings of homely utilities of house and field and farm, and displays as a contrasting theme an illustrative title-page in which Indians and early French settlers are portrayed engaged in active combat with all the decorative pattern of a Bayeux tapestry. Thus early did the artist indicate his preoccupation with things historic.

One of the finest illustrations in colour, composition and design is the full-page pen-and-ink drawing by D. F. Thomson, entitled THE SURVEY PARTY, suggested by the "Field Notes of Mr. Augustus Jones, the principal surveyor in the country from 1792 onward." We have but to look at this drawing and others by the artist to receive a great impression of distinction. Here is pure line work with all the effect of a painting in tone and colour. In this highly sensitive picture, in which every stroke of the pen is made to count, the drawing of the detail, often more suggestive than actual, is done with evident pleasure to the artist. It has the breadth of style and the calligraphic ease which distinguishes the work of the masters. Throughout, the drawing is intensely expressive. Obviously, too, there is enjoyment in the actual touch of pen to paper which was always characteristic of Thomson and is always special to great art. It is like the touch of a sympathetic musician. It is line drawing at its best—spontaneous, free, delightful, but with the effect of each detail carefully studied and fore-ordained, we may be sure, so that each line, form and shadow falls into place with the smoothness and inevitability of a well-ordered design. Here is natural thought, wedded to natural skill and close observation. A sign of the presence of fine art is the accommodation of style to theme. The drawings of Thomson have the faculty of seeming contemporaneous with the subjects they depict. In his emotional use of light and shade he imparted to his black-and-white drawings much of the charm and refined feeling by which they still attract and instruct the student.

Other notable drawings in the *Ninety-Eight* calendar are: OUT FROM THE FOREST, by C. M. Manly; THE OLD HORSE BOAT ON TORONTO BAY, by W. Bengough, in which crayon and pen-and-ink are skilfully blended; *1837*, by C. W. Jefferys, showing a squad of rebels drilling in a secluded field with pikes and ancient muskets; EARLY SETTLERS CLEARING LAND, by F. H. Brigden, in which, it must be confessed, there is little to forecast the mastery of the later Brigden; THE TRAPPER, by John Cotton; and A CHRISTMAS PARTY, by D. F. Thomson, who painted water-colours of the north country worthy to rank with those of his successor, Tom Thomson.

With the advent of the calendar for *Nineteen Hundred* there is evident a notable advance in the quality of the drawings shown. This issue is described as "A Canadian Calendar for the Year, with

PLACID WATERS: NORTHERN ONTARIO [1907]

DAVID F. THOMSON

notes and pictured things, suggesting the impress of the Century on the land and its people." The cover design, in pale blue and sepia, by R. Weir Crouch, employs the white trilium as the main floral motif. Prophetic as well as retrospective are the contents of this issue: THE GOLDEN NORTH, 1900, and THE MINES, 1900, by Jefferys; HISTORY AND PROGRESS, by C. M. Manly, depicting the Old Fort, Toronto, against a background of factory chimneys; THE DESERTED RACE, showing a herd of buffalo ranging the western plains, and THE ROUND-UP, both by F. H. Brigden; THE SAW MILL, by D. F. Thomson; THE PLANTING OF THE ORCHARD; AN OLD HOMESTEAD, NOVA SCOTIA, by W. D. Blatchly; THE KING'S HIGHWAY and THE QUEEN'S HIGHWAY, by D. F. Thomson; TRANSPORTATION, 1900, by C. M. Manly; THE IMMIGRANTS OF 1830 AND 1900, by C. W. Jefferys; WINTER FASHIONS, MONTREAL, by Brigden, completes the toll.

Canadian village life formed the theme of the *Toronto Art League Calendar* for 1901, with numerous illustrations better on the whole than any which had hitherto appeared. The quality of the pen-work displayed had steadily, and, it would seem, consistently, improved. Robert Holmes was showing an increasing interest in flowers as decoration, as is evidenced by the title-page. A centre panel depicts an old clapboard house of the early nineteenth century. Within an open doorway the figure of a woman stands half in shadow. Wooden steps divide a garden plot in which sunflowers form a large part of the design. The effect of afternoon sunshine upon the walls of the house and upon the garden is enchanting in its directness and simplicity, far surpassing in exquisite craftsmanship and beauty any previous essay of the artist. Within the side panels, against a background of red, dandelions and maple branches form a pleasant pattern. A scroll at the top of the design contains a lettered inscription; unfortunately neither scroll nor letter are happily conceived or competently executed. Somehow the work of the League was nowhere so deficient as in its lettering; and it must be admitted that contemporary artists in black-and-white do little better. Handlettering still remains the bane of the ordinary commercial designer. But if the lettering was sometimes weak, the drawings themselves were faithful documents of Ontario's fast vanishing village life. To fidelity to fact was added beauty and delight in transcription.

To this issue of 1901 D. F. Thomson contributes A LAKE

WESTON FROM ACROSS THE VALLEY

[From the Toronto Art League Calendar, 1901]

FRED H. BRIGDEN

ONTARIO FISHING VILLAGE, said to be a winter scene at Port Credit, and THE RAILROAD STATION, of which the old wooden station, the adjacent water tower and the horse-drawn bus form the chief elements of the composition. Scattered by a vagrant breeze, snow sifts from the roof of tower and station, as the hotel bus that meets all trains, mounted on runners, plunges through the mounting drifts, laden with passengers and luggage. The locality might be Listowel or Brussels, or indeed any of the wayside towns along the route of the old Grand Trunk in the nineties. Fragrant memories of old-time village life are vividly recalled by THE CHURCH SOCIABLE, another pen-and-ink drawing by Thomson, in which the artist has admirably caught the spirit of wholesome fun and infectious gaiety which animates the scene. The composition as a whole lacks the element of contrast, as well as that elimination of non-essential details, which give point and emphasis to Thomson's view of a pine-studded hillside under snow on the opposite page. Something of this artist's masterly handling of the pen is seen in Fred Brigden's WESTON FROM ACROSS THE VALLEY, THE POST OFFICE, THE PRINTING SHOP (showing the interior of an old-time weekly newspaper office) and ACROSS THE FIELDS, which he has drawn with skill and feeling. The technique of W. W. Alexander provides further evidence of an improved draughtsmanship, which normally derives from a close association with others similarly engaged. In CHÂTEAU RICHER, QUEBEC, and in A FRENCH CANADIAN VILLAGE SCHOOL, a vista of a winding waterside street, with beached boats and clustering houses, we discern the studied placement of "colour" and whites to form a picture lifelike and agreeable. However much it may be influenced by others, the style is indisputably that of William Alexander, sympathetic, flexible and imbued with the spirit of confident craftsmanship. C. M. Manly's drawings, UP THE HILL TO SPRINGFIELD, and THE YARD OF THE MONUMENT INN AT QUEENSTON, are likewise examples of free, accurate and intelligent draughtsmanship. Possibly, in parts at least, Manly errs on the side of over-elaboration of detail; but his work is almost invariably characterized by careful handling and good taste. ST. ANTOINE, RICHELIEU RIVER, QUEBEC, and SUNDAY MORNING, IN A FRENCH CANADIAN VILLAGE, by C. W. Jefferys are, as might be expected, admirable, displaying as they do sound drawing and a fine feeling for line and colour. His grey harmonies are enlivened with accents of black and medium tones imparting to his drawings a distinction which proves him to be a close observer and inspired interpreter rather than an imitator of nature. It thus requires no special acuteness to perceive in the artist in black-and-white the sensitive perceptions of the colourist. An excessive use of red as contrast throughout the *Calendar* mars

A FRENCH-CANADIAN VILLAGE SCHOOL

[From the Toronto Art League Calendar, 1901]

W. W. Alexander

perceptibly what is otherwise an exceptionally creditable production.

A manifest tendency toward decoration, over-elaboration of statement and a fussiness of format detracts from the favourable first impression of the 1904 *Calendar*, which is notable chiefly for the introduction of several new and important contributors, as well as for its attempt to portray "some of the characteristic landscape features of Canada." A. A. Martin furnishes a page drawing of a snow-laden pine branch treated decoratively; and Arthur C. Goode's CASTLE MOUNTAIN IN THE ROCKIES is a free, spirited drawing, notable in style and arrangement.   Other new-

UP THE HILL TO SPRINGFIELD

From the Toronto Art League Calendar, 1901]

C. M. MANLY

comers to the 1904 *Calendar* are Thomas G. Greene and Norman Price, who are made conspicuous by good work.   Greene's pen-and-ink drawing, HARVESTING, CENTRAL ONTARIO, reveals a genuine knowledge of natural forms and is marked by freedom, breadth and vigour. The cloudy sky, always a difficult subject, is particularly well handled in its suggestion of grey amorphous masses in motion and delicately modulated tones. Norman Price's FRUIT FARM IN THE NIAGARA PENINSULA, and a smaller panel untitled, are distinguished by their *plein-air* atmosphere

HARVESTING, CENTRAL ONTARIO
[From the Toronto Art League Calendar, 1904]
THOS. G. GREENE

and sense of the artist's intense enjoyment in the landscape forms. Price's line admirably suggests the force and swirl of the wind and the delicacy of a calm, contemplative setting: the broad definition of form and the realism that is felt rather than seen. In all his work, there is a tender grace of line and form, a quality, however, most exquisitely expressed in D. F. Thomson's drawings,

of which the present issue contains one of his most typical [in ON
THE LOWER ST. LAWRENCE, depicting a delightful spring morning
with apple orchards in blossom, the river and a church steeple in the
middle ground, and dark wooded hills in the distance. The soft air of
June can be felt in one's face, while resilient to the foot is the fresh,

THE ST. LAWRENCE BETWEEN MONTREAL AND QUEBEC

[From the Toronto Art League Calendar, 1904]

CHARLES W. JEFFERYS

young turf. With something more than superficial cleverness the
artist has suggested the poetry and the jocund essence of springtime. A rare emotional expressiveness gives live to the beautiful
drawing by C. W. Jefferys, THE ST. LAWRENCE BETWEEN MON-
TREAL AND QUEBEC. Here is broad and simple composition, with
a unity of impression and the vitality of draughtsmanship that
makes this artist's work so interesting and distinctive.

So the series of Art League *Calendars* comes to an end, and the League itself, figuratively, if not literally, goes out in a blaze of glory. Nevertheless, the League has left to us a legacy of fine work and a worthy tradition. Both were to be carried on, as we shall see, by similar organizations to which it gave birth. Meanwhile, it may be remarked in passing that a salient feature of illustrative drawings of the present day is, that design, pattern and decoration are seemingly of more importance as pictorial motives than dramatic or poetic expression. With the illustrators of the eighties and nineties it was of course otherwise. Expression came first, yet design was always present, controlling emotion unobtrusively. Comparison is suggested as a means of proving this point. An older generation will need no such confirmation.

One thing which undoubtedly helped the members of the League in their endeavours to perfect their skill was their practice of making each day produce its sketch: *Nulla dies sine linea* was their motto; and it is on record that they lived up to it.

The art of Upper Canada had by now attained a continuous existence of nearly seventy years. That it was not wholly Canadian is true. Other races had unconsciously assisted in its development. Purely native painters in the past had been, as in 1905, a sparse minority. Their day, however, was dawning. To review briefly, at this stage, the successive movements leading up to the revolutionary changes in art which were to come with the close of the Victorian era would doubtless prove interesting and perhaps instructive.

It was not, indeed, until after the turn of the century that the application of the graphic arts to industrial design and the development of advertising illustration began to be at all noticeable. Prior to this period such publications as the *Canadian Magazine*, revived in 1893, and *Massey's Magazine*, with which it was subsequently merged, also the *Canadian Illustrated News*, the *Dominion Illustrated Monthly*, the weekly *Globe* and the Toronto *Saturday Night* gave employment to our artists and commercial designers. During the early nineties the inception of the new movement was first felt, and illustrations and designs by such men as A. H. Howard, Arthur Heming, C. W. Jefferys, Fred H. Brigden, A. C. Goode, John Innes and H. W. Murchison found place in our periodical literature. From the magazines and newspapers to the advertising pages of these publications was but a brief transition,

FISH SHANTIES AT BRONTE

J. E. H. MacDonald

Thoreau MacDonald

and with the growing use of advertising the services of the artist became progressively enlarged, until today the combined earnings of the artist and the commercial illustrator, usually attached to an engraving house or, as often happens, working on his own, represent an expenditure of many thousands of dollars yearly. Naturally,

with the constant employment of the artist has come a greater
mastery of his mediums, and an enhanced skill far surpassing in
both quality and execution the sometimes crude and often mediocre
work of the eighties and nineties.   Canadian graphic art, it will be
seen, has come into its own and need not shrink from comparison
with similar work elsewhere.

But in the field of industrial design there was and still is vast
room for improvement as the mediocre quality of many of our

National Gallery of Canada.

WINTER IN THE CITY

LAWREN HARRIS

present-day commodities attest.   In mechanical construction
design has improved greatly, as witness for instance the motor car.
But in furniture, silverware, textiles, lamps, fireplaces, pottery,
small houses and similar things of common utility there is still
evident an unreasoning devotion to ornate and often ugly forms.
In only one department is there a noticeable rapprochement
successfully accomplished between the designer and the machine,

and that is in printing. This point I shall discuss later at some length.

The founding of the Ontario Society of Artists, in 1872, and the Royal Canadian Academy, in 1879, were each to mark a decisive step in the annals of Canadian art, as in a restricted sense did the Toronto Art Students' League whose formation in the middle eighties was to impart new life and vigour to local art. The League had a life of almost twenty years—from 1886 to 1904. During this period some of the nation's most prominent artists were at one time members of it. Its formation, of course, was suggested by the Art Students' League of New York; but unlike that organization it never developed into a purely teaching institution and was not conceived from the first on so elaborate a scale. Yet its influence was widely felt, so much so that it is doubtful if any similar organization in Canada, not excepting the Ontario Society of Artists, or the Academy, has to its credit such a beneficial and lasting effect upon Canadian art as had the Art Students' League of Toronto during its lifetime and for some years after.

Offshoots or lineal descendants of the League were numerous. Among the most notable were the Mahlstick Club, the Little Billee Club and the Graphic Arts Club. These were in reality nothing more than studio clubs designed to bring the members together in drawing and sketching classes, and dues were merely enough to cover model fees and incidental expenses. The Mahlstick Club, which had rooms in the St. James Building at the south-west corner of Adelaide and Church Streets, later removed to 75 Adelaide Street East, near the old General Post Office. An invitation card, printed to resemble birch-bark and bearing an illustration by Arthur C. Goode of an Indian drawing, a design on a bearskin, urges the members in Hiawathian metre to:

> Sling the ink and war-paint,
> To our Pow-wow bring this totem.

Since the notice is of the "3rd Annual Exhibition," and the date is "May 5, '02," we may safely assume that the organization of the Club took place in 1899, the last year of the old century. A number of the members of the Toronto Art League, it seems, were also affiliated with the Mahlstick Club, among them Robert Holmes, Fred Brigden, Charles Jefferys, J. W. Beatty, A. A. Martin, T. G. Greene, D. F. Thomson and W. W. Alexander. Other members were T. W. McLean, J. E. H. MacDonald, W. Wallace, Fred S. Haines, A. H. Robson (artist and author), Norman Price and Neil McKechnie. McKechnie lost his life while canoeing with T. W. McLean and three friends on the Metagami River; the canoe struck a rock in the rapids and McKechnie, who was unable to swim, drowned. All five men were spending a vacation in the Northland, acting meanwhile as government fire-rangers. Strangely enough, a tragedy in the same region was to claim the life of another artist, Tom Thomson, some years later.

The activities of the Mahlstick Club included drawing from the model (either nude or in costume) three evenings a week and a composition class on Saturday evenings. Frequently the life and costume classes were varied by the introduction of memory drawing and fifteen-minute sketches from the model. J. W. Beatty and J. E. H. MacDonald attended the composition class occasionally, probably during 1901. Martin, Greene and Price then proceeded to England for further study, while Goode went to New York and Maguire married and moved to Winnipeg. About 1903 the Club, having served its purpose and having lost most of its members, closed its doors at 75 Adelaide Street East and ceased to function.

S. H. Howard, son of A. H. Howard, R.C.A., and formerly a writer on the Toronto *Daily Star*, attended the composition classes quite regularly, but *wrote* while the others drew. William Wallace, who had been a staff artist on *Saturday Night*, went to England at the same time as Martin, Greene and Price, who were to found the Carlton Studio of London, of which Martin and Wallace in course of time became sole owners and remain so to this day. Arthur Goode soon tired of New York and left to join the London group, later joining the advertising department of the London *Times*. Goode died some years ago of a heart attack while swimming. He was not only a perfect swimmer, but a finished boxer, and boxed regularly with John Scholes, of Toronto, prior to Scholes' winning the world's amateur championship.

Throughout the lifetime of the Mahlstick Club it was customary, following the composition class on Saturday nights, to hold a sing-song and assault-at-arms. Boxing, fencing and sometimes singlesticks made up the impromptu programme. Since there were no shower-baths available, one was improvised by having one of the members stand on a chair and sprinkle the perspiring athlete with a watering-can. There must have been good plaster in the old building, for there were never any complaints from below. Finally the doubtful conveniences of a somewhat decrepit building were enhanced by the installation of a jerky, slow-moving elevator; but it availed little. With the passage of the years the old building has since gone the way of many another losing venture; and the space where it once was is now a parking lot. In the olden days all the members' bicycles were parked in the lower hall.

For several years the Mahlstick Club held annual exhibitions. A fair number of persons laboriously climbed the four flights of stairs, whether for the sake of art or the Bohemian hand-out, the members never knew; but it is extremely doubtful if any sales were ever made. Criticism among the members of the season's work, followed by an informal hour or two of singing, reciting and story-telling, with refreshments, was about the nearest thing to the atmosphere of the Latin Quarter the artists of the time were able to achieve. The Club went out of existence, or was resolved into the Graphic Arts Club, about 1903.

During this brief period [in 1898] a smaller art organization was formed, obviously inspired by du Maurier's *Trilby*. This was the Little Billee Sketch Club, which met over McConkey's restaurant, King Street West, on the site of the present Canadian Bank of Commerce. It included among its membership Fred S. Haines, Dalton Brown, Edward Laur, T. G. Greene, Fergus Kyle, Bert Sloan, Neil McKechnie, A. C. Goode, Norman Price, Carl Beal, William Wallace, A. A. Martin, J. E. H. MacDonald and John Conacher, who afterwards went to New York where he worked on *Life* and *Judge* and made drawings in the manner of Charles Keene. The life of the Club was very brief, probably not more than two years.

At this time also the Royal Canadian Academy conducted what was known as the Academy life class, in rooms over the old Princess Theatre, King Street West, in quarters occupied by the Ontario School of Art and Design, now the Ontario College of Art. The building has since been demolished by the extension of University Avenue from Queen to Front Streets.

Following the demise of the Mahlstick Club, the Graphic Arts Club came into existence. It may be said to stem directly from the Toronto Art League, from which it gained much of its first membership. Organized about 1904, it had amongst its founder-members such well-known artists as Charles W. Jefferys, later president, J. W. Beatty, T. W. Mitchell, J. D. Kelly, Ivor Lewis, Walter Duff, T. G. Greene, Robert Holmes, F. H. Brigden, T. W. McLean, C. M. Manly, Neil McKechnie, and A. H. Robson, who held the office of president for fourteen years. At first the members of the new organization met in different studios, but subsequently they engaged rooms on Melinda Street, immediately behind the *Telegram* building, and were there during the great fire of April, 1904.

Life classes at this time were not carried on; in fact, the Graphic Arts was then much of a social club. D. F. Thomson had by this time gone to Boston to join the art staff of the Forbes Lithographing Company, and W. D. Blatchly, who had been active in the older organization, died before the members moved in. Later the Club removed to 70 Victoria Street, thence to the Yonge Street Arcade, and then to the Lombard Building, next the morgue. There followed a series of migrations to quarters in the Arts and Letters Club, Elm Street, to the south-eastern corner of Lombard and Victoria, and finally to Tom Greene's studio in Grenville Street.

From the Royal Canadian Academy the Club was able to procure a grant for the purpose of conducting a life class, which it did during its tenancy in Lombard Street. The class was continued until the grant was revoked when the Club moved to a private studio, thereby breaking the agreement under which the grant was conceded. Later members of the Club included: Ivor Lewis, H. W. Cooper, J. E. Sampson, L. A. C. Panton, Eric Heathcote, Malcolm Gibson, F. S. Challener, S. S. Finlay, Arthur Gresham, Gersham Campbell, Darby Moore, Leo Butler, David Balfour, Harold McCrae, Lorne K. Smith, Laura Gibson, Aubrey Liversedge, Stanley Turner, Frank Carmichael, Arthur Lismer, Robert Johnston, Franz Johnston and many others down to the present day. A list of every artist of note who at one time or another has been a member would be too long to include here.

As the Canadian Society of Graphic Arts, a name it had used for some years, it was incorporated in 1933. But the old club spirit never survived the incorporation, and almost the only function now left to it is that of exhibiting the members' work, which now has a much more important place than formerly. Exhibiting at regular intervals public and private exhibitions of the members' work, the original Graphic Arts Club resembled the Pen and Pencil Club of Montreal, though its membership perhaps was not so rigidly confined to those artists who had acquired public recognition. Today the Canadian Society of Graphic Arts has a membership that literally extends from Halifax to Victoria. In fact, almost two-thirds of the total membership live outside Toronto.

ON THE DON: TORONTO
W. F. G. GODFREY

Ivor Lewis has long since transferred his affections to the little theatre movement, where his skill as an actor has added lustre and distinction to that group. His uncanny facility in make-up, of old men especially, may fairly be attributed, in part at least, to his training as an artist with the first Graphic Arts Club, of which he was for many years an enthusiastic member. Eric Aldwinckle of the present-day society is not only an artist and designer of originality, but he is likewise a non-professional actor of quite professional skill. He, like Lewis, is also engaged in the work of the theatre at Hart House, and is frequently called upon to play a prominent part in its productions.

Members of the present-day Society of Graphic Art comprise men and women well known in the field of painting, designing, advertising, illustration and interior decoration, notably: Leonard Hutchinson for his delectable colour-prints from woodblocks; Charles Goldhamer for his graphic pencil drawings of scenes in Old Ontario and Nova Scotia, valued as historic documents as well as for their more immediate aesthetic qualities; Carl Schaefer, recent winner of the Guggenheim Foundation Award, for his highly individual water-colours and pen drawings of scenes in and around Toronto; W. F. G. Godfrey, for his woodblock prints of memorable beauty; and similarly Eric Bergman of Winnipeg, using the same medium to produce skilfully handled prints of landscape and botanical subjects in the tradition of Thomas Bewick and Eric Ravilious. These and others such as Donald McKay, Halifax; Miller Brittain, St. John; Grace Fugler, Hamilton; Viola Depew, Stoney Creek; William H. Howard, Toronto, and Charles H. Scott of Vancouver are doing collectively much to maintain and advance the standard of artistic practice throughout the country. To contemplate its present point of development, therefore, is to realize that the first Graphic Arts Club, in laying the foundation of the Society three decades ago, builded better than it knew. A thirtieth anniversary is a landmark in the life of any society, and thus the value of its achievement can be to some extent measured. Today the Society is strongly organized, functioning through its own annual exhibitions in Toronto and other Canadian cities and through the Graphic Arts Section of the Canadian National Exhibition, which this club fostered and developed.

During his lifetime Albert H. Robson rendered conspicuous and valuable service to Canadian art as a member of the council and vice-president of the Art Gallery of Toronto, when he served on that body as the representative of the Graphic Arts Club. He was president of the Club during its formative period, and is reputed to have been largely responsible for its achievements in connection with its annual exhibit at the Canadian National Exhibition at Toronto.

As art director of Grip Limited, an engraving-house in Toronto, he came into close contact with J. E. H. MacDonald, Tom Thomson, Frank Johnston, Arthur Lismer and other commercial artists, some of whom were afterwards to organize the Group of Seven. Robson himself was an artist in black-and-white and in colour; occasionally he contributed to public exhibitions in Toronto, Montreal and elsewhere. Active in the field of Canadian letters, he was the author of *Canadian Landscape Painters* and of a series of monographs dealing with the lives and the work of notable Canadian painters. Nor was his interest confined to the pictorial arts. Under his influence there was a healthy and sustained support, through the agency of the little theatre movement, given to the promotion of a native drama and literature as well as art. Appointed by Lord Bessborough, Governor-General, as one of the

THE RHYTHM

ERIC BERGMAN

original governors of the Dominion Drama Festival, Albert Robson served for three years as president of the Ontario Regional Drama Festival. From 1935 to 1937 he was president of the Toronto branch of the Canadian Authors' Association, and was a member of the National Executive. He was also a member of the Authors' Club of London, England, a past president of the Bach Society and a founder of the Arts and Letters Club, Toronto. His death, in 1939, at a comparatively early age, was a serious loss to art and literature in Canada.

6

An earnest attempt to promote the cause of Canadian art was made in 1907 when, through the efforts of Edmund Morris, well known for his authentic Indian studies, many of which are now to be found in the collection of the Royal Ontario Museum, the Canadian Art Club came into being. As a direct result of this move such men as Horatio Walker, Homer Watson, Curtis William-

CABIN IN THE LANE

The British Mortgage and Trust Corporation, Stratford, Ontario.

HOMER WATSON

son, Franklin Brownell, Archibald Browne, W. E. Atkinson, James Wilson Morrice, William Brymner and Edmund Morris banded themselves together to hold annual exhibitions of purely Canadian paintings and sculpture. Homer Watson was elected president, with Curtis Williamson as secretary.

With the exception of Brownell and Browne, these men were

73

born in Canada, and all entered into the spirit of the venture with courage and determination. The organization was definitely a club. There was no official recognition, no government bonus. The members had to subsist by themselves with the aid of whatever outside patronage they could enlist. Fortunately, this support was made possible by the accession of D. R. Wilkie, a wealthy banker, who was made honorary president, a position assumed following Mr. Wilkie's death, in 1915, by Sir Edmund Osler, M.P., a man of public spirit and a discriminating collector. Although the Canadian Art Club was not acknowledged to be a secession from art bodies already established, it was in reality a revolt from the lack of public interest in the arts in general in Canada. This, and a professed abhorrence of the low standards governing selection of contributions allowed by other art organizations, were mainly instrumental in bringing the new society into existence. The members felt that there was no honour in having a picture hung or a piece of sculpture placed locally; and, in order to have a Canadian exhibition where there would be at least an attempt made at fixing a standard, they would set standards of their own. At first they had no difficulty in fixing a standard, because the standard was already fixed by the character of the men admitted to membership. That is, a painter was not admitted unless qualified; and once admitted, his work was accepted as a matter of course.

When the time came for holding an exhibition, the eight original members resolved that it would be unwise to exclude everything but the work of their own brushes. Although they may not have been aware of the fact, they followed a precedent set, in 1848, by the English Pre-Raphaelite painters headed by Holman Hunt and J. E. Millais, and, in 1874, by a group of seven painters—Renoir, Monet, Sisley, Pissarro, Moriset, Cézanne and Guillaume. This latter group held a collective exhibition, but came to the opinion that they should not allow cleavage between their own and the conventional work to be too sudden or too great. Therefore they invited, as a means of easing the transition, exhibits from Degas, Boudin, Latouche and Bracquemond.

Similarly did the Canadian Art Club. They invited exhibits from Maurice Cullen, W. H. Clapp, St. Thomas Smith, Laura Muntz and Robert Harris of Montreal; Charles P. Gruppe and Arthur Crisp of New York; James L. Graham of Toronto; and the sculptors Henri and Philippe Hébert of Montreal. And for members they even went further afield. They took in Phimister Proctor, one of the foremost sculptors of New York; Walter S. Allward, a distinguished sculptor of Toronto; John Russell and Clarence Gagnon, both young painters working chiefly in Paris; and J. Kerr Lawson of London, England. Gagnon, who joined the Club as an etcher, soon began to enter paintings.

Although things went comparatively well for a time, with pictures sold and members encouraged, there were breakers ahead. Morris, the mainstay of the new Club, had meanwhile become a member of the board of directors of the Art Museum, later the Art Gallery of Toronto. The result might have been foreseen: the Club, already under obligation to the Museum for gallery space, came more and more under the influence of that organization, and lost its former independence. The Art Museum was responsible also for the defection of one member, John Russell, who, disappointed and irritated by the failure of the Gallery to hang suitably his portrait of Goldwin Smith, resigned. Even a tardy government grant of five hundred dollars, which it was assumed would be an annual grant, failed to revive a waning enthusiasm. The sudden and untimely death of Edmund Morris by drowning, while yet in his early forties, removed forever the motive power which had operated to keep the Club alive. In 1915 the members finally decided to disband. Although its life was brief, the Canadian Art Club did much to arouse a strong national spirit among our artists and to stimulate them to look inward rather than outward for the source of their inspiration. It was a healthful influence and, while it lived, beneficial to artist and layman alike. It bred a self-confidence in Canadian art, especially among the older official bodies, such as the Ontario Society of Artists, that had hitherto been lacking. Canada aesthetically was beginning to find her feet.[1]

It would seem strange, had we not many personal experiences of the mutations of human progress, that events, which appear to be epic and epochal, have a habit as time recedes of diminishing in vitality and importance. So true is this, and so common, that it requires here neither argument nor evidence to sustain it. It need occasion no astonishment therefore, that the Group of Seven, which was to usher in a new movement in Canadian painting, has become

[1] See Chapter on The Canadian Art Club: *Fine Arts in Canada*, by Newton MacTavish (Macmillan.)

almost legendary within a comparatively brief space of less than two decades.

It seems somehow to be commonly assumed, that the Group of Seven movement sprang full panoplied from the brow of Jove. Of course it did nothing of the kind. Various important influences were at work in the world of thought and art to foreshadow this movement, for in former times as well as in later days the event blossomed when the time was fulfilled. It never happens otherwise. Specifically it may be said, that the flowering of the Group of Seven in the second decade of the present century marks, as is generally agreed, one of the major events in the history of art in Canada. It is easy to exaggerate the extent of the movement itself; it is easy to dwell too exclusively on the bright side of its results; but the undoubted fact of its importance still remains. The Group marked the culmination of all the progressive and converging influences of painting in Canada for the past hundred years.

A new world was opened. As Sir Robert Falconer writes in the *Cambridge History of the British Empire:*

Over poetry and the fine arts in general there moved a creative breath as the day of the new Dominion dawned. Impelled by the spirit of their own homeland, a group of young men began to come into their power during the nineties, the best known among whom were Charles G. D. Roberts, Bliss Carman, Archibald Lampman, Wilfred Campbell, and Duncan Campbell Scott. These formed the vanguard of the new movement in Canadian art and literature. Although the art of Canada extends over a period of more than one hundred and fifty years, we have seen that it was really continued as an influence in communal life into the English settlement of Canada in the late eighteenth and early nineteenth centuries.

Most of the early painting was done, as we have seen, by artists who had migrated to Canada from Europe and New England and, having brought with them their material outlook and national traditions, painted the Canadian scene coloured by their previous life and training. These pioneer artists were followed in turn by native-born painters who themselves were to turn to European *ateliers* for light and guidance. There they were to acquire not only the technique of their art but their most characteristic subject matter as well. Meanwhile, the foreign-taught Canadian artist, apart from a few notable exceptions, saw little to attract him in his native countryside. He simply was not interested; and since interest must of necessity precede execution, threadbare themes painted abroad, both landscapes and interiors, continued to cover the walls of our public galleries and wealthy homes to the almost total exclusion of canvases descriptive of the Canadian scene. This snobbishness, for much of it was nothing else, had another unfortunate effect, and explains in part the practice of the native artist who sought subjects abroad rather than at home: It caused the picture-buyer to prefer the products of the foreign painter. Much worse, it caused, among others, such painters as Horatio Walker, Paul Peel, Blair Bruce, and James Wilson Morrice to seek abroad in foreign lands the living denied them at home.

This lamentable situation, insofar as it affected Canadian art, persisted during the seventies, eighties and nineties, until the dawn of the new century, when the liberating influence of the French Impressionists turned the thoughts of the Canadian painter to the pictorial possibilities of his own land. Men who had acquired a fine technical background by study abroad, had returned to paint with enthusiasm the subjects of their native Province. Perhaps it was because attractive pictorial material was so abundantly at hand that the work of our landscape painters of the early part of the present century so quickly reflected a note that was distinctly Canadian. The rolling plains, the Rockies, the Indian life, the sleighs, the ancient houses and bush, so fascinating to Kane and Krieghoff fifty years earlier, were freshly delineated with a feeling for characterization and sound artistry by men technically equipped to make them into things of lasting beauty and interest.

This growing interest in the Ontario and Quebec landscape as a source of pictorial material had its influence in time on a small group of commercial artists working for the engraving-house of Grip Limited in Toronto. The name of the company, it may be explained parenthetically, was derived from a humorous and political illustrated paper called *Grip*, which had been started in 1873 by John W. Bengough, one of Canada's early cartoonists. In course of time and subject to the usual vicissitudes of fortune, the paper languished and in 1894 died. However, the art and engraving department continued under the old name as Grip Limited. With the passing of the years, this company grew in size and importance and became a large employer of artists for the production of illustrations and designs.

About the year 1905, then, a group of artists working for an engraving-house began to take an interest in landscape painting as a recreation from the daily grind of commercial work. Partly through contacts with the Mahlstick Club, of which some had been members, and partly through the influence of work done by members of the Toronto Art League, but mainly through the practical encouragement and support of Dr. James M. MacCallum of Toronto, this local group began week-end sketching trips and spent their holidays in parties of two or three in Northern Ontario. The experience of a group on one of these outings is vividly and humorously described by J. E. H. MacDona'd in "A.C.R. 10557," which appeared in *Lamps*, published by the Arts and Letters Club of Toronto, in 1919. The cryptic letters and numerals which form the title were taken from the red box-car of the Algoma Central Railway, occupied by the sketchers during their trip.

Enthusiasm as a result of these explorations in the Northland grew, and a number of men were shortly found in the Grip organization who were not only rapidly improving their technique as part-time painters, but were also working from a distinctive Canadian point of view that was eventually to flower in a definite art movement. Of the men who were thus soon to become actively identified with this development may be mentioned J. E. H. Mac-Donald, Arthur Lismer, Frank Carmichael, F. Horsman Varley, Tom Thomson, T. W. McLean, Frank H. Johnston and W. Smithson Broadhead. There were others; but these artists were the men who did most to promote a new or, as some prefer to call it, original interpretation of the Northland. From a strictly utilitarian point of view at least the idea was excellent; their adventuring in Northern Ontario had developed in these men fresh conceptions of design as applied to commercial publicity. The railways were demanding bright attractive folders and posters, a demand inspired by similar work in England, portraying the pictorial charm of our Northern districts, and these artists in their eager enthusiasm were able to interpret something of the true spirit as well as the physical beauty of the country.

The opening of the Northland of Ontario as a source of fresh material for the landscape painter may be largely attributed to the spirit of adventure which animated J. W. Beatty. In the first decade of the new century Beatty went north to sketch: at first alone, then later with Tom Thomson. Several years were to elapse before the Group of Seven were to rediscover the new country. Usually regarded as a strict traditionalist, he was in reality a forerunner of the Canadian movement in painting. But the movement was to go beyond him, or, perhaps it would be more correct to say that, although he saw much to admire in the new school, he

MORNING: ALGONQUIN PARK

J. W. BEATTY

National Gallery of Canada.

found himself unable to accept its teachings unreservedly. Fond as he was, however, of Northern Ontario, with its wild and picturesque vistas, its fresh and virgin beauty, his chief interest remained in the cultivated countryside of central Ontario; though he went on many sketching trips to Algonquin Park, to Quebec and to the Rockies, the fruits of these visits are to be seen in some of his finest canvases: IN THE LAURENTIANS (owned by the Department of Education) for one; and THE EVENING CLOUD OF THE NORTHLAND (owned by the National Gallery, Ottawa) for another.

The story of Beatty's life reads like a page from Samuel Smiles. He was born in Toronto in 1869. His formal education was slight, for he quit school after a few years, determined to paint. As with Krieghoff and Verner, a period of soldiering interrupted his training as a student. He volunteered and served in the Riel Rebellion of 1885, and in 1889 joined the Toronto Fire Brigade of which he was a member till 1900. In his spare time—the peculiar nature of his duties left him with an ample supply—he drew and painted under the direction of William Cruikshank and F. M. Bell-Smith, sound if not brilliant men. In the meantime, by dint of self-denial and the strictest kind of economy, he managed to save a sum sufficient to take him abroad, where he studied under Jean-Paul Laurens and Benjamin Constant at the Calorossi and Academie Julien in Paris. On coming back to Canada his work began to attract attention and win official recognition. In 1901 he was elected a member of the Ontario Society of Artists, and within a few years an associate of the Royal Canadian Academy. In 1906 he was able to go to Europe again, this time for a period of three years. He studied with Burroughs in London, and again at Julien's, and travelled through Spain, Belgium, Holland and England, sketching as he went. Like Gagnon he tried his hand at etching, but it proved only a minor diversion in his career.

In 1912 he began to teach painting at the Ontario College of Art—although he had conducted outdoor sketching classes some years before—and continued until the end an active member of the staff. In 1913 he was elected to full membership in the Academy; and, having previously been rejected for active service, he went to France in 1917 to paint for the Canadian War Memorials, with F. Horsman Varley, A. Y. Jackson, James Wilson Morrice, David Milne, Homer Watson and others. When the Ontario College of Art opened its summer school in Port Hope, Beatty took charge. Later he took over the school himself and conducted it until his death. Here and also as instructor at the Ontario College of Art for nearly three decades, he exercised a marked influence on a long line of students, including such well-known painters as Herbert S. Palmer, Manly Macdonald, Franklin

Arbuckle, Evan Macdonald, Peter Sheppard and Doris Gillespie, most if not all of whom were awarded medals and scholarships.

Throughout a long and active life as artist, he remained constant in his preoccupation with landscape painting, the treatment of which he varied from time to time by introducing the human figure, or as is sometimes seen in the early European sketches of his student days, cattle and sheep. His painting shows a steady development from the grey and sombre harmonies of the French and Dutch landscapes to the rising lyrical notes of the full palette of his finely orchestrated studies of his later Northern Ontario days when he was obviously influenced by the pure, strong, singing colours of Tom Thomson and the Group of Seven. Active to the last, he died after a brief illness in the early autumn of 1941. "Self-educated and self-supporting from his boyhood days, even when he changed his mind, there was no middle course, and he expressed himself accordingly." There is no hint, however, of this combative attitude in his pictures, which, in their placid interpretation of nature, are strangely at variance with his forceful direct and emphatic personality. In general, however, his reasoning on art was orthodox: he spread no heresy and begat no schisms.

His work is to be found in the National Gallery, the Provincial Department of Education, Toronto, the Ontario College of Art, the Art Gallery of Toronto, and in numerous private collections. His students showed their appreciation of him as a teacher by purchasing his AUTUMN: ALGONQUIN PARK, and presenting this fine canvas to the Art Gallery of Toronto as a tribute to his memory. A combined memorial exhibition of the paintings and etchings of Clarence Gagnon and J. W. Beatty, held in the Art Gallery of Toronto in October, 1942, attracted much attention. A memorial exhibition of Beatty's work, less representative on the whole, was held at the Eaton Galleries shortly after his death.

To return to the Group. Its artistic importance made up as it was of Frank Carmichael, A. Y. Jackson, J. E. H. MacDonald, Lawren Harris, Arthur Lismer, F. Horsman Varley and Frank H. Johnston, was enhanced greatly and suddenly by the discovery that Tom Thomson, who had gone his own way, was developing an artistic talent far beyond anything that had been anticipated by members of the Group. Much of Thomson's early success may be ascribed in no small measure to the sympathetic advice and financial help of

Dr. James MacCallum of the University of Toronto, who was later similarly to assist J. E. H. MacDonald when that painter stood in need of a helping hand.

Now the great merit of Thomson's discovery, if discovery it can be called, is not that by his remarkable painting he initiated modern art as we know it in Canada. Credit for that must go first, to the French Impressionists, and equally to Van Gogh and Cézanne, and also and more especially perhaps to the Scandinavian painters who exhibited at Buffalo in the early years of the century. But he seems to have been the first man in Canadian art to see or put into practice the theory, that artistic salvation was not to be found in changing the painter's subject, though that consideration may have influenced him, but in changing his method of looking at and rendering the visible world. He began trying to paint what he saw.

At any rate the times were ripe for revolt, and had the Group not come when they did their places would almost inevitably have been filled by other young men. As it was, we may say that some if not all of the Seven were revolutionists simply because they were temperamentally unwilling to paint in the older manner, and not because they were unable to do so or too indifferent to learn it. Johnston, upon the whole, it may be said, was never a very ardent member of the Group. The movement was, in his facile and delightful career, a mere episode. Perhaps he gained something from its fresh outlook; perhaps he did not, we cannot tell. His subsequent work affords no clue or indication.

The credo of the Group was set forth in a foreword to the catalogue of its first exhibition of paintings in the Art Museum of Toronto, May 7 to May 27, 1920. The text was written by Lawren Harris, to whose energy and enthusiasm the Group largely owed its existence:

The group of seven artists whose pictures are here exhibited have for several years held a like vision concerning art in Canada. They are all imbued with the idea that an Art must grow and flower in the land before the country will be a real home for its people.

That this Art will differ from the Art of the past, and from the present day Art, of any people; superseding nothing, only adding to what has been done. Also it seems inevitable when something vital and destructive arises it will be met—

(1) by ridicule, abuse or indifference.
(2) The so-called Art lovers, having a deeply rooted idea that Art

is a matter of picture buying through the medium of the auctioneer or dealer, will refuse to recognize anything that does not come up to the commercialized, imported standard of picture-sale room.

They prefer to enrich the salesman than accept the productions by artists native to the land, whose work is more distinctive, original and vital, and of greater value to the country.

(3) The more sophisticated will meet it with: "If you have no traditions, no background, no Art is possible." How then do traditions arise? Or they will say that anything produced will shortly die and be superseded—which is to say that nothing has been or ever will be worth the doing. They will say anything that sounds erudite, patting their own backs at the expense of Art and country.

Finally: A very small group of intelligent individuals, realizing that the greatness of a country depends upon three things: "Its Words, its Deeds and its Art." Recognizing that Art is an essential quality in human existence they will welcome and support any form of Art expression that sincerely interprets the spirit of a nation's growth."

Then the manifesto goes on to add:

The artists here represented make no pretence of being the only ones in Canada doing significant work. But they do most emphatically hold that their work is significant and of real value to the country. They also hold with A. E. Russell[1], the Irish writer, "that no country can ever hope to rise above a vulgar mediocrity when there is not unbounded confidence in what its humanity can do." And that, if a people do not believe they can equal or surpass the stature of any humanity which has been upon the world, then they had better emigrate and become servants to some superior people.

A word as you view the pictures. The artists invite adverse criticism. Indifference is the greatest evil they have to contend with. But they ask you—do you read books you already know? If not, they argue, that you should hardly want to see pictures that show you what you can already see for yourselves.

Now this statement by the Group is important for two main reasons. It marked the first time in Canada that any group of artists had proclaimed its belief in native art as native art; and, secondly, it detailed, though not always in logical or lucid terms, the common faith by which this group of seven artists was animated. That the tone of the manifesto is at times somewhat supercilious, and that there is implicit a rather heavy and amusing assumption of superiority, is by the way. The fact must be confessed, that with a slight sense of amusement there is mingled a feeling of admiration for these men who were to undertake a new venture in the interpretation of the Canadian scene. In all

[1]George W. Russell (A.E.), Irish painter, writer and lecturer.

sincerity, and on the strength of their youthful ardour, they dared to be themselves, to transcribe Nature as they saw her, saw her under Canadian skies, in the changing Canadian seasons; and it will no longer be denied, I think, that such honesty of purpose, firmness of mind and steadfast resolution are to be accounted unto them for righteousness. The stagnant waters of Canadian art at the time, as contemporary exhibition catalogues show, much needed the freshness of a stirring breeze. The Group supplied the invigorating and life-giving element; and there has been since then no dead or miasmatic calm. Thus, the early twenties were to see a rebirth of a fresh, vigorous and healthful impulse in Canadian landscape painting.

True, the change did not take place overnight. Much hostile and even venomous professional opposition and newspaper criticism were encountered. Into the details of this bitter polemic we need not here enter; a full account of this period of the Group's progress is to be found in F. B. Housser's book on the movement, as well as elsewhere.

The work of the Group is now history. Little can be added which is not already known. Like the pre-Raphaelite and later insurgent movements in art, there were three progressive stages through which it passed, namely, that of surprise, that of opposition, that of acceptance. Today the work of the Group is generally accepted for what it is: a revolutionary movement designed to turn men's thoughts from the past to the present and the future. "Like all revolutionaries, however, the Group may have been inclined to hold tradition too lightly, and to mistake a propaganda for a gospel. But happily their evident sincerity matches their undoubted ability," and in seeking the true index of the Canadian Northland they have not been turned aside by its often stark and forbidding reality.

Some exceptions there are, of course, and always will be. Yet, generally speaking, the work of the Group reaches a high peak of achievement, of which the isolated examples seen from time to time give but faint indication. Assembled as they sometimes are in one exhibition, notably as in 1937, the mass effect is startlingly impressive. Here is nature as nature transmuted by the poetic instinct of the painter.

One willingly surrenders, for instance, to the magical lure of A. J. Casson's CLEARING AFTER RAIN, now owned by the National

Gallery, in which trees and sky and river form an exquisite harmony of tender colour and moving form.   It expresses a delicate, dreamy mood, as befits a springtime theme; and yet, withal, it is virile and robust in handling, as one feels, or seems to feel, the urgent breeze upon his face and savours the clean, sweet smell of growing things.

National Gallery of Canada.

CLEARING

ALFRED JOSEPH CASSON

SPRING and AUTUMN HILLSIDE, by Frank Carmichael, are revelations of glowing, jewel-like colour to those who know this artist chiefly by his pale and sombre vistas of Northern Algoma, with their bleak and depressing solitudes, markedly stylized in form and pattern.   Ordinarily he paints with broad strokes, in flat subdued tones, and in much of his work the decorative motive predominates.

Those who know the work of Lawren Harris only in his later period, his progress marked by conventionalized icebergs and formalized trees and hills, will find a different painter, and I for one prefer to think a better, in GREY DAY IN TOWN, ALGOMA SWAMP and ELEVATOR COURT, HALIFAX. These paintings show the artist in probably the most promising period of his career, before he had superimposed upon his natural genius a barren and self-conscious style.

Design dominates, as a rule, the composition of A. Y. Jackson, though seldom does he let it get out of hand. Typical of his best because of his evident mastery of form and colour, light and air, are LAURENTIAN HILLS and THE ST. LAWRENCE IN WINTER. Jackson enjoys the distinction of being the first Canadian painter to be represented in the Tate Gallery of London. Another, though later, is James Wilson Morrice. Jackson's painting, HALIFAX HARBOUR, was bought by the Gallery after the Wembley Exhibition of 1924.

The manner of Arthur Lismer, now associated as instructor with the Montreal Art Association, is strikingly shown in his RAIN IN THE NORTH COUNTRY, which also reveals to a marked degree the influence of Tom Thomson, commonly, though mistakenly, regarded as the real founder of the Group. Lismer's painting, however, in both colour and design, has deteriorated in the past few years, with a tendency to become crude and chaotic, but as a draughtsman in black-and-white, and in caricature particularly, he displays extraordinary skill and fecundity. His painting, SEPTEMBER GALE, in the National Art Gallery, Ottawa, is undoubtedly his most important achievement to date. In addition, he has to his credit a number of canvases interpretative of the Canadian landscape, highly decorative in design, in which the forms are briefly summarized but not always successfully realized. It is chiefly as a teacher of new and vitalizing ideas that he is likely to make his most useful and lasting contribution to Canadian art.

Mention has previously been made of F. Horsman Varley, who, until his departure for Ottawa, was a teacher at the School of Decoration and Applied Arts, Vancouver. It may be added, however, that during the war of 1914-1918 he was artist in the War Records Office. He went to Flanders, where his war experience brought forth several important canvases, notably FOR WHAT?, a bitter comment on the futility of war, THE GAS CHAMBER AT SEAFORD and DEAD HORSE CORNER, MONCHY. All of these exemplify the characteristics of great painting: line, mass and colour are combined with passionate intensity to express an emotion; an intelligent use of means by which the artist has striven

J. S. McLean, Esq., Toronto.

AN AUTUMN HILLSIDE

FRANKLIN CARMICHAEL

to lift art above mere representation. The result, aesthetically, is most gratifying, which probably accounts for their enthusiastic reception by the English critics when exhibited in London. His later West Coast sketches, done while in Vancouver, particularly of Howe Sound, are well designed, judiciously simplified, drawn with feeling and painted with a respect for the medium employed—an achievement worthy of attention, as indeed most of Varley's essays are.

A capable and ingenious designer and commercial artist, Frank Johnston has pursued a course which has seemed erratic. An original member of the Group of Seven, he soon severed his connection with the Group to follow his own inclinations. These led him first to become principal of the Art School at Winnipeg, instructor in the Ontario College of Art, and later to journey in

FALSE BAY: CAPE OF GOOD HOPE
ARTHUR LISMER

Northern Ontario for subject matter. For a time he used tempera as a medium almost exclusively, but afterwards returned to the use of oils. He has painted in various parts of Ontario, Quebec and in the West, including the Rockies, but more recently he has sought subjects for his brush in the North Country which he has depicted with considerably less breadth of detail than that characterizing his sketches in tempera. These latter paintings also betray evidences of having been influenced, especially in the snow scenes,

National Gallery of Canada.

A NORTHERN NIGHT

FRANK JOHNSTON

by the technique of Choultsé, the Russian painter, which causes them to verge uncomfortably on the artificial and affected. His work, however, continues to display a fine sense of design and vigour of treatment; his skill in the management of light and shade for emotional effect has given his pictures a strongly decorative quality. A native Canadian painter, Frank Johnston received most of his art training in Toronto, although he also studied for a time at the Pennsylvania School of Art in Philadelphia. During the war, 1914-1918, he was attached to the Flying Corps by the Canadian War Records Office, and painted a number of decorative and moving episodes of the Air Force in training. Of late years he has conducted a summer class in painting and sketching at his home near Midland, on Georgian Bay.

7

Tom Thomson, it has been said by one who knew him well, was a natural painter. However that may be, it is very questionable, if not highly improbable, that Thomson would have arrived at the place he did in Canadian painting had it not been for the direct encouragement and financial aid he received from others: most of all from Dr. James MacCallum. He it was who discerned in the first efforts of the struggling young painter evidences of a genius which, under sympathetic appreciation and intelligent criticism and direction, was to grow into something infinitely finer and richer than even he had suspected.

It may be mentioned in passing that Dr. MacCallum was and, happily, still is, a patron of the arts of a kind familiar enough in European capitals before the present war, but rare enough here, whose interest in painting especially took the very practical form of assisting in various ways those painters who were thought to stand most in need of such aid. His friendship for such artists as Tom Thomson, J. E. H. MacDonald, Lawren Harris and A. Y. Jackson is fairly well known. Not so common is the knowledge that he assisted these painters with useful advice and often with his means. That is to say, he bought their pictures and recommended their purchase by others; he received them into his summer home on Georgian Bay, which they made their headquarters during the outdoors painting season; and from his long and intimate knowledge of the district, he was able to name likely spots for sketching. With these painters and others less familiar, he has maintained for much of his life a footing of friendly informality

Dr. J. M MacCallum, Toronto.

THE PINE ISLANDS

Tom Thomson

in which all are believed to have found a common source of pleasure and inspiration. One of the fruits of this association was the erection in 1925 of the Studio Building in Severn Street, Toronto, devoted exclusively to the use of artists, and is without parallel in Canada. The project was the result of a collaboration between Lawren Harris and Dr. MacCallum, both of whom were responsible for its design and supervised its construction.

It was in the late summer of 1912 that Thomson and Mac-Callum first met. Thomson had returned from a sketching and fishing trip to the Mississauga forest reserve, bringing back with him a number of rapid oil impressions of its wooded and rocky shorelines. The chance encounter, which occurred in the studio of J. E. H. MacDonald, may best be described in Dr. MacCallum's own words:

> The door opened and in walked a tall and slim, clean-cut, dark young chap who was introduced to me as Tom Thomson. Quiet, reserved, chary of words, he impressed me as full of resolution and independence. After he had gone, I told MacDonald of how I had heard of him, and asked him to get some of his sketches so that I might get an idea of what the country was like. This was done, and as I looked them over, I who had known the north since the days when Collingwood and Orillia were the railheads, realized their truthfulness, their feeling and their sympathy for the grim, fascinating northland. Dark they were, muddy in color, tight, and not wanting in technical defects; but they made me feel that the north had gripped Thomson as it had gripped me when, as a boy of eleven, I first sailed and paddled through its silent places. Some of the sketches, fished up from the foot of the rapids [Thomson and his companion Smithson Broadhead had been upset.] I bought. The money was received with the remark, "That will let me buy more paint."

Meanwhile Tom Thomson went back to the engraving-house to resume his work as a commercial designer, making folder and catalogue dummies and hand-lettered advertisements, in which branch of art he was in no sense a competitor of MacDonald. His work here, although respectable enough, was for the most part undistinguished. With the coming of spring, however, Thomson once more became free to roam and sketch at will. When autumn came again, he returned to the city, bringing with him the harvest of his knowing hand and observing eye. To quote Dr. MacCallum again:

> The north country gradually got him, body and soul. He began to paint that he might express the emotions that the country inspired in

him: all the moods and passions, all the sombreness and all the glory of color, were so felt that they demanded from him pictorial expression. He never gave utterance in words to his feelings of the glories of nature. Words were not his instruments of expression: color was the only medium open to him. Truthfulness was his one aim and goal. When I demurred to anything he had painted, he was content to say merely: "Yes, it is just like that." Of all our Canadian artists he was the greatest colorist: not from any desire to be original or to make sensation did he use color. His aims were truthfulness and beauty: beauty of color, of feeling, and of emotion. To him his most beautiful sketches were only paint. He placed no value on them—all he wanted was more paint so that he could paint others. He enjoyed appreciation of his work; criticism of it he welcomed; but its truthfulness was unassailable, for he had seen it. Those of us who camped or canoed with him soon learned that he never painted anything which he had not seen. He was not concerned with any special technique, any particular mode of application of color, or of this kind of brushstroke or that. Was it true to nature, the technique might be anything. A study of his pictures will show that the technique varied as the subject varied. Drawing was the expression of form and form might be expressed by any method so long as the form was true. Untrained in the schools, he had to devise his own technique. His color was varied, brilliant and beautiful, but used so as to express some emotion or feeling. His color sings, not in ragtime, but in the Hosannas of the joy and exultation of Nature.

Thomson began painting out-of-doors about 1910 and continued until his death in 1917. At first, as we have seen, his sketches were dull, tight and timid, showing little, if any, of that effulgent and glowing colour, later to distinguish his manner, but none the less revealing an intimate feeling of the country. His first large canvas, A NORTHERN LAKE, painted from a sketch and exhibited at the 1913 Exhibition of the O.S.A., was bought, let it be said to its credit, by the Provincial Government of Ontario.

In the fall of 1913 Thomson returned from a sketching trip to the north, expecting to resume his duties as commercial artist at Grip Limited, who had meanwhile obligated themselves to keep his job open for him. They did not; and Thomson, without funds or immediate prospects of any, was hard put to make a living. Fortunately, at this point Dr. MacCallum, his friend and mentor, came to his assistance and soon a financial arrangement was effected whereby Thomson was to keep on painting and the doctor was to be reimbursed with pictures sold to him at prices set by the artist. By this time Thomson's painting had greatly improved; for he now "sought to depict lightning flashes, moving thunderstorms, trees with branches lashing in the wind." These sketches, shown to A. Y. Jackson, so interested him that he asked to meet Thomson, and ended by inviting him to share his studio with him.

At the next O.S.A. exhibition, in 1914, Thomson showed two pictures, one of which, MOONLIGHT, EARLY EVENING, was purchased by the National Gallery, Ottawa. This marked the beginning of his rise to fame, a fame which was to extend in the process of time far beyond the borders of his own country.

The basic knowledge of design obtained through his training as commercial artist explains much of the decorative beauty of composition and arrangement which so distinguishes his painting. In this respect Tom Thomson and J. E. H. MacDonald were linked by a common interest. Both were designers by training and practice, and both approached the problem of landscape with a finely discriminating knowledge of form and arrangement. Although MacDonald felt the appeal of a wide diversity of subject material, Thomson, on the other hand, concentrated his attention on the Northern Ontario wilds, with a devotion that was complete and unwavering. Both of these men made important and enduring contributions to the art of Canada. The work of both was alive with charm of design and beauty of colour. Thus profound knowledge of design, as will be seen, played a great and essential part in the work of each.

From year to year Thomson grew in the capacity to summarize, in the beauty of his colour arrangements, in confidence and ease of execution, and in brilliancy of technique. His acute sense of design and colour "wove enchantment into a sketch, never cluttering or confusing it, but rather integrating it with a richer simplicity and a more subtle significance." This concentration of purpose, together with his natural genius and an intimate knowledge of his subject, are shown in probably more than four hundred sketches, and perhaps twenty large and finished canvases, which he left. There were, it is fair to conjecture, possibly as many slight or experimental pictures as well.

But it is to be remembered that Thomson led the vanguard of the new movement in Canadian art. He it was who "painted a world of phenomena of colour and of form which had not been touched by any other artist." His sketches are a complete encyclopedia of all the phenomena of Algonquin Park and, aside from their artistic merits, have a historical value which demands "that they should be preserved in our National Gallery." Happily this wise admonition has been obeyed, to the extent that the National Gallery now includes in its Canadian section no less than five large canvases and twenty-five sketches by Thomson, with in course of time the prospect of many more sketches and finished paintings to augment the present collection. Besides the sketches mentioned, Thomson is now represented at Ottawa by MOONLIGHT, EARLY EVENING; NORTHERN RIVER, SPRING ICE, THE JACK PINE and AUTUMN'S GARLAND.

In July, 1917, he died, suddenly and tragically, bringing to an end a life short of complete fulfilment.

Upon a cairn at Canoe Lake, erected by Dr. J. M. MacCallum, assisted by J. W. Beatty, R.C.A., who did the actual work of construction, is a plate, whose design and words are by J. E. H. MacDonald, R.C.A., "his friend through the years of aspirations and accomplishment." It reads:

TO THE MEMORY OF

TOM THOMSON

ARTIST, WOODSMAN AND GUIDE

WHO WAS DROWNED IN CANOE LAKE, JULY 8TH, 1917. HE LIVED HUMBLY BUT PASSIONATELY WITH THE WILD. IT MADE HIM BROTHER TO ALL UNTAMED THINGS OF NATURE. IT DREW HIM APART AND REVEALED ITSELF WONDERFULLY TO HIM. IT SENT HIM OUT FROM THE WOODS ONLY TO SHOW THESE REVELATIONS, THROUGH HIS ART; AND IT TOOK HIM TO ITSELF AT LAST.

Tom Thomson, it should be explained, had worked as a fire-ranger and guide in Algonquin, and had become, in consequence, thoroughly intimate with that region. He was, besides, like many another artist, a fly-fisherman of exceptional skill.

Tom Thomson is represented in the following public collections: the Art Gallery of Toronto; The Ottawa Normal School; the Montreal Art Association; Hart House, University of Toronto; the Home and School Association, Sarnia, Ontario; the Ontario Agricultural College, Guelph; Queen's University, Kingston; and the National Gallery of Ottawa. Undoubtedly the largest collection of his works, privately owned, is that of his brother, George Thomson, O.S.A., Owen Sound, Ontario; and that of Dr. J. M. MacCallum, Toronto.

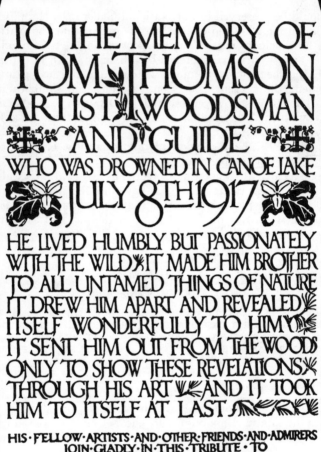

TO THE MEMORY OF
TOM THOMSON
ARTIST WOODSMAN
AND GUIDE
WHO WAS DROWNED IN CANOE LAKE
JULY 8TH 1917

HE LIVED HUMBLY BUT PASSIONATELY
WITH THE WILD IT MADE HIM BROTHER
TO ALL UNTAMED THINGS OF NATURE
IT DREW HIM APART AND REVEALED
ITSELF WONDERFULLY TO HIM
IT SENT HIM OUT FROM THE WOODS
ONLY TO SHOW THESE REVELATIONS
THROUGH HIS ART AND IT TOOK
HIM TO ITSELF AT LAST

HIS·FELLOW·ARTISTS·AND·OTHER·FRIENDS·AND·ADMIRERS
JOIN·GLADLY·IN·THIS·TRIBUTE·TO
HIS·CHARACTER·AND·GENIUS

HIS·BODY·IS·BURIED·AT
OWEN·SOUND·ONTARIO·NEAR
WHERE·HE·WAS·BORN
AUGUST,
1877

DESIGN FOR
THE TOM THOMSON MEMORIAL

ALGONQUIN PARK, NORTHERN ONTARIO

J. E. H. MacDonald

It is logical and perhaps inevitable that J. E. H. MacDonald, having taken upon himself the study of design for the greater part of his life, should have kept the decorative idea uppermost in his painting. This result indeed might have been expected, since during his lifetime he was justly regarded as a decorator and designer and was widely known for the fine and true quality of his work.

After a time, however, his sense of design was more marked and his colour more powerful and brilliant. He became increasingly preoccupied with composition, with line and form and mass, which led him to forsake in the end his first direct and unaffected style for a technique based upon formal and arbitrary arrangement. His art became self-conscious and much of its natural beauty fled. MacDonald, however, seems to have grasped the principles of the new school—insofar as it can be said to have any clearly-defined principles—much more completely and surely than others of its disciples, possibly more vociferous but less gifted. In 1916, when one of his important canvases, THE TANGLED GARDEN, was exhibited by the Ontario Society of Artists, its daring colour and design brought forth a storm of abuse from the public and newspaper critics, who doubtless were better informed on the technique of baseball than of art. The clamour did serve a useful purpose, however, in that it drew attention to the work of the new movement. Criticism has been made that the pigment is too fat; the French use the word *gros*, for which we have no exact equivalent: I did not find it so. In fact, the entire colour-scheme has the richness, luscious colour, soft tones, the breadth and subdued fire of an old tapestry—much of which is doubtless due to MacDonald's pronounced flair for design and colour as displayed in the compositions of his later years.

At any rate, a series of large canvases of the North Country followed, among them THE SOLEMN LAND, then sketching trips to Nova Scotia, to the Rockies and, finally, to the Barbados, with numerous sketches and larger canvases. Of these, his final work, there is little to be said.

His records of the Rockies, both in sketch form and among his more important canvases, are rather too suggestive of the sort of thing transportation companies affect to be altogether satisfying. None the less, technically they are far above the ordinary commercial poster or coloured illustration. Many of the smaller

National Gallery of Ca[*]

MARCH EVENING: NORTHLAND

J. E. H. MacDonald

sketches, done at white heat, are delightfully free and spontaneous in the suggestive handling of the Canadian autumn scene, the Barbados beaches and the all-pervading light. So much so that their translation to the larger canvas frequently adds nothing to their value or their interest. There is, however, much to indicate that, as the years go by, MacDonald will be remembered as one of the few great designers Canada has yet produced. Even today he stands a foremost figure in Canadian art; a painter who had a sound sense of design, a fine passion for colour and the ability to discover dramatic material in his own country.

More than most artists, MacDonald was a man of varied talents; and more than most men, he was the perennial student. Not only was he distinguished as a painter and designer, but he was an accomplished author of both prose and verse; not only a public lecturer and writer on art and cognate subjects, but he was for several years instructor and principal of the Ontario College of Art of which institution he had once been a pupil. Formal recognition as an artist was accorded him when he was elected, in 1909, a member of the Ontario Society of Artists, and again, in 1931, when he was elected to full membership in the Royal Canadian Academy of Arts. He had been honoured with an Associate membership in 1912. As a designer MacDonald stood alone. Whether it were book-jackets, title-pages, memorial tablets, murals, heraldic forms or commemorative windows, he displayed a versatility, invention and technical skill that amounted to genius. Typical of his work as book designer are the jacket and title-page designs of Archibald MacMechan's books, *Old Province Tales*, and *The Book of Ultima Thule*, and *West by East*, which he himself planned and composed. As a memorialist, his tablet to Tom Thomson will stand for all time as an impressive example of dignified and chaste simplicity; as a muralist, his compositions in the Anglican Church of St. Anne's, Toronto, in the Concourse Building and in the Clarendon Apartments, Toronto, are handled with an admirable regard for the purpose in view as well as a sincere respect for his materials. The same may be said of his treatment of heraldic devices in which modern feeling is tactfully blended with a sense of what is due to tradition. Moreover, his extraordinary skill as an all-round designer has been a guide and inspiration to artists who have followed him. Had he chosen to apply himself exclusively to typography it is possible, even probable, that he would have made a name for himself comparable to that of Frederick W. Goudy, Bruce Rogers or T. M. Cleland in the United States, for he was letter designer as well as artist par excellence.

As a writer MacDonald is remembered for his contributions in prose and verse to *The Canadian Forum*, *The Rebel*, *The Lamps* and similar periodicals; all done with distinction and charm and a sensitive feeling for words. His verse, as in *West by East*, which takes for subject matter the familiar sights and sounds of the Ontario countryside, is marked by close and thoughtful observation and deep understanding and sympathy with nature. Living as he did in the historic little village of Thornhill, MacDonald wrote and spoke from a long and intimate experience of rural life in accents tender and wistful of its more homely and primitive side which is today all but a memory. Whatever his importance as a writer, it will be as artist that he is likely to be remembered, and it is fortunate indeed for Canada that he is worthily represented in the National Gallery by no less than twelve important canvases as well as a group of ten sketches typical of some of his best work. The major works comprise IN THE PINE SHADOWS, MOONLIGHT; THE SHINING RIVER, SPRING; SNOWBOUND; MARCH EVENING, NORTHLAND; ASTERS AND APPLES, one of his few still-lifes; CATTLE BY THE CREEK; THE SOLEMN LAND; SEASHORE, NOVA SCOTIA; BATCHE-WANA RAPID; AUTUMN IN ALGOMA (presented by P. D. Ross, Esq., LL.D.); GLEAMS ON THE HILLS; THE TANGLED GARDEN (presented in memory of Richard Southam, Toronto). There is, meanwhile, comfort in the thought that MacDonald's son, Thoreau, as designer, continues to follow in the high tradition established by his father, and that without sacrifice of his own individuality or integrity. His work, like his father's, is similarly distinguished by its fine taste, originality and the surpassing skill with which it is done.[1]

Now it need hardly be said that any attempt to appraise the influence of the Group of Seven upon Canadian art as a whole can only be done intelligently, fairly and logically from first-hand knowledge. And first-hand knowledge means, if it means anything at all, a careful and conscientious inspection of pictures painted by members of the Group. Fortunately, this course is made easy by the presence of these paintings in various large centres of population throughout the country, supplemented by periodical travelling exhibitions sent out from the National Gallery at Ottawa. Although one may not be able consistently to commend all that the Group has done, there is yet much that remains deserving of honest praise. For one thing, these painter-adventurers had the courage to be themselves. In a day when mass thinking and mass action were by no means dormant, they invited, even challenged, adverse criticism. Well, as the written record shows, they were not ignored. Yet in spite of much hostility, or because of it, they survived, which after all is the crucial test. About their work lingers no stale and stuffy odour of the studio, but rather the brisk,

[1]See *Thoreau MacDonald*, by E. R. Hunter. The Ryerson Press, 1942.

eager, bracing air of Canada's lakes and rivers, fields and forests. These men, then, were the pictorial prospectors of Canada's vast Northland, and much of what they discovered there has made us conscious, as we had not been before, of the richness of our heritage.

All the same, it may be well, if for nothing more than the sake of novelty, that we hear the case for the other side. In "Art—Canada Hits Back" [London *Mercury*, December, 1938], Paul Oppé reviews the Century of Canadian Art Show at the Tate Gallery, presenting the English or European point of view.

Like the Americans, whose work was to be seen in the spring at the Wildenstein Galleries, the post-War painters of Canada claim to have cut adrift from Europe. The most patriotic of them, however, could scarcely persuade themselves that they are free from European attachments, and they must not complain if, when their pictures come over, the points of similarity are more immediately noticed than the features which promise or already mark a divergence. It is easy enough to recognize the traces of Van Gogh or Cézanne in the more recent pictures, and still more the influence of the almost ubiquitous colour print from Munich or Vienna. Where there is a divergence we do not naturally assign it to some local characteristic of topography or vision. We are far too much accustomed in modern painting to stylized exaggeration of form and structure for the sake either of rhythm or absence of rhythm, and to combinations of colour which are introduced for their own sake and without any reference to nature. In Canada, of course, the realistic reference must be much more powerful, but in this country we cannot substantiate any new or disconcerting features by our own experience as, for example, we have come to accept Van Gogh's rendering of Provence under a mistral. Nor, so far at any rate, does there seem to be anything with such force of colour, design or realism that it can impress itself as a new vision, as Van Gogh's has done on thousands who know nothing either of Provence or the mistral.

Those who have been to Canada, however, tell us of an autumn when the blaze of colour is so intense that it can scarcely be tolerated, of range after range of featureless hills which spread endlessly like a wilderness of dark foliage, of a hard bright toneless atmosphere at some seasons, and at others of vast opaque clouds which are unparalleled for heaviness by anything in Europe. No doubt the new painters in Canada are right in deciding that the old European conventions of painting are powerless to make pictures of these. At any rate, the earlier part of this exhibition, while it shows some highly accomplished painters such as Brownell, Hébert, Cullen, Gagnon and Morrice, contains nothing which might not have been produced, say in the Highlands of Scandinavia by natives of those countries. The newer forms of technique have certainly freed the painters to attack a new type of subject, just as in Europe they have enabled pictures to be made of the material which would have proved deterrent to an older generation. The weapons may have been forged in Europe, but if they find them suitable for use on their own soil and for their own purposes, the Canadians may have justified themselves in forgetting whence they were derived.

Their leading painter, Tom Thomson, died too early to have a part in the movement, and he was too short-lived to do himself full justice. It is unfortunate that the exhibition does not include any of the direct sketches from which his few large pictures were composed. In these the gaily coloured decorations no doubt owe something of flatness and want of depth to the Canadian atmosphere, but for us it is only part of a semi-oriental convention. His somewhat complicated technique adds the process-like effect. Of his successors, Arthur Lismer and Franklin Carmichael began by introducing an element of greater solidity into static compositions on Thomson's lines, while Alexander Jackson and James MacDonald seem to have led the movement towards enlivening their compositions by emphasis on waving and rolling lines. The clear atmosphere of Canada is no doubt reflected in the former by strong, rather harsh colouring, while the latter largely restricts himself to the somewhat soupy browns and reds of its darker days. Both of them, with Lismer and many others, seem to seek with their flat and heavy colouring something of a woolwork effect which is by no means unknown in Europe, but is so much pronounced in this Canadian movement as almost to constitute a national characteristic. On the other hand, Charles Fraser Comfort, whose large portraits in water-colour are among the most noticeable pictures in the exhibition, has a neater and more restrained note in his little picture of pill-box houses against a wide expanse of sea, and the most striking painter of the group, Lawren Harris, has simplified his Arctic landscapes under a slaty light until his rocks and promontories are fluted and scalloped into metallic shapes.

By comparison with much of the work that was produced in England during the same period, these Canadian pictures have a note of freshness and vigour. The painters have managed to retain in their maturity much of the quality of good student work. They strive too much for effect, and have a confidence which owes more to fashion than they know themselves, but they show a brave effort to achieve something which they have observed for themselves, though it may as yet be beyond their grasp. Possibly their over-assertion may be due in part to isolation and a lack of a congenial atmosphere. Conditions in Canada must be still harder for painters than they are here. But with greater encouragement at home it is to be hoped that the master painter will arise to fuse the material and the manner together into a convincing unity. It might be as well to go back a little way and, instead of producing drop scenes and woolwork, to follow up the line indicated by Carmichael's Light and Shadows, in which an attempt was made to combine the solid forms of mountains with the depth of a three-dimensional picture. As it is, however, we are told that Harris has now turned to purely abstract painting, and there are indications even in the selection of the Tate that, for all their detachment from Europe, the youngest generation of Canadian painters is already imitating those among their dotard elders who seek to renew their youth by crawling on all fours.

The full genesis of this new style of Canadian painting, as presented by the Group of Seven, since expanded into the Group of Canadian Painters, will not be apparent for many years to come.

C. A. G. Matthews, Esq., Toronto.

HOMEWARD AS THE EVENING FALLS

J. SYDNEY HALLAM

Contemporary analysis is often untrustworthy and I for one do not propose to attempt it. But from the evolution of the Group's own style we can at least guess what has been stirring. An abandonment of the traditional and academic practice of detailed, representation, together with a free inquiry into the divers motives and revolutionary theories and formulas of the last three decades of nineteenth-century art, and a selection from these periods of what seemed most useful, have at last been co-ordinated by these Canadian painters into a synthesis that is neither archaic nor pastiche. Modern taste is in love with the formal and, in a sense, with the austere, but it also demands a certain grace and deftness of touch. Anything approaching the heavy-handed in painting, as in letters, is abhorrent. Thus the landscapes of the Group, reminiscent of nothing in the past—I speak now of art in Canada—have

Art Gallery of Toronto.

BEFORE RAIN: PARRY SOUND
CARL SCHAEFER

resulted in a clear break with the older ideas, in colour, form and representation, upon which most Canadian painting had hitherto been based.

Formed, in 1925, to encourage and foster the art of water-colour painting in Canada, the Canadian Society of Painters in Water Colour has been nation-wide in its activities, with the result that since its inception the art has received great stimulus. Exhibitions of the Society's work, sponsored by the National Gallery at

Ottawa, have been sent across Canada, to Great Britain and to the United States. The interest thus awakened has led a rapidly increasing number of painters to explore the possibilities of this medium of expression.

New methods of technique have been experimented with and developed. As a result of this revival, an ever-increasing group of artists are painting in water-colour, for the most part with freshness, sparkle and a new intensity of feeling. In the process, many prejudices have been broken down. Thus painting in water-colour as a polite accomplishment has gone; and the day of the serious and intelligent worker in the medium is here. The policy of the Society is flexible and encourages all forms of experiment in water-colour, from the tinted drawing made popular by Rowlandson, to the later and more robust methods of expression as advanced by Charles Comfort and Peter Haworth.

It scarcely need be said, that the understanding and appreciation of good pictures comes primarily through the experience of seeing them. By its periodical exhibitions throughout Canada, the Canadian Society of Painters in Water Colour has done a distinct service to its community, in which the best of contemporary water-colour painting has been offered to public view without reserve. By this means, as one of its presidents half-humorously remarked: "It has served those who are finally conscious that art is not imitation, as well as those who say, 'I don't know much about Art, but I know what I like.'"

Among its members are to be found such painters of reputation as Charles W. Jefferys, Fred. H. Brigden, Walter J. Phillips, Charles Comfort, Peter Haworth, Carl Schaefer, Paul Alfred, Conyers Barker, Franklin Carmichael, Alfred J. Casson, Fred. G. Cross, J. S. Hallam, A. C. Leighton, Arthur Lismer, T. W. McLean, Will Ogilvie, J. E. Sampson, George A. Reid, Owen Staples and W. A. Winter—sufficient proof, if proof were needed, of the representative nature and importance of this comparatively youthful society in the art life of Canada.

A water-colourist, working independently, is James Blomfield, who finds congenial subjects at his own doorstep. Excepting those derived from residence or visitation elsewhere in Canada, most of his themes are found in Toronto and its vicinity, as his titles indicate: OVER SCARBOROUGH BAY, A SUMMER MORNING, ACROSS DANFORTH MEADOWS, THE CREDIT RIVER, OLD TRINITY

National Gallery of Canada.

A PORTRAIT OF THE ARTIST

AS A YOUNG MAN

FRANÇOIS MALEPART DE BEAUCOURT

106

CHURCH, TORONTO, and EVENING ON THE BROAD WALK: CENTRE ISLAND. Here the older purlieus of downtown Toronto, Scarborough, and the shoreline of Bronte have presented inviting material of which he has taken full advantage. Certain it is that his water-colour drawings, though moderate in size, even small, exhibit a breadth of treatment and a freshness of approach not often seen. In such poetic studies as THE POPLARS OF PARKDALE, WATERSIDE HOUSES, A FLIGHT OF HOMING DRAGONS, depicting a broken range of purple-tinged clouds floating across a luminous evening sky, and in THE LITTLE BRIDGE he displays a marked virtuosity in the varied and fascinating use of clean translucent washes. A nature painter with a genuine love of all natural phenomena, Blomfield studies closely the changing skies, the play of light and shadow on distant landscape, reflected sunlight on quiet waters, and the shimmering haze of autumn that softens and refines colours and contours. And in these familiar neighbourhood scenes he interprets so well he wields a dexterous and a knowing brush flowing with joyous colour.

8

Among the early artists of Quebec, the earliest recorded name is that of Beaucourt or, to give him his full and high-sounding appellation, François Malepart de Beaucourt. For a time it was thought that Paul Kane was to be distinguished as being our first native-born artist, until it was discovered that he owed his birthplace to Ireland. However, that distinction, in any event, would have been reserved for Beaucourt, who was born at Laprairie, Quebec, about the year 1735. The son of the Chevalier de Beaucourt, military engineer under Frontenac, and Governor of Montreal, young de Beaucourt studied in France and, returning to Canada, he painted for many years after the Conquest; but the unsettled state of the country induced him to go to Russia, where he painted for some years. He again returned to Canada and died at the beginning of the last century. Little of a definite nature is known of his career, and examples of his work are rare. One of his few known canvases (it may or may not have been painted in Canada), formerly in the McCord Museum of McGill University, Móntreal, and now in the National Gallery, Ottawa, portrays a smiling negro wench with a bowl of exotic fruits. The whole composition is suffused with a soft mellow glow, whether due to age or the artist's intent, is impossible to say. In technique the portrait faintly recalls Gauguin. It is thinly painted. A less well-known portrait by Beaucourt is that of JOSEPH PEPIN (1770-1842), militia major, sculptor and architect.

Besides Beaucourt, any group of early Quebec painters must of necessity include the names of Joseph Légaré, Antoine Plamondon, Théophile Hamel, Napoléon Bourassa, Joseph Adolph Rho and Charles Huot, with possibly Antoine Falardeau. Perhaps three, at most four, of these names are familiar to artists in Canada, still fewer to the ordinary layman who knows them not at all, yet these Canadian painters of French descent are, for the most part, deserving of a better reward than the total oblivion that threatens to overtake them.

Of all our early painters, affirms Georges Bellerive in his series of monographs, *Artistes-Peintres canadiens-francais*, Joseph Légaré is certainly one who merits the major consideration of his fellow countrymen. Indeed he is the only artist of Quebec who has by his works won the admiration of his contemporaries without having had the advantage of studying in Europe under the direction of recognized masters, and without even having had teachers of standing at home to advise and direct him. Alone he had to perfect himself in his art; but by the force of native energy, of perseverance, and of long years of study and practice, did succeed at last in attaining success.

Such in bare outline is the life story of Joseph Légaré, artist, patriot and, in its most respectable sense, politician. Born on March 10, 1789, at Quebec, Légaré began while still in his twenties to copy the paintings to be found in the churches and religious institutions of his native city. This self-imposed discipline occupied many of his first years as a student painter. In 1832, however, he reproduced on canvas episodes of the great cholera epidemic in Quebec. These were followed, in 1845, by FAUBOURG ST. ROCH, and also a companion piece, FAUBOURG DE ST. JEAN-BAPTISTE, showing devastation caused by the fire of that year. Historically, if not aesthetically, these pictures today have an especial interest and value as authentic and vivid records of the time. Other paintings were his studies of Indian and habitant life, as well as Quebec landscapes. Among his pictures of Indians and

Indian life to be found in the collection of Laval University are: LE DESESPOIR D'UNE INDIENNE, which in 1826 was awarded a medal by the Society of Arts in Montreal; LE MASSACRE DES HURONS PAR LES IROQUOIS; and UN PORTRAIT DE JOSETTE OURNÉE, daughter of an Abenaquis chief. Of the numerous landscapes painted by Légaré, four are to be seen at Laval. These are: LE BASSIN DE LA RIVIÈRE ETCHEMIN; LES CHUTES NIAGARA (just when Légaré visited the Falls is not recorded; this picture, therefore, though of course not necessarily so, may be a copy); LES CASCADES DE LORETTE, and those of the Jacques Cartier River; LE ROCHE DE PERCÉ; and LES MARCHES NATURELLES, on the river Montmorency, which encroaching industry has since caused to disappear. Of actual scenes of Canadian life, meaning of course life in Lower Canada, four canvases only are recorded: LES ANCIENS CANADIENS, and UNE SCENE D'ELECTION AU CHÂTEAU-RICHER, owned by Laval University; and two other canvases, LA PROCESSION DEVANT L'ÉGLISE DE GENTILLY, and LA BATAILLE DE STE.-FOY, both privately owned. Also in the possession of Laval University at Quebec are three historic portraits of importance: LORD ELGIN, former Governor-General of Canada, QUEEN VICTORIA (presumably after Winterhalter); and GEORGE III, after Allan Ramsay.

Légaré was not only an artist, but he was also a member of the Legislative Council and a senator, a distinction which he shares with the painter David. During his career Légaré managed to form, it is said, probably the richest collection of paintings and engravings known to exist in the country at that time. These were exhibited publicly in 1838 and again in 1852. Finally they were acquired by Laval University following the artist's death in 1855.

Antoine Plamondon was born in 1802, at St. Roch, Quebec, where his father kept a grocery. In 1826, after a brief period of tuition in the studio of Légaré, he went to Paris to study, where he had as instructor Paul Guerin, one of the masters of the French school. Quitting Paris after a time, Plamondon journeyed to Rome, Florence and Venice, where he employed himself, as was the custom of the day, in copying the works of the early Italian painters. In 1830 he returned to Canada and was appointed professor of drawing at the Seminary of Quebec. His studio at the Château Haldimand was on the site of the present Château Frontenac. It was there that many of his religious paintings were done.

The copies of paintings by Raphael, Nicholas Poussin, da Vinci and Van Loo were subsequently destroyed by fire. Nevertheless, the greater portion of his works still remain, distributed over many places, including Laval University, the Hôtel-Dieu, the General Hospital at Quebec, and in the chapel of the Jesuit Fathers in Upper Town, Quebec. Plamondon's work is also to be seen in the old church at Ste. Anne de Beaupré, in the church of St. Anselme and of St. Peter on the Island of Orleans, as well as in other churches of the district. In the Parliamentary Library at Quebec is preserved a portrait by Plamondon of Zacharie Vincent, last survivor of the Huron tribe at Lorette, who died in 1886. This canvas, entitled ZACHARIE VINCENT, THE LAST OF THE HURONS, won a gold medal from Lord Durham in a public competition, in 1838, held by the Literary and Historical Society of Quebec.

Other important pictures attributed to his brush include: PORTRAIT D'UN JEUNE ÉCOLIER (1852), now in the collection of Laval University; GROUPE D'ENFANTS; PLAMONDON JEUNE ET SES DEUX JEUNE FRÈRES (1853); and LE JOUEUR DE FLUTE. This last-named painting owes its origin to the arrival at Quebec of *La Capricieuse*, the first French warship to visit Canada since the Conquest. In subject matter it recalls the JOUEUR DE PICOLO by Edouard Manet in the Louvre at Paris. A large canvas, LA CHASSE AUX TOURTES, painted by him in 1869, forms part of the permanent collection of the Art Gallery of Toronto. Bold in conception, vigorous in treatment, though somewhat stilted in composition, it is a striking example of the popular story picture of the Victorian period.

Towards 1860 Antoine Plamondon was engaged to paint the portrait of the Honourable Joseph Cauchon, who was to become in 1867 Lieutenant-Governor of Manitoba. In 1874 he painted a scene of the trial of General Bazaine, which was bought by the Honourable M. De Bouchéville, then Premier of Quebec. Another subject done at this date, possibly a copy, was ANDROMAQUE ET SON FILS DEVANT PYRRHUS. A period of ecclesiastical painting followed until 1882, when at eighty years he turned aside to paint a portrait of himself, which is reputed to be one of his best works. The colouring is still fresh, and the features serene, dignified and imposing.

Plamondon had the honour of being the first French-speaking Canadian to be admitted a member of the Royal Canadian Academy at its foundation in 1880, to figure in a picture of the celebrities of Canada in 1864, and to be compared at his death to the Italian (later English) painter, Fuseli, by Pierre Georges Roy, provincial archivist. One of his paintings, THE PORTRAIT OF A NUN, is owned by the National Gallery at Ottawa. He died at Neuville, Quebec, in September, 1895, aged ninety-three.

No less interesting, certainly no less productive, is the career of Théophile Hamel, who was born November 8, 1817, at St. Foye, where his father was a farmer on a modest scale as most of the farmers of the Province were and are. At the age of seventeen young Hamel entered the studio of Plamondon. In 1843 he left for Europe, where he continued his studies at the Academy of St. Luke, Rome. He then visited successively Florence, Bologna and Venice, and later Paris, where he copied a number of paintings in the Louvre. Hamel also spent some time in Antwerp, where he had as fellow-students De Keyser, Van Lerius and Portaels, who afterwards became the instructor of the Canadian painter, Eugene Hamel, R.C.A.

In 1846 Hamel returned to Quebec. Here he painted a portrait of himself in the garb of an artist, wearing a beret and holding a palette and brushes. This canvas, one of thirteen now owned by Laval University, is said to be one of the artist's best works. Later Hamel undertook to visit professionally Montreal, Toronto, Kingston and the United States. At Montreal, in 1847, he did a large canvas for the main altar of the Church of Notre Dame du Bon-Secours, which represents the Sisters of Charity ministering to the victims of typhus, or what was more commonly known as "ship fever," as brought to this country by immigrants of the thirties and forties.

Hamel's greatest glory was to have been charged by the government of the Province of Quebec, at the time of the Union, to do the portraits of the members of the Baldwin-Lafontaine ministry and the Speakers of the Legislative Council and Assembly before and after the Union of Upper and Lower Canada. These portraits included, among others, those of the Honourable Sir David Smith, Sir William Campbell, Sir Louis-Hippolyte Lafontaine and Denis Benjamin Viger of the period of the Union; and the Honourables M. Panet, De Lotbinière and Louis Joseph Papineau of the period before the Union. All these canvases, unfortunately, were destroyed, partly by the fire which consumed the first Parliament Buildings at Quebec in 1854, and the remaining pictures by fire which later razed the second Parliamentary edifice.

In his portraiture, Hamel gives evidence of searching for character in his sitters. Certainly as a craftsman he was far in advance of his predecessors in Quebec, and it may well be in Canada. As a mark of recognition for his skill as a painter, the Chamber of Arts and Manufactures of Lower Canada awarded a medal to Théophile Hamel at the Industrial Exhibition held on the occasion of the visit of the Prince of Wales to Canada in 1860. Ten years later he was to die, "bearing with him to the tomb," as his biographer testifies, "the respect and esteem of all his contemporaries."

Antoine Sebastian Falardeau, born on August 13, 1823, in one of the oldest settlements of Quebec, Cap-Sauté, was the son of Joseph Falardeau, who at the age of thirteen fought in the ranks of the Voltigeurs of Chateauguay under Colonel de Salaberry in the War of 1812. His father wished to make his son a farmer, but the son had other ideas; he wished to paint. And so he applied to Théophile Hamel, who gave the young Falardeau some advice and lent him some sketches to copy. After a time Falardeau went to Florence and then to Parma to study, and copied the works of the old masters in Milan, Bologna, Venice and Naples. There he took part in an international competition for the best copy of SAINT JEROME by Correggio. Falardeau's copy is still believed to form part of the collection of the Museum of Parma. However that may be, the Parma Academy of Fine Arts awarded Falardeau first prize and admitted him to their number as an honorary member. In further recognition of his ability as a painter, the Duke of Parma made him a chevalier of the Order of Saint Louis. So highly was the painting valued, that England (the details are no more explicit) is said to have offered two million francs for its possession. In any event, the interest it aroused was so great and the crowds so numerous, that the authorities of the Museum were compelled to open the doors of the galleries on Sundays to satisfy the public curiosity.

The period was the early fifties, when interest in religious painting was at its height and the Pre-Raphaelite movement in England was upsetting conventional ideas of painting. Falardeau came back to Canada to receive the homage of his countrymen. He did not remain long, however, but returned to Italy, where, in 1889, as the result of a tragic accident, he died. At the moment

112

when he was crossing on horseback one of the bridges of the Arno, his horse took fright and threw him into the river, where he was drowned. He was buried at the cemetery of San Miniato at Florence.

Although Falardeau produced considerable work, little of it is original. His paintings in Canada are few and these imitative. Three only are known to exist here: LE CHRIST EN CROIX, after Raphael, in the Seminary of Quebec; LA BAIE DE CASTELMARE, after Salvator Rosa (done in Florence in 1855), in Laval University; and a copy of a self-portrait by MADAME VIGEÉ LE BRUN, owned by P. B. Casgrain of Quebec.

Of his work, the Abbé Casgrain says in part. I venture to translate:

He excelled in perfection of finish, in the poetic feeling of his execution. His miniatures are true in tone, and pure in line; luminous in quality, fresh and harmonious in style, and often of a ravishing naïveté. We have been able to admire especially the merging of these brilliant qualities in the little pictures that he has shown here.

On August 27, 1916, there died at Lachenaie, Napoléon Bourassa, at the advanced age of eighty-nine years. Thus was recorded in a brief obituary one of the most distinguished figures in the annals of Lower Canada. Although he is for our present purpose listed as painter, Bourassa was also an architect, a writer of parts, a musician, a sculptor and possessed beside something more than a layman's knowledge of law.

At the College of Montreal, Bourassa followed a classical course, but later studied for the bar. It was not very long, however, before he perceived that his vocation was not the bar, but art. For the arts he felt a real aptitude; and so, despite parental objection, he soon apprenticed himself to Théophile Hamel as student. Then followed the customary period of four years abroad. In 1856 Bourassa returned to Canada and, following an exhibition of his work, was employed for the next six years making portraits.

At this time group teaching of the arts in Montreal was confined to the Council of the Arts and Crafts, an English school, founded in 1857, which only opened its library to the Société des Artisans Canadiens-français in 1865. However, the Art Association of Montreal, founded in 1860, of which the members with few exceptions were English, evinced a spirit of generosity and friendliness toward its French-speaking compatriots by inaugurating its first exhibition of paintings in the rooms of the Artisans Canadiens-français.

Bourassa, believing that such expedients were neither sufficient for his purpose nor especially fruitful in results, sought to popularize art among the people by precept and example. He became teacher of drawing, in 1868, without salary, at the Société des Artisans Canadien-français, where he taught classes in the evenings. Three years later a union of that society with the Council of the Arts and Crafts, brought him exactly three dollars a night. In 1868 he insisted upon the primary utility of a knowledge of drawing in an article published by the *Revue Canadienne*, under the title: "Du developpement du gôut dans les Arts en Canada."

L'enseignment de quelques specialites utiles, particulièrement de l'art fertile du dessin, ne se fait encore nulle part, de manière à offrir quelques resultats satisfaisans.

Then he went on to say how he grounded his pupils in the principles of art, by carrying out under his direction the execution of murals in churches of the near-by parishes of Montreal, notably in the Chapel of Notre Dame de Lourdes. There his pupils acquired that personal experience in doing which he deemed no less essential to their proper education than oral instruction. Let us please to remember also, if we wish to know how farsighted Bourassa's methods were, that the time is 1868, not 1942. And yet what system of teaching could by any chance be more plausible, more logical or, if you like, more in the spirit of our day? Bourassa concludes his article, apparently one of a series, by saying:

Eh, bien! si un des articles de ce programme improvisé dans un reve n'est pas tout a fait realizé, je veux dire la fondation de l'école d'art par la pratique, par la production de l'œuvre même, il y a au moins ici la preuve que la chose est non seulement possible, mais qu'elle est la seule veritablement efficacé dans les conditions de notre société.

In 1870 the Art Association of Montreal invited him to exhibit a number of his paintings, among others LA MISE AU TOMBEAU and LA MORT DE SAINT JOSEPH. One of his portraits was specially signalized by the critic of the *Canadian Illustrated News:* "M. N. Bourassa's portrait of an ecclesiastic is in every way a fine painting. The artist has remarkably succeeded in throwing expression into the features."

Three years before this, Bourassa had been elected a member of the Society of Canadian Artists, which had for its aim the sale of members' pictures. In 1874 he became instructor of modelling and director of the School of Design. In 1877 the provincial government confided to him the task of enquiring into conditions as they existed in the schools of arts and crafts in France. His report, as submitted upon his return, suffered the fate of many another report; it was buried in the fyles of the ministerial office. The time had not yet arrived to consecrate to art, public funds required for what was conceived to be more pressing needs.

Napoléon Bourassa, in 1880, became one of the founder-members and vice-president of the Royal Canadian Academy of Arts, and was deputed to deliver one of the principal addresses at its inauguration.

It was said of Bourassa that he had all the talents, and so it would seem. By competent authority, he was regarded as one of the best writers of his time. His romance of Acadian life, *Jacques et Marie*, is filled with moving passages of idyllic prose. Although not a composer, he was a musician, and the laws of harmony, of which he possessed an innate sense, were familiar to him. He would also háve made, had he willed it, a fine sculptor, as his bust of Louis Joseph Papineau bears witness. An excellent draughts-man, he preferred architecture to sculpture. The chapel of Notre Dame de Lourdes, Montreal; the church of Sainte Anne, Fall River, Mass.; the monastery of the Dominican Fathers and the chapel of the Religieuses de la Presentation at St. Hyacinthe, all testify to his skill as an architect, despite an amplitude of conception often too vast for the resources of the country at that time.

However, "son œuvre rest, apres sa mort, utile à ses conci-toyens: cela, suffirait à sa memoire." He is represented in the National Gallery, Ottawa, by his LEGENDE DU BERCEAU, a diploma picture.

An artist of Quebec of little fame and yet, I think, not unworthy of record, was Joseph Adolphe Rho, who like his fellow artist, Bourassa, was a man of parts. The reason why Rho is not better known outside his native Province is, we may suppose, because he devoted his working life largely, if not almost alto-gether, to the painting of religious themes. Following in the tradition of Louis Jobin, he engaged in the carving of religious subjects for the parish church, for he was sculptor as well as painter. In the district of Three Rivers, and even throughout the Province, his reputation in both these forms of art would appear to have been considerable.

Rho was born at Gentilly, Quebec, in April, 1835, and died at Becancourt, Quebec, in August, 1905. Between these years he managed to turn out a respectable body of work, which, if not of a high order, proved at least that he was a journeyman of the soundest kind. Joseph Rho was quite definitely a man of resource — a substantial achievement in this day of intense specialization — which alone entitles him to recognition. Besides being a sculptor of merit, he was an architect, a carpenter, a machinist, a blacksmith or metalworker and a fertile inventor.

Tous les genres de travaux, says his biographer, semblement lui être devenus familiers, et tout est éxécute avec une justesse de coup d'œil, une promptitude qui jettent dans l'éstonnement tous ceux qui le voient à l'œuvre.

Thus the worthy example set by Cellini is reflected in the earlier artists of the country; the later ones somehow seem to have lost something of this fine facility.

Like a number of his confrères, Rho practised sculpture before taking up painting. He had had the early advantage of instruction from a competent master in drawing and perspective. Knowing something already of sculpture, photography, geometry and perspective, Rho wished to supplement this knowledge with a period of study in Europe. He went to Paris, where he was assisted by the Canadian painter, Charles Huot, who directed him to the galleries of the Louvre, of Versailles, of the Luxembourg and of the Écoles des Beaux-Arts, where his work was warmly praised. In portraiture, in which he excelled, Rho was noted for his ability to obtain a close likeness of his sitter, whether in crayon, in pastel or in oils.

During the period from 1885 to 1903 Rho sculptured all three statues in wood for the façade of the church of Yamachiche; he executed all the sculpture for the church of St. Elphege of Nicolet; and he carved two statues in wood for the college of St. Gabriel, which were placed on the façade. His best work in sculpture is said to be a reproduction in relief of LA CÈNE, by Leonardo da Vinci, which ornaments the main altar of the parish church of Jacques Cartier in Quebec. In painting, among many others, we may cite as representative of his best style LE BAPTÈME DU SEIGNEUR, a canvas given to a church in Jerusalem by a body of Canadian pilgrims. Above all, however, Joseph Rho was a portrait painter, and in the district of Three Rivers his work is still to be found in the possession of the older families. Among the early painters of Quebec his life seems to have been one of the most productive as well as, with the notable exception of Bourassa, the most singular.

Now it may be asked, and with some show of reason, I think, Why did these men of Quebec, these painters and sculptors often endowed with superior gifts, why did they then choose to maintain the tradition of two hundred years by copying the work of their predecessors, talented and famous though they were? The answer, it seems to me, lies in the conditions by which they were surrounded. In this case Diderot's maxim applies admirably: *Le milieu explique l'homme; l'atelier commente l'œuvre.* The truth of the matter is, that Quebec at this period had few art classes of her own; in all but the more thickly populated centres there were no picture collectors of any account; teachers were scarce and these when found by no means always competent. Such a condition left the schools and galleries of Europe almost the sole resource of the aspiring student. Accordingly, when his means permitted, he went to Paris and to Rome and to Venice, and found as others before him had found, students copying the work of the old masters; so he, too, copied. The net effect was that, though in course of time he achieved a fair control of colour and form, he seldom achieved anything else. The great masterpieces overawed him, and left him less and less inclined to attempt original work of his own. To try his fledgeling wings in mounting flights seemed beyond his capacity; he gave himself no chance to develop his gift for original design.

Another factor was the tendency of the ecclesiastic of Quebec (with his thoughts on the splendour that was the Mother Church's in the gorgeous days of the Renaissance, when the great masters of the period were at her command), to desire to revive something of that glory in his own time. And so the Quebec artist – painter or sculptor – was constrained by the duty he felt he owed to his Church to exemplify his devotion by embellishing her walls and sanctuaries with subjects taken from the famous churches and chapels of great cities of the Old World. Thus the practice began

117

and so it has continued. The old masters became not guide-posts, but hitching-posts.

Now there is no reason why an artist should not work for the Church as he would for another client. But there is every reason why (and I wish especially to stress this point), if he wishes to advance as an artist, that his work, whatever it may be from its conception to its completion, should be his own, and not that of another painter, however famed or however sanctified by time. The thing, then, that has hampered religious painting in Quebec is not that it was religious, but rather that it has failed to escape from a nostalgic historicity which has bound it to a purely imitative expression in which there is no health and no progress. Such restriction, it need hardly be said, was unknown when the originals were painted. No similar restraint was imposed upon El Greco, on Murillo, or on Michelangelo; and most certainly not on Rubens; and it interposed not at all on the work of Raphael. These men were masters of their *métier* and supreme in their field; then why should not our Quebec painters of ecclesiastical subjects enjoy a like freedom of action?

Certain it is if our Quebec religious painters are to become masters in their own right and give to the Church the full benefit of their originality and training, then they must perforce enjoy the same freedom to improvise and design that their more illustrious predecessors in other countries were granted. Mastership implies nothing less; and is to be achieved on no other terms.

Born in Quebec in the same year as Allen Edson, Henri Julien achieved some reputation chiefly as a cartoonist, though he painted in oils and water-colour. His pictures, which are often sketches, lacking the fullness and finish of more deliberate work, depict the life of the habitant with vigour and feeling. In 1871 he accompanied the Red River expedition as illustrator.

For more than twenty years he was, before the general use of photo-engraving, chief illustrator of the Montreal *Star*, and during this period made a name for himself by his caricatures of contemporary politicians. It is perhaps a misnomer to call them caricatures, for many of them betray but little tendency toward acromegaly. Though full of humour and spirit, they are mostly free from the violent distortion and pitiless exaggeration which mark the work of later men such as Sam Hunter, John Collins, Ivan Glassco and John McLaren. Julien's BYTOWN COONS, a series of political cartoons levelled at Laurier and his ministers, evoked lively interest when published in the late nineties, though they would scarcely excite comment now. Fashions in cartoons have changed; today we demand a style more dramatic and emphatic. Julien did not live to see the change of trend, for he died in Montreal, in 1908, at the comparatively early age of sixty-two. His water-colour sketches of French habitant life are characterized by humour, sympathy, vivacity and facile rather

HABITANT PLOUGHING, QUEBEC

CHARLES HUOT

National Gallery of Canada.

than brilliant drawing. His *forte* was rapid sketching, and his best and most typical work was done in the daily round of his duties as a newspaper artist.

If we except Charles W. Jefferys, and perhaps F. S. Challener, Canada has few historical painters. Among the artists of French Canada only one, Charles Edouard Huot, is known as a painter of historical subjects. Born in Quebec city about 1850, young Huot studied as so many Canadians did at the École des Beaux-Arts, Paris, where he was a pupil for years under Cabanel. He exhibited at the Salon at the age of twenty-one, and was awarded Honourable

Mention at the Paris Exposition of 1876. Let it be remarked here that they were Canadian landscapes and not, as has so often happened in similar instances, views of the French countryside. At the Universal Paris Exposition of 1878, he exhibited his SCENES CANADIENNES. After this his progress was rapid, for we read that, in 1888, he was awarded a silver medal at the Black-and-White Exhibition in Paris.

Upon his return to Canada, Huot painted several historical canvases, a number of religious pictures and several mural compositions for the House of Assembly at Quebec. Among other things he brought back from France materials, documents and sketches for a large composition destined for the Legislative Council-room, entitled THE FIRST SESSION OF THE SOVEREIGN COUNCIL UNDER THE FRENCH RÉGIME IN 1663, over which the Governor of New France, M. Saffray de Mesy, and Monseigneur de Laval presided. On the wall of the Legislative library he painted LA PREMIÈRE SCÉANCE DU PARLEMENT CANADIEN. This latter mural represents, as the title implies, the inauguration of the first legislative assembly composed of representatives elected by the people under the provisions of the Quebec constitutional government. The scene takes place in the chapel of the former archbishop of Quebec, and occupied by the government since 1778.

The poet, Louis Fréchette, a close connection of the painter, made this first historic composition the subject of a minute study or critique in a journal of the day. In it he observed that the work lacked authority, probably a case of the writer regarding the painting from the literary point of view. However true or wide of the mark it may be, we do well to remind ourselves that Fréchette was no stranger to the fine arts, since he had ample opportunity while in Paris and London to study the most characteristic, which is to say the best, works of the ancient and modern masters. Moreover, the severe discipline and preparatory training imposed upon the painter is in no wise different or relaxed for the poet. Invention, imagination, structure and a sense of rhythm and colour are component parts of the products of both. And the principles of criticism which might apply to the one might as aptly apply to the other. Fréchette's verdict then would seem to have some basis of reason whatever one might be tempted to think of it at this distance.

Fortunately, this detraction, if it be called a detraction, does not impair the reputation of Charles Huot as a religious and historic painter of marked distinction, as the regard in which he is held both here and abroad attests. Huot, moreover, brought a well-stored mind to his task, for he had lived and studied and worked in Spain, Germany and Italy, and for almost fifteen years in France. During his stay in Paris he executed numerous illustrations for the publishers Hachette, Firmin-Didot and Delagrave. Such drawings as LA MOULIN DE LA CALETTE and EXCAVATIONS,

Carnegie Institute, Pittsburg.

PLOUGHING AT DAWN

HORATIO WALKER

BASILICA OF MONTMARTRE, are characterized by feeling and vigour, warmth and intelligence. His painting of the Jacques Cartier House, in the Quebec Provincial Museum, indicates a style marked by breadth, strength and simple beauty.

In the early eighties came a gradual and general awakening to the immense material riches of the country, as yet not fully explored, whose living symbols were the fur trader, the timber cruiser, the miner, the migratory settler, the North-West Mounted Police, the cattle rancher, the wheat farmer and the prospector.

The artist, for the moment concerned with their outward significance, found in them ready and prolific material for his pencil and his brush. In Quebec, on the Isle of Orleans, the Ontario-born Horatio Walker was to engage in putting on canvas for more than fifty years those scenes of habitant life which have become part of our most cherished possessions.

Unquestionably the handling of his subjects shows the influence of Millet, but above all they bear the impress of the painter's masterly skill and powerful personality. A Walker painting would be recognized for what it is even though it bore no signature at all. It is no credit to Canada that the genius of Horatio Walker was first recognized in the United States, where he was from the beginning highly appreciated and richly rewarded. But the story is an old one, and likely to stale by repetition. In the same Province at the same time, assisting in the development of a Canadian school of painting, were William Brymner, Suzor-Côté, James Wilson Morrice, G. Horne Russell, Maurice Cullen, F. S. Coburn and, somewhat later, Clarence Gagnon.

Like other Canadian painters of the period, Cullen went abroad to study, where he was for several years a familiar figure in the ateliers of Paris, as was also James Wilson Morrice. Upon his return to Canada, Cullen applied himself so diligently and sympathetically to the interpretation of the Canadian landscape as to win a considerable international reputation as a painter of superior talent. At his death, in 1934, he bequeathed to us a large body of exquisitely fine work, indigenous to the country and testifying to the painter's attachment to his native land in a manner that recalls West's remark to Constable, that he must have greatly loved the English landscape, he painted it so well. No one, I think, can contemplate Cullen's THE ICE HARVEST or MARCH EVENING, LAURENTIANS without being profoundly conscious of his sensitive observation of Nature, and his superb ability to translate to canvas her varying moods.

Though an expatriate by choice, James Wilson Morrice was no less a Canadian in his fondness for his native soil. His recurrent essays on his infrequent trips to Canada show him at his best as a painter of Quebec scenes, both of urban and rural life, which no one depicted more sympathetically or more knowledgeably than he. His paintings of habitant life in handling and colour occasionally recall Horatio Walker. The influence, if any, was probably unconscious, since Morrice of all Canadian painters was strikingly individualistic in his point of view and in his technique. In the main his style is markedly personal, the true expression of a man, directed by a selective and discriminating eye which tends to reduce the subject in hand to broad masses and simple planes. The chief charm of his canvases lies in their lovely subtleties of colour and felicitous arrangement. As a colourist, Morrice causes his paintings to glow with light and sunshine, and always a joyous note pervades, as if he took a sheer pagan delight in the changing

THE VALLEY OF THE DEVIL RIVER   *National Gallery of Canada.*
MAURICE CULLEN

beauty of the world outdoors. His is a simple art, to the unthinking or unknowing deceptively simple; but it will be found upon examination to contain all the elements necessary to a full sensuous enjoyment of his work.

In the category with Morrice, but more closely akin in personal style to Cullen, is E. Suzor-Côté, who as a Canadian of French parentage devoted his days to reproducing on canvas his beloved Laurentians and the valleys and plains below, both in the heydey of summer and when the countryside was under snow. Suzor-Côté was also a sculptor of high capacity. One recalls his models

123

La Mussée de Lyons, Lyons

EFFET DE NEIGE, CANADA

JAMES WILSON MORRICE

in clay of MARIA CHAPDELAINE, of the INDIAN WOMEN OF CAUGH-
NAWAGA, as being among the finest things that Canadian sculpture
has yet produced   But these and others of the habitant country
were largely a labour of love, for Canadians are not yet patrons of
the pictorial arts, let alone the less obvious art of sculpture.
Fortunate indeed are the persons or the institutions that possess

them.   Suzor-Côté is a conspicuous exception among our established native-born artists as one who had the capacity to work
in both pigment and clay with equal facility.   Thus his position
among Canadian artists is shared probably by only one other

Vancouver Art Gallery.

CAUGHNAWAGA WOMEN

Aurèle de Foy Suzor-Coté

artist of our day—Cleeve Horne, who is both a painter and sculptor
of marked ability.

I have tried to measure the influence of the Quebec group of
sculptors and painters upon Canadian art.   By illustration and
citation it has been shown that the artist of French Canada,
whatever may have been his medium, his *genre*, or his intent, did

125

to some extent encourage by his example his contemporaries in the fine arts labouring in the Canadian field elsewhere. There were others, among them the sculptor Henri Hébert, who with his brothers Philippe and Adrien formed a triumvirate of the arts quite as unique in their way as Suzor-Côté was in his. For the moment we are concerned with Henri. Of him as perhaps the most recent of the trio, Jean Chauvin, in 1928, wrote: "L'art décoratif est devenue la grande preoccupation du moment. De tous nos artistes Henri Hébert est celui qui peut-être sent cet art le plus profondement et l'exprimi le mieux." Doubtless there is room for a difference of opinion here. It must be admitted that this view expressed by a compatriot is valuable, not because it is in any sense final, which of course it is not (since no assessment is), but rather because it is the considered opinion of one well acquainted with Henry Hébert and his work and in a position to speak of it with some authority.

Of Hébert's work as a sculptor much has been said in honest praise.

His SIR ANDREW MACPHAIL, physician and man of letters, is, to translate M. Chauvin, a remarkable bust, which with that of ALPHONSE JONGERS, the portrait painter, and of the organist MARCEL DUPRÉ, are sufficient to confirm the reputation of Hébert as our *maître bustier*. They have never been so well done. . . . Above all he seeks to achieve something more than a photographic resemblance, in favour let us say, of a reflection of the psychological, or, as it is commonly phrased, the soul of the sitter.

Henri Hébert has also by turns been etcher, pastellist and engraver; but it is with clay that he works with the utmost skill and pleasure. Bas-reliefs executed for the remodelled Moyse Hall of McGill University denote the sculptor's fixed regard for the classical tradition. The principle of wilful distortion and exaggeration upon which modernistic art is largely based has no place in his *modus operandi*. His art is purely representational, yet his range is wide and his manner versatile. Nowhere possibly is his response to the new movement in art more evident or handled with greater skill, tact and intelligence than in his treatment of *1914*, a feat of graphic and dramatic symbolism challenging in its admirable simplicity. DANSEUSE AU REPOSE and the FLAPPER are similarly works of a man who is master of his medium. Philippe, his father, and possibly the more conventional of the two, is chiefly remembered for his MAISONNEUVE MEMORIAL, his statue of SIR

GEORGES ÉTIENNE CARTIER, and his highly imaginative memorial to the French-Canadian poet, OCTAVE CRÉMAZIE.

Adrien Hébert is a painter of the quay and the city—familiar scenes which the artist, with a keen awareness of modern life, with his gift of translation and with his penetrating and fresh vision of things, seems to show us for the first time. His pictures of ships are portraits of ships, a subject in which the artist excels, and on which he has for some years exerted his skill as a painter of the waterside. But these are not sailing ships of sail; they bear us to no far-off adventures. Instead of a sea-chanty, we hear the voice of the siren. Their destination, too, is fixed: within a fortnight they shall twice cross the ocean. They are huge and powerful and overawing, often inspiring as the traffic of commerce seldom is. They have also a certain austere beauty, for they have much of beauty in themselves; in the contents of their cargoes is the stuff that dreams are made of, and in their line and form inhere the traditions of the sea. Thus Hébert comprehends them, thus he depicts them in the harmonious proportions of a modern and highly efficient structure. In 1923 he studied in Paris with some masters of the French modern school: André Favory, Charles Jacquemot, Marcel Roche, to name only a few. In spite of this modernistic training in which the rational so often plays a small part, Hébert is not embarrassed by any pictorial theory. Painting what he sees around him, the objects and people of our time, he departs radically from the principle of distortion and deformation of modernistic art, as his MONTREAL HARBOUR and THE SMITHY clearly reveal.

9

Other men in the Quebec group whose work is widely known are Frederic Simpson Coburn, Charles W. Simpson, Albert Robinson and Laliberte the sculptor. Strangely enough, Coburn did not take up the study of painting until 1914. Until then, and during a period of some twenty years, he had been engaged as an illustrator. Today scarcely a Canadian painter enjoys a higher reputation. His early illustrations were drawn in black-and-white for William Henry Drummond's book of verse, on the habitant,

A ROAD IN THE WOODS

FREDERICK SIMPSON COBURN

Noël au Canada, a novel by the French Canadian poet, Louis Fréchette, and Drummond's *Johnnie Courteau* and *The Great Fight*. Next he illustrated the works of Edgar Allan Poe for Putnam's of New York. He illustrated the verse of Tennyson, of Oliver Goldsmith and of Robert Browning, as well as other books by

128

English and American authors. A period of long and arduous study had prepared the artist for this task to which he brought a keen, sympathetic mind and a disciplined hand.

Born in Upper Melbourne in the Cantons of the East, he early registered as a student of the Council of Arts and Manufactures at Montreal. He next pursued his studies in New York under Carl Becker; at Berlin and at Paris in the studio of Gerome; at the Slade School in London, under Henry Tonks; and lastly at the Institute des Beaux-Arts in Antwerp, under Julian de Vreendt, where he had as a fellow the Canadian painter, James L. Graham. At Antwerp he won a scholarship good for three years. He prolonged it for twenty years, and only quitted Antwerp when war broke out. Since then he has applied himself to painting only, dividing his time between his studio at Richmond and his studio, or rather a *pied-à-terre*, in Montreal. Coburn's canvases are familiar to all lovers of painting. His favourite subject perhaps most often seen shows horses, usually a white and a bay, or oxen hauling a sled heavily laden with logs and driven by one of his cherished habitants on its way toward the river. Groupings of fir saplings as in CANADIAN WINTER, violet or mauve, underline in the distance the soft inflections of the mountains and the snow, with their blue shadows brilliant under an azure sky. Usually there is a road in the clearing where the painter has captured that light which vibrates in the woods as in THE PASTURE HILL, or HEALE VALLEY, and is softly reflected in his animals, snow and trees. Again there are summer landscapes with toilers in the fields in which the whole composition is bathed in warm, luminous sunshine. The canvases of Coburn, having regard to his earlier training, are invariably distinguished by fine draughtsmanship. He is not only a painter, but an etcher, an engraver on wood, proficient of course in black-and-white when the pencil and the crayon take the place of the brush and the palette. His drawings for L'ASSASSINAT DE LA RUE MORGUE, executed with two crayons, a black and a red, have all the freshness, lightness, delicacy and charm of pastel colouring. He evidently regards a subject as an opportunity to produce effects of light and subtle colour harmonies. The subject may be, and sometimes is, repeated, but the light which illumines it rarely is.

Contemporary with Coburn were men of the Quebec group likewise distinguished for their varied talents and solid contribution to Canadian painting. Their names are familiar to all who profess an interest in our native arts. All were members of the Royal Canadian Academy, though possibly at this date that distinction may be to some a doubtful recommendation. However, at the time of their election it was not so. The Academy rallied beneath its banners the foremost men of the arts in Canada. Among them in Quebec, besides those previously mentioned, were William Raphael, Charles S. Millard, Edmond Dyonnet, John Hammond, though by adoption he belongs to New Brunswick, Robert Harris, Clarence Gagnon and Charles W. Simpson. Of this group of painters only Simpson and Gagnon showed themselves in any sense free of European domination: the rest followed the well-trodden path of academic convention. There may be, and doubtless is, a reason for this religious adherence to established forms. For one thing, there was in Quebec, outside Montreal, where the population is not so homogeneous, an entire absence of art schools and clubs devoted to art where free discussion and friendly intercourse (as well as frequent opportunities for exhibitions) would have done much, in this formative period of Canadian painting, to foster and maintain an independent point of view in relation to the arts.

"À Quebec," says Jean Chauvin, "ni marchands de tableau, ni Salons, ni sociétés artisque." The visitor, he naïvely adds, remained astonished! Finally a group of artists was formed under the name of the Société des Artistes de Québec. However, Henry Ivan Neilson, the etcher, having been able to recruit but five artists, soon lost interest in the society he had founded, and of which he had been elected first president, and resigned. There had existed an important art school directed by the sculptor, Jean Bailleul. Later it had been rumoured that the government was to establish next at Quebec a museum of fine arts. Happily, unlike many another laudable government project, the effort did not die aborning, and Quebec City now possesses a civic gallery of Canadian art for the instruction and edification of student and visitor alike.

Because of the absence of art schools in Quebec, the young artist of sufficient means and ability went to Europe for his training. In the studios of Paris and Rome and Antwerp "he learned to paint according to conventions then in vogue, and upon his return to Canada continued painting, like his brethren in Ontario, according to these conventions." Thus there were not many Canadian artists of this day who were able to throw off the influence of the European schools by which they were obsessed, and "to realize that the landscape around them possessed a character and a glory so intensely its own that the European traditions of that day [the grey day of brown underpainting, a technical device of the time which Sir Wyly Grier once described as 'painting with brown soup'"] were not applicable to its brilliant sunshine and vivid colouring. Circumstances seem to have conspired to defeat these early artists. Canadians of a generation ago, brought up in an atmosphere of staunch British traditions, did not especially desire pictures of the Canadian scene, even native-born Canadians did not, for that matter, but rather of the Old Land, and, failing that, then of Dutch landscape. If Canada was to be painted at all, then the more it resembled the Old Land the better. In this the scattered patrons of the arts were aided and abetted by the dealers, who, true to their natural instinct, were inclined to give the public what it wanted. Nevertheless, this former generation did paint Canada and, gradually freeing themselves from the stultifying influence of European schools, realized more and more her character and splendour. These earlier painters in time "opened the eyes of the public to the fact that the country of their adoption possessed qualities so lovable and intimate, so happy and familiar, that the pictures of it might give them more pleasure than those of the land they had left behind." Possibly instrumental toward this change of attitude was an increased knowledge and deeper appreciation of the Canadian seasons and their effect upon the Canadian landscape.

One of the foremost of these men of the Quebec group was William Brymner, sometime President of the Royal Canadian Academy, whose long, patient and earnest effort in behalf of Canadian art won for him the gratitude of his countrymen and the formal recognition of his King. For many years he lived and worked in Montreal, where he rendered invaluable service in conducting, as headmaster, the life classes of the Montreal Art Association Schools. For subject matter, as painter, he explored the countryside of the old Quebec settlements and realized much of the old world sweetness that clings around them. Of his style there was little that was novel. His work was distinguished chiefly by its sincerity and honest craftsmanship. There was no conscious striving after the strangeness of new colour; but the simple truths of Nature's changing expression were presented with a steady, sober earnestness which remains where mere superficial brilliance soon loses its power to attract and charm.

In his later period Brymner painted several studies of the Atlantic from the site of historic Louisbourg on Cape Breton Island, and a number of extremely fine canvases of fog-enshrouded

INCOMING TIDE, LOUISBOURG
WILLIAM BRYMNER

seas and sheep-cropped uplands were the result. His individual appreciation of Nature's more sombre moods won for him wide recognition. At the Pan-American Exposition, Buffalo, in 1901, he won a gold medal; and, in 1904, the award of a silver medal at the Louisiana Purchase Exhibition at St. Louis. Besides having been conspicuous as a landscapist, William Brymner during his lifetime was also a portrait painter of distinction. His death, in 1925, was a severe loss to Canadian art which he had by his teaching and example done so much to develop and foster. Among his more notable students were Clarence Gagnon, Paul Barnard Earle, James L. Graham, Randolph S. Hewton, H. Mabel May, Lillias

WINTER IN THE LAURENTIANS
FARQUHAR McGILLIVRAY KNOWLES

Torrance Newton and Charles W. Simpson – sufficient evidence of his skill as a painter and of his influence as a teacher.

John Hammond, though born in Montreal, lived during most of a long life at Sackville, New Brunswick, where he took for subjects of his brush the rolling farmlands and seafaring life of that maritime Province. He also painted numerous scenes in Nova Scotia; and the Tantramar Marshes below Sackville formed the theme of a number of his more salient canvases. Usually he worked in low-toned harmonies of colour, and his paintings are notable for their air of soft, quiet charm and deep and inviting tranquillity. Like Hammond, Percy Woodcock showed a marked predilection for the silvery green marshlands of rural Quebec, in whom they found precisely the interpreter they needed to record their gauzy mists and dew-pearled mornings.

So accustomed are we to the presence of Alexander Young Jackson in Ontario, we are apt to forget that by birth he really belongs to the Quebec group of artists. Born in Montreal in 1882, he studied first at the evening classes of the Council of Art and Manufactures, Montreal, under Edmond Dyonnet, now secretary of the Royal Canadian Academy; later at the Art Institute, Chicago, under Clure and Richardson; and finally at the Academie Julien in Paris, under Jean-Paul Laurens. He was elected a member of the Ontario Society of Artists in 1914, associate of the Royal Canadian Academy in the same year, and to full Academy membership in 1919, from which he resigned in 1933. At its Centenary Convocation in 1941, Queen's University conferred upon him the honorary degree of LL.D. During the first Great War Jackson was twice wounded while fighting with the Canadian infantry in France. He was afterwards appointed an official artist for the Canadian War Memorials. Nowadays Jackson devotes himself exclusively to landscape painting, and within this limitation finds a wide variety of subject matter and constant change of mood.

Early influenced by the work of James Wilson Morrice, and later by the technique and point of view of the French Impressionists as well as Rockwell Kent, Jackson has, however, developed a quite definite personal note in his art. In nearly all his compositions one may observe a preoccupation with design as design which occasionally merges into over-emphasis. When undulating lines are carried to the skyline, and clouds become as weighty and as substantial as the earth below, it may well be time to ask whether this underlining of pattern is not being carried too far in representational painting. Yet there are compensations, and these significant. Jackson has a fine sensitivity to tonal values; he is a subtle colourist. Few painters can capture the lure of the Laurentians and the Quebec country and waterside with the same skill, truth and sincerity which mark even his rapid out-of-doors sketches. The lyrical rhythm and flow of his compositions, and the directness and simplicity with which he puts down essential details, prove him to be a painter of rare technical ability and sound sense.

Whatever ideas Jackson has to express he expresses bluntly and honestly, without rhetoric but certainly not without imagina-

The National Gallery.

THE *BEOTHIC* AT THE BACHE POST, ELLESMERE ISLAND

A. Y. JACKSON

tion. That Canada is still a vast wilderness of forest, plain and hills, with a fringe of rugged civilization which battles stoically and at times a little grimly, and still more tragically, for existence on the frontier must be patent to all. "Thus his painting conveys a sense of its boundless distances, its hard and massive architecture, its sharply accented rhythms." It is this back country which

135

appeals most to Jackson – Georgian Bay, the far Northland and rural Quebec – and it is a consolation as well as a source of pride to Canadians that he is able to interpret for the present and the future a land so inexhaustibly rich in character and of such infinite variety in natural and austere beauty. For Jackson apparently has the same devotion to the soil and is subject to the spell of the countryside as any habitant of generations of land-owning ancestors.

Not even F. S. Coburn, justly noted for the excellence of his Quebec scenes, can make lake, hill and plain as memorable as does Jackson, who eschews the merely picturesque and comes to close grips with reality. Light effects have interested him greatly, and he has contrived to make them fit into his compositions and to effect contrasts that a less skilful painter might have been content to present through greater variety of colour. As evidence of his skill one might cite Laurentian Hills and Early Spring, Quebec, both sombre scenes with subdued light reflected on melting snow. Both are notable for originality of arrangement, a rhythmic flow of lines and masses, and a fine sense of structure. His First Snow, Georgian Bay, one of his early canvases, showing inlet, marshy land and November sky, is exquisite in its tonal harmonies. More conventional in treatment than much of his later work, it marks a transitional stage in his development as a landscape painter. In all Jackson's painting the prevailing note is competence, which upon occasion can mount to technical performance which is really brilliant. Edge of the Maple Wood, now the property of the National Gallery, Ottawa, was painted in Sweetsburg, Quebec, in 1910, shortly after his return from study in Europe. This painting attracted the attention of J. E. H. MacDonald and Lawren Harris and led eventually to Jackson's going to Toronto to ally himself with the Canadian art movement then in process of formation. Following the Great War, the movement took tangible form in the Group of Seven, of which Jackson was one of the original members and an enthusiastic missioner. As an indication of its growth, the original seven have since become the Group of Canadian Painters with a membership of twenty-eight, holding periodical exhibitions at the Art Gallery of Toronto. Jackson's influence on Canadian art has been pronounced and wholesome, not only in his native Province of Quebec, but throughout the whole Dominion. Besides his ENTRANCE TO HALIFAX HARBOUR in the Tate Gallery, London, four of his paintings hang in the National Gallery at Ottawa; and one each in Sarnia, Kitchener and Hart House, University of Toronto, in addition to those in private collections scattered throughout the country.

HORSE-RACING IN WINTER

Art Gallery of Toronto.

CLARENCE GAGNON

Another Quebec artist whose reputation extended beyond the borders of his native land is Clarence A. Gagnon. As an etcher, painter and illustrator he held an enviable position. His work in any one of these mediums has been of sufficient importance to deserve special and extended treatment. Born in Montreal, in 1881, of French-English parentage, he was educated in the schools of Quebec, later studying drawing and painting under William Brymner of the Art Association of Montreal. In 1904 he went to Paris where, as many another Canadian student had done before him, he worked under Jean-Paul Laurens at the Academie Julien. Although Gagnon subsequently visited every country in Europe except Russia, he always remained Canadian both in his work and outlook. "From 1909 onward the Baie St. Paul district had been his favourite sketching ground. There he was a familiar figure to the habitants and the trappers, with his sketching materials in a rucksack on his back and a fishing rod or gun in his hand. Clarence Gagnon first attained international recognition for his etchings, and in this medium he is represented in many of the important public collections of Europe. As a Canadian painter Gagnon stands easily among the first. Along with Maurice Cullen and Suzor-Coté he did much to awaken Canadians to the beauty and brilliancy of colour and light in the Canadian scene. His influence here proved widespread and profound. Upon his return from his earlier trips abroad, Gagnon painted vivid, colourful pictures of rural Quebec, radiant with light and atmosphere. He applied the new theories of *plein-air* painting to the scenes he knew and loved, and in so doing enriched the art of Canada. With the ripening of his technical skill came a gradual unfolding of his powers as an artist. He moved toward greater simplicity of design and decorative pattern, and brilliancy of colour."

His personality, as reflected in his work, became more clearly defined, and something more nearly related to the spirit and tradition of our French Province stands revealed. In many, if not all, of his paintings will be found exemplified the life of the people at work in the fields, clustered around the parish church after Mass, spending time in tuneful mirth, receiving the Curé on his parochial visits, or racing horses over the ice on a clear, cold January day: to Gagnon all these things were but symbols of a living, organic whole —the cycle of the family, the parish, the province. His intense love of the simple, ordered life of the habitant, and his close knowledge of the rural customs of his native Province, make him in all ways their faithful and sympathetic interpreter. The explanation is simple: he himself was of the people. For three hundred years his family had been *enracine* in the soil of French Canada. He knew, therefore, the outer semblances as well as the innermost thoughts and aspirations of the countryside. There is insight, sympathy and understanding implicit in every stroke of the brush, in every line of the needle.

In later life Clarence Gagnon devoted much of his time and talent to book illustration, and in this field he added materially to his already considerable reputation. In 1928 Mornay of Paris published *Le Grand Silence Blanc*, by Louis F. Rouquette, for which Gagnon drew the illustrations. The success of this work was followed by a superb edition of Louis Hémon's classic of French Canadian frontier life, *Maria Chapdelaine*. For five years Gagnon worked on this book, and fifty-four illustrations in colour, of exquisite and astonishing beauty, were the result. These were reproduced in colotype with marvellous fidelity to the originals. In this series of pictures, for pictures they are, Gagnon found ample scope for the expression of his intimate and comprehensive knowledge of the peasant life of French Canada.

In 1938, by a piece of great good fortune, the entire collection, with a demonstration of the manner of their reproduction in plate form, was exhibited at the Art Gallery of Toronto, where many came to see, to wonder and admire. More recently still (1940) Gagnon drew a series of illustrations in colour for W. H. Blake's fishing classic, *Brown Waters*, which has now become, like its predecessors, a collector's item. Proof is thus afforded, if proof were needed, that Gagnon was a sensitive and knowing artist, a most competent and understanding chronicler of our time. Canada no less than Quebec is immeasurably the richer for the rare gift he possessed of bringing beauty out of common things. He was truly representative of the Quebec group of painters at its best. In 1942 Clarence Gagnon died, and one might say that his memorial was everywhere, even in the renaissance of Quebec handicrafts, though greater than all else was the example and the inspiration he left to his people.

Frank Hennessey, whose death in the autumn of 1941 brought to a sudden close a brilliant career, was a painter of fine taste and sensitive perception. His mastery of the crayon made his pastel landscapes memorable for their solid virtues of glowing colour and confident treatment of mass and line and atmospheric effect. His handling of A ROAD IN THE WOODS and WINTER DAY, scenes in the Laurentians, are typical of the countryside which supplied him with much good material. Born in Ottawa in the early nineties, and largely self-taught in art, Hennessey was a conscientious and industrious painter who showed consistent development of a natural talent which at last gained for him a wide reputation both here and abroad. In 1932, he was elected to membership in the Ontario Society of Artists. Two years later he became Associate of the Royal Canadian Academy; and, in 1941, almost coincident with his death, he was raised to full membership. Although he painted in all seasons, latterly in oils, spring and autumn and

A ROAD IN THE WOODS
FRANK HENNESSEY

winter engaged his interest chiefly. His favoured sketching ground was the Gatineau country, with now and then a brief excursion to Gaspé where the rugged country exactly suited the breadth and vigour of his brushwork. The habitant at work in the bush, cutting wood or sap gathering; farm chores and such homely tasks as soap making in the old-fashioned rural way, also supplied him with congenial subjects. He is represented in the National Gallery by WOLF CROSSING A LAKE, a pastel painting which was shown in the Canadian collection at Paris in 1927. Outside

Canada he is represented in public and private collections in England, France, Australia, New Zealand, the United States, Germany and Japan. When only fourteen, he accompanied Captain J. E. Bernier to the Arctic Circle, acting as assistant naturalist and artist to the expedition. Between 1913 and 1915 he was associated with the Geological Survey of Canada. In 1921 he was

QUEBEC FROM LEVIS

Robert W. Pilot

National Gallery of Canada.

appointed to the entomological branch of the Department of Agriculture for the Dominion. A memorial exhibition of his works was held at the galleries of J. Merritt Malloney, Toronto, in April, 1943.

A one-time pupil of Maurice Cullen, and a native, as was Cullen, of St. John's, Newfoundland, Robert W. Pilot was elected in 1934, at an early age, a full member of the Royal Canadian

Academy. This unusual honour was not unmerited, for Pilot even by that time had achieved something of an international reputation. He had exhibited throughout Europe, in Morocco, in South Africa, Australia and in the United States. Like so many Canadians, he had studied at the École des Beaux-Arts, Paris. Subsequently he went on a sketching trip through France, Italy, Spain, Morocco and England. Like his foster-father Maurice Cullen before him, he has since done much to lead the public toward "an appreciation of that still white beauty which lies over a snow-laden country." His paintings of Quebec City, Lévis, Perth, Ontario, and the Ontario and St. Lawrence shoreline are memorable for the surpassing beauty of their arrangement, colour harmonies and brushwork finely expressive of his intense and ardent feeling for his subject. Twice in succession he has won the Jessie Dow prize for painting awarded by the Montreal Art Association. He is worthily represented in the National Gallery by his QUEBEC FROM LÉVIS. Oil is his favourite medium, but on occasion he ventures into etching and other forms of engraving. At present he is an instructor in painting at the Montreal Art Association School of Fine Arts.

In the years when Ontario and Quebec were making history in the arts, the artists of the Maritime Provinces were no less active. Rarely, however, if ever, for a period of almost a century was there a direct relationship between the two parts of the country, widely separated as they were by vast distances and lack of ready communication. Indeed, so late as the year 1914, the roll of the Royal Canadian Academy of Arts fails to show the name of a single Nova Scotian painter, although there had been one or two from New Brunswick. Happily this unfortunate omission has since been remedied, so that today at any rate the Maritimes are represented in that supreme art body by at least two painters of ability and distinction: Elizabeth Styring Nutt, director of the Halifax School of Art, and Stanley Royle, instructor in art at Mount Allison University, Sackville, N.B. Both artists have managed to record on canvas the beauties of the Atlantic seaboard and, as their work shown at the annual Academy exhibitions attests, have handled their various subjects, whether landscape or marine, with intelligence, taste and skill.

10

From its foundation, in 1749, Halifax was notable for its culture and its learning. Peopled as it was by soldiers, sailors, administrators, teachers, artisans, parsons, shopkeepers, it also had its share of ancient families gently reared, who, at the time of its settlement, had come in response to the lure of a virgin land. However, for a time at least, such non-utilitarian matters as the fine arts were not even considered. Since, among conscious aesthetic pursuits, only architecture, which supplied roofs and walls, had a place in Nova Scotia's early economy, we should expect only that economy to flourish when architecture widened with Nova Scotia's social development. It did. But, unlike architecture, literature and the arts had to wait for several generations before they brought forth on the one hand such men as Thomas Chandler Haliburton and Joseph Howe, and, on the other, Robert Field and William Valentine. The colonists' first work was to cut clearings from the primæval wildness whereon to build their habitations and forts to protect themselves against the marauding Micmacs who infested the surrounding country. Naturally, under such raw and exiguous conditions, interest in the fine arts did not flourish but definitely languished. For the newly arrived settlers these were plainly times of uncertainty and peril.

Halifax and St. John and Charlottetown then, and for many years after, must have presented a rough and unattractive exterior to the tutored eye of the cultured European or New Englander used to an older and more gracious environment. The amenities of architectural design were almost unknown, for there could have been no substantial public buildings: the houses were little better than temporary habitations erected for protection against the weather. So beset by poverty, harassed by dread and faced with the stern necessity of earning a living, the early settlers of the Maritime Provinces had little time and still less inclination to obey the scriptural injunction to consider the lilies. For the time, at all events, anything resembling a systematic cultivation of the fine arts did not exist.

As with Upper and Lower Canada, so with the Maritime Provinces, the first persons to engage in any kind of art in Nova

143

Scotia, and still more particularly in Halifax, were the officers of the army and navy Of the men of the service, Halifax, like Quebec, Montreal and Toronto (York), had its fair share. Among them are chiefly remembered Richard Short, who, as purser of H.M.S. *Prince of Orange*, was with Wolfe at Quebec, Joseph F. W. Des-

National Gallery of Canada.

THE NORTH WEST ARM: HALIFAX

ELIZABETH STYRING NUTT

Barres, the Honourable Richard Bulkeley, Provincial Secretary, the Honourable Hibbert Newton Binney, first cousin of the native Canadian painter, Gibbert Stuart Newton, G. J. Parkyns, J. E. Woolford, Lieut. Robert Petley, William Eagar and William Henry Bartlett. The activities of these men, who for the most part followed art as an avocation, and only incidentally as a means of

livelihood, covered the period from about 175?
altogether something more than eighty years, or ι
of the Frenchman Daguerre turned the fickle taste
the newer method of portraiture. The comparative ci.
the daguerreotype was no doubt a factor in promoting th

Of this group of topographical artists, Short, Petley, I
Bartlett were probably the most proficient, as indeed the   re the
best known.   Certainly their work which remains to   ode
exhibits a surprising degree of competency.

The painstakingly accurate sketches or, to be more precise,
drawings, for they are much more detailed and exact than a sketch
would suggest, these drawings of Halifax and later of Quebec, in
1761, by Richard Short, are sufficiently familiar to students and
collectors of Canadiana to need but brief mention here.   It is
particularly interesting to note, however, as indicative of Short's
ability as a draughtsman, that these Halifax impressions afterward
formed the basis of a number of paintings by Dominic Serres,
sometime member of the Royal Academy and marine painter to
King George III, which were later engraved on copper by eminent
English and French engravers and published by Short in London,
March 1, 1764, with a dedication to the Earl of Halifax.   These
prints were subsequently reissued by John Boydell of Cheapside,
London, in 1777.   Today the first edition is extremely rare.   Four
of the 1777 prints are reproduced in Bourinot's *Builders of Nova
Scotia*.   In the National Archives at Ottawa are three prints of the
1764 edition and six of the 1777 issue.   Pictorially as well as
historically these views of Short's are by far the most important
prints of Halifax and Quebec that have appeared, both for fullness
of detail and accuracy of drawing.   Besides the Halifax plates,
already mentioned, Short made a series of twelve drawings of
Quebec at the close of the siege.   These prints, published at
London in 1761, are to be seen in the J. Ross Robertson Historical
Collection at Toronto; as well as in the Sigmund Samuel Collection at the Royal Ontario Museum, where they seem to convey
the very flavour of the period.   Many of the prints are reproduced
in Dr. Samuel's book, *The Seven Years War in Canada* (Ryerson).

I have treated of Short rather minutely because his, in many
respects, is the story of the rest of the topographical artists who
were his contemporaries, or who followed him during the intervening years.   From about 1787 to about 1817, a pencil, brush and

chess club was active in Halifax. As its president it had the Honourable Richard Bulkeley, the versatile, inept, and aristocratic secretary of the Province. Apparently this was the first organization of which there is any trace of anything like an art club in Nova Scotia. An existence of about thirty years would seem to

A HARBOUR SCENE: HALIFAX

Peter Sheppard

justify an expectation of more knowledge concerning its activities than is now extant.

Some time early in the 1800's the silhouette began to compete with the portrait painter for the patronage of the town. The silhouette makers of course were those itinerant artists who delicately cut profiles from black paper, many of them in highly ingenious style. They flourished from 1806 until about 1845, when this kind of rapid portraiture was driven from the field by the introduction of photography. Silhouettes, then as nowadays, for the old art has since had a brief revival, show the portrait, full length or bust, as black on a white ground, but a few show the silhouette white on a black background. Some were ornamented or highlighted with brush strokes of bronze. Silhouettes were produced with the assistance of various instruments especially contrived for the purpose, but the more skilful practitioners disdained such aids, preferring to work with scissors alone. William King, it would appear, first introduced this inexpensive but dainty art to Halifax in 1806. He was followed in June, 1808, for a brief interval by Samuel Moore, who worked in the long room at the Golden Ball, Sackville and Hollis Streets, and charged two shillings a portrait.

In the field of formal portraiture, that is, portraits produced by oils or water-colours, there were in Halifax at this time several prominent and highly talented executants. One of the most gifted of the group was Robert Field, an English painter of some renown, who came to Halifax in the spring of 1808 and remained for about ten years. He worked in both oils and water-colours, and was besides an accomplished miniaturist. He was, as records extant show, the first painter of miniatures in Nova Scotia, as he was also the first engraver. Since he is by far the most competent portrait painter ever to work in Eastern Canada, some particulars of a career by no means undistinguished would seem to be called for.

Born in Gloucester, England (the conjectural date is 1770), Robert Field as a young man went to London to be educated as a painter. About 1792 he decided to visit Baltimore, and sailed on the ship *Republic*. Evidently a man of enterprise, he painted a miniature of the captain on the voyage across. One may assume, though there is no actual evidence to confirm it, that at least part of his passage money was paid in this way. From Baltimore, Field went to New York and Philadelphia, where he worked for a time painting very good miniatures, which at the moment were his chief occupation. Sequier, in his *Critical and Commercial Works of Painters* (1870), tells us that Field painted "clever portraits which in style and lightness of pencilling remind us a little of Hamilton."[1]

During his visit to Philadelphia, in 1795, Field found plenty

[1] William Hamilton (1751-1801), English Miniature-painter.

to do. Among other commissions he engraved a portrait of President George Washington, after an original painting by Walter Robertson, an Irish miniaturist who had accompanied Gilbert Stuart to America. A year later he was in Baltimore, where Thomas Twining in his *Travels in America One Hundred Years Ago* records having sat to Field for his miniature. Field also made an engraving of the Chandos portrait for the first American edition of Shakespeare's works published in Philadelphia. His portrait in oils of Charles Carroll of Carrolton, one of the three American commissioners sent to Canada in 1776 by the Continental Congress to treat with the Canadians, later engraved by Longacre, may be assigned to this period. In his journal for July 1, 1810, John Pintard notes that Field was in Washington City and painted miniature portraits of Washington for fifty dollars apiece.

Rembrandt Peale, the American painter, in an entertaining story of his friend Robert Field, explains that "Field was an Englishman, who painted in beautiful style and commanded good prices."

In 1805 Field moved to Boston, and frequented the gatherings at the home of Andrew Allen, the British Consul. He was constantly occupied. Charles Fraser records his meeting with Field in the latter part of the year 1806 in a letter to a friend: "There is a miniature painter there named Field who associates with the best circles: He is a fine artist. I received many attentions from him." While in Boston, Field published two engravings, one in 1806, after Trumbell's portrait of Alexander Hamilton, and another, in 1807, after Gilbert Stuart's study of Thomas Jefferson.

Acting upon the advice of Sir John Wentworth, Lieutenant-Governor of Nova Scotia, it is said, Field sailed for Halifax. In the Halifax *Royal Gazette* of June, 1808, appears this announcement:

> Robert Field, at Alexander Morrison's, book seller, intends during his residence in Halifax to exercise his profession as portrait painter in oils and water-colour, and in miniature, where specimens of his painting may be seen and his terms made known.

Whereas in the United States Field had worked largely in miniature, his pictures in Halifax were mainly important canvases.

Under Wentworth's patronage, Field was soon commissioned to paint many of the most notable men of the town. Somewhat as Kneller had done for the famous Kit-Kat Club, he painted kit-kat portraits (that is to say, portraits of less than half length but including hands) of the wealthy members of the old Rockingham Club. These paintings hung for a time about the walls of the clubroom in the Rockingham Inn, near Wentworth Lodge on Bedford Basin, on the outskirts of Halifax.

Among his Halifax portraits the most pretentious ones were a full-length of Governor Sir George Prevost (1808-1811), and of his successor, Sir John Coape Sherbrooke (1811-1816), both probably painted for the Government House in Halifax. The Prevost portrait, "finely composed and executed," was later engraved and published in London, in 1818, by S. W. Reynolds, the eminent mezzotinter; a copy may be seen in the Halifax Legislative Library. The portrait of Sherbrooke, though "a good likeness and dignified, was not quite so fine a production." Tradition has it that Sherbrooke, who was irascible, got tired of posing for the painter and, when the face was finished, told him to fill in the rest of the figure as best he could. Field himself engraved in line and stipple and coloured "a degenerate variation" of the Sherbrooke canvas, and published the print at Halifax in June, 1816. Unfortunately very little idea of the original may be gained from the engraving, since Field, taking a painter's license, changed the posture of the figure, introduced fresh accessories, omitted the background and sacrificed altogether the repose and dignity of the sitter. Both paintings now hang on the walls of the Halifax Club.

One of Field's best portraits is said to be that of his patron, Lieutenant-Governor Sir John Wentworth, painted for the Rockingham Club, probably about 1808. This picture, which now hangs in the Government House in Halifax, depicts Sir John in his old age. On the o'her hand, Copley's portrait of him at Portsmouth, N.H., shows him in middle age when Governor of New Hampshire from 1767 to 1775, or in the period immediately preceding the American Revolution. Field's delineation of Bishop Charles Inglis of Nova Scotia, justly considered one of his very finest performances, now forms part of the permanent collection of the National Portrait Gallery of London.

When, in 1848, this portrait of Inglis was shown in Halifax at an art exhibition held on October 3, 5 and 7, it was described by *The British Colonist* as "a jewel of a picture (evidently the reviewer was Irish)—one of Field's very best performances. The Bishop was a fine, majestic looking old man. He is represented in his canonicals." Then, exalted by the splendour of the canvas before him, the critic concluded: "This is one of the best works of art in the country." Doubtless he was right. For this tribute, which at first seems excessive, is really not so when we remember how little first-rate painting was to be seen in Canada at this time. Judged even by the standards of a later day, the general effect of the canvas is most impressive and creditable, and testifies eloquently, if mutely, to the extraordinary ability of Field as a delineator of human character.

Field's portrait of John Lawson, the founder of the Halifax family of that name, is described as "a fine piece of work, with some good tender colouring in the face." It was later poorly engraved in miniature on the first bank-notes of the Bank of Nova Scotia, of which institution a son, William, became first president in 1832.

Besides these pictures, Robert Field while in Halifax painted portraits in oil of such notable men of the community as: Sir Alexander Cochran; Sir Edward Parry, the Arctic explorer, probably done when Lieut. Parry visited Halifax about 1818 on board the *Niger;* Commissioner John Nicholson Inglefield of the Naval Yard; the Honourable Richard J. Uniacke; the Honourable Michael Wallace; the Honourable Lawrence Hartshorne; the Honourable Charles Morris 3rd (1759-1831); the loyalist Adam DeChezeau, the elder; the Reverend Dr. Archibald Gray and Mrs. Gray; Andrew Wright and his sister, Mary; Dr. William J. Almon; the Honourable James Fraser; Judge James Stewart; William Bowie, who was killed in a duel with Richard J. Uniacke, Jr., in 1819: a striking piece of characterization though scarcely to be thought so from the poor reproduction which appears in the *Annals of the North British Society.* Others who sat to Field were Dr. John Haliburton, father of Chief Justice Thomas Chandler Haliburton, the latter better known perhaps as the author of *Sam Slick;* Captain Maynard, R.N., Rear-Admiral Herbert Sawyer, as well as many other men of substance and historic interest. All of which suggests that, measured by the yardstick of commercial success, if by no other and more exacting standard, Robert Field did well for himself. Altogether during his stay of about ten years in Halifax, it is estimated that he painted no less than one hundred and fifty portraits. His extreme prolificacy seems to have been only equalled by that of George Theodore Berthon

WILLIAM LAWSON

ROBERT FIELD

The Bank of Nova Scotia, Halifax.

working at a somewhat later date in Upper Canada. On occasion, and because of the scarcity of canvas during the war years of 1812 to 1815, a lack to which our artists of this year of grace, 1942, are subject and for the same reason, Field resorted to tin plate instead of the customary fabric whereon to paint his sitters, notably in the case of the Morris and DeChezeau portraits. But since the practice of painting on metals such as tin and copper, and even cardboard, was fairly common among the painters of the period, this enforced departure from customary practice should not be considered in any sense "reprehensible," as it has been.

As we have already noted, Field now and then descended to the painting of miniatures; and it is on record that he showed the same skill and dexterity in the production of these as in his larger pictures. Witness the miniature of Captain Nicholas Thomas Hill depicting him, at the age of thirty or so, in the uniform of a member of the Royal Staff Corps, of about 1817. Here we have "a very beautiful piece of work, nobly designed, boldly executed, the hatching being not overclose or niggled," and the whole "excellently coloured." This portrait, a thing of charm and beauty, passed in course of time to Captain Hill's son and, much later, in 1913, became the property of Miss Grace Hill, of Vancouver, B.C., a descendant of the original owner.

Halifax tradition has it that Field was somewhat of a dandy, and wore Hessian boots, with tassels at the tops. Dandy or no, Robert Field evinced a manly patriotism by joining in July, 1812, the First Company of Volunteer Artillery under the command of Captain Robert Tremain. William Dunlap, the American dramatist, painter and historian of the arts, who knew Field, described him as "a handsome, stout, gentlemanly man, and a favourite with gentlemen."

During the year 1818 Field exhibited in the Royal Academy at London when he was listed as a portrait painter of Halifax. In the following year he died. His death is thus recorded in the Nova Scotia *Royal Gazette:* "Died at Jamaica, August 9, Robert Field, an Eminent Artist very much regretted." And so he was; for of all painters who came to this country, and especially to the Maritimes during the early part of the nineteenth century, Robert Field, by all accounts and by the evidence of his own handiwork, was one of the greatest, if not the greatest, in fine craftsmanship and rich, artistic resources, that we have seen. So it is that in the annals of Canadian art the name of Robert Field stands deservedly high.

Gilbert Stuart has been recorded as having lived and worked for a time in Halifax. Unhappily for the interest that naturally attaches to such a belief, there is no trustworthy evidence to support it. Neither of his biographers, G. C. Mason or Lawrence Park, insofar as can be discovered, indicated that he even set foot in Canada. And so we have to dismiss, albeit somewhat reluctantly, this beautiful legend as having no basis in fact, and as being, in short, purely apocryphal. The matter is of no great moment. Even the legendary account gives Stuart no more than a few years in Nova Scotia, much too brief a period to have enabled him to leave any visible impress upon the art of that Province, to say nothing of the Maritimes generally. That being so, what then becomes of the attribution to Gilbert Stuart of the portrait of James McGill in the library of McGill University? Here is posed a nice question for the antiquarian to answer, if he can.

We now come to the advent of what may be called the minor professional artists in Nova Scotia, men of respectable skill but of no great reputation. In this group might be included George McCrae, from Edinburgh, who painted oil portraits in Halifax from about 1783 until his return to Scotland in 1802. Little is known, however, of his work, nor is there any available record of the canvases done while in Halifax. John Poad Drake, a young English artist who came to Halifax in 1815, is remembered chiefly for his excellent full-length painting of Chief Justice S. S. Blowers (1797-1841) in his official scarlet robes and wig, which was ordered by the magistrates and grand-jurors of the County of Halifax. The picture until 1919 hung in the Province Building, but is now in the County Court House. It was apparently the only portrait he painted in Halifax. Drake was an artist of some note, who was born near Plymouth, Devonshire, in 1794, and died at an advanced age at Fowey, Cornwall, in February, 1883. He was a descendant of John Drake, a cousin of the famous admiral. Having painted the portrait of Justice Blowers, he visited Montreal where he painted an altarpiece, and then went to New York where his picture of NAPOLEON ABOARD THE BELLEROPHON was exhibited. Like many another artist before him and since, Drake was of a mechanical turn of mind and spent much time in inventing new devices and improving upon old devices. Among other things to his credit, he is said to have discovered, in 1835, the principle of the Snider-Enfield rifle.

Almost as famous as Robert Field, and certainly not far behind him in technical accomplishment, was William Valentine, who from about the first quarter of the nineteenth century until his

153

death in 1849 pursued his profession in Halifax. Next to Field he was to achieve the most success as a portrait painter in Nova Scotia. Often as his name may be heard, not very much is definitely known regarding his career. Certain facts, however, are available. It is definitely known, for instance, that he came to Halifax in 1813, about the time Field is supposed to have quitted the town for England. His age was twenty. Without friends and without orders he turned to the trade of house painting and decorating for a livelihood, forming a partnership with one Bell under the firm name of Bell and Valentine, until May, 1824, after which he did business alone. About the year 1830 his ability as an artist began to be recognized, and from then until 1849 increasing commissions kept his brush busily employed. Among the more important canvases executed by him during these years was a portrait of the Honourable William Grigor, M.D., first president of the Halifax Mechanics Institute which the painter presented to the Society. A companion portrait of another president, Andrew McKinlay, is believed to be the last painting Valentine did. The former picture is the better in pose, the latter in colouring, bearing evidence of a more mature style.

In 1836 William Valentine visited London, where he divided his time between study and painting copies in oils of three successive presidents of the Royal Society, namely, Dr. William Hyde Wollaston (after John Jackson, R.A.), Sir Humphrey Davy (after Sir Thomas Lawrence, P.R.A.), and Dr. Davies Gilbert (after Thomas Phillips, R.A.), the originals of which hang, of course, in the rooms of the Society in London. The Wollaston, Davy and Gilbert portraits became the property of the Halifax Mechanics Institute, and with those of Grigor and McKinlay passed in trust to the Provincial Museum, where they now hang; they are among the best of Valentine's work. His studies in England had given him a more delicate sense of tone and colour, and his subsequent paintings were much the better for it.

Valentine's revealing and firm characterization of the Honourable Samuel G. W. Archibald, Master of the Rolls, a three-quarter length, in black gown, painted about this time (Archibald died in 1842), is a masterly piece of work, one of his very best originals, and a fine likeness as well. It shows the jurist in his palmy days, and the peculiar expression of rich humour which lightened up his fine countenance when addressing an audience is vividly conveyed by the artist. When shown at an exhibition in Halifax, in 1907, it was complimented as being from the brush of Sir Thomas Lawrence. Formerly in the possession of the Province House, it was later transferred to the Barristers' Society to be hung in the Halifax Court House where it now is.

On March 9, 1837, Valentine published in the *Novascotian* a notice expressing his gratitude for the patronage with which he had been honoured since his return from London to Halifax, and stating the terms on which he was prepared to execute paintings. These charges were: £1 10s. for profiles in oil, 11 x 13 inches; £3 for the same style, 16 x 19 inches size; £10 for three-quarter size (25 x 30 inches); £15 for kit-kat (28 x 36 inches); and £30 for half-length (42 x 56 inches). That is, he got fairly good remuneration for his work, if there was enough of it, which probably there was not. Other painters had worked in Halifax for longer or shorter periods during his time; but there is no doubt that he obtained the best of the local patronage during the thirties and the forties, in which period he had grown to be a professional portrait painter of some reputation. It was the hey-day of his artistic career, his best original work having been done after 1836.

Science, however, was about to invade the field of portraiture, for in January, 1839, Daguerre's experiments in photography were made public and, in the same year, Talbot published his mode of multiplying photographic impressions by means of a negative photograph, the Talbotype or calotype (on paper), the patent being dated February, 1841. Very soon the new process found its way to Canada, and in October, 1840, daguerreotypes were taken in Quebec. Having first, it is said, received instructions from Daguerre himself in Paris, Valentine sometime about 1844 introduced the new daguerreotype process into Halifax, thus becoming the first photographer in the Maritimes, and in doing so became as painter his own most formidable competitor. His fortunes, too, as an artist, in consequence were to suffer seriously, although it is questionable whether the blow would have been long delayed.

A large number of Valentine's photographs in their ornate velvet-lined, clasped cases still linger about Halifax; but without the photographers' imprint as is now the custom. His artistic skill permitted of posing his subjects with some taste, a thing that was made difficult by the long period of exposure that was at first necessary and the cumbersome apparatus then required in the posing of the sitter. At the same time, he was still eking out his earnings as an artist and photographer by practising the humbler but perhaps more lucrative trade of house, sign and ornamental painting. Parenthetically, there is much in this latter experience of Valentine's in Halifax that recalls a similar training undergone at a much later period by John Arthur Fraser, John Hammond and Henry Sandham with Notman's of Montreal and Toronto. Both were to find in photography a temporary means of livelihood as well as a helpful technical assistant.

The end came to Valentine in circumstances singularly depressing. A fire occurred at his studio in Bell's Lane, which resulted in the destruction of some of his finished and unfinished pictures; others were stolen in the confusion. He did not long survive the shock, and on December 26, 1849, he died in Halifax, after having lived there for thirty-one years, some eighteen or twenty of which were devoted to the production of paintings of varying degrees of merit. His age was fifty-one. The period from about 1837 to almost 1844 represents the time of his greatest artistic activity. A short obituary notice in the *Novascotian*, written doubtless by his friend Joseph Howe, truly says that "few men have lived in this community more deeply respected or died more deeply regretted." His humble tombstone is hidden away in a little iron-railed plot in Camp Hill Cemetery, justly offering that he was "much respected as a worthy man, a skilful artist and a Christian." "The day will surely come," says Harry Piers in his excellent essay on the artists of Nova Scotia, "when Halifax will be pleased to erect a befitting monument over his last resting place in God's Acre, but the simple inscription on the present stone cannot be bettered."

Almost solely a portraitist in oils, William Valentine painted, besides the canvases already mentioned, the following persons: John Howe (d. 1835) father of Joseph Howe (of which there is a replica in Montreal); the Reverend Matthew Richey, M.A. (afterwards engraved in stipple by T. A. Dean); John Sparrow Thompson (father of Sir John Thompson; said to be one of Valentine's best portraits; reproduced on page 459 of J. Castell Hopkins' *Life and Work of Sir John Thompson*); Sir William Young, the Honourable John Black; Chief Justice Sir Brenton Haliburton, Captain Thomas Maynard, R.N., of Windsor, N.S.; Samuel Sellon of Liverpool, N.S. (said to be a very fine piece of work). He also painted about 1832, a portrait of Lila, daughter of W. B. T. Piers, representing her as a child of about four years of age, holding a bunch of grapes, this being the only child's portrait by Valentine on record. It was vivacious and well executed. Valentine also painted a few miniatures, finished in a very smooth style, and without any noticeable effects of stippling, unless examined under a lens. In this respect they resemble the still smoother workmanship of Gillespie (who worked in Halifax in 1829), but are more strongly coloured in the flesh. The style, however, differs entirely from the bold, decisive stippling which marked Robert Field's miniature painting. After the grandiose manner of Haydon, Valentine attempted historical subjects such as KING JOHN SIGNING MAGNA CHARTA, THETIS PRESENTING THE VULCAN-WROUGHT ARMOUR TO ACHILLES and a companion picture to the "Achilles." These three canvases are probably copies since the composition of one at least "seems almost too good for a painter who did not devote much attention to such representations." Several of Valentine's canvases are said to be in Windsor and other provincial towns. Following the practice of many English painters of the time, many of his pictures he left unsigned. During his life in Halifax, it is estimated that Valentine must have painted almost one hundred and fifty portraits in all.

The first woman painter in Nova Scotia, that is to say, professional artist, was Miss Maria Morris, afterwards Mrs. Garrett T. N. Miller. She was born at Halifax, in 1813, a member of a cadet branch of the well-known Morris family of that place. Her early tuition in art she acquired from W. H. Jones in 1829 and 1830, and further, in 1833, "availed herself of an eminent professor for the last nine months." The eminent professor was L'Éstrange (given name unrecorded), an English portrait painter in oils, a miniaturist and an instructor in painting, who practised in Halifax from about 1832 until at least 1834. It is not known whether his merit as a painter was equal to his modesty as a man, for he announces in *The Novascotian* that "his style of copying nature in her richest attire has been acknowledged by the best informed artists in Great Britain." A decent reticence, we may suppose, prevented the disclosure of their names.

W. H. Jones, formerly of Boston and Philadelphia, taught classes in Dalhousie College on the Parade, where he had as pupils a number of notable persons, including Lady Mary Cox (daughter of William IV and Mrs. Jordan) as well as Maria Morris, the flower painter. Apparently this was all the formal instruction Miss Morris ever received in elementary art, for in December, 1833, she re-opened her school of drawing and painting at her residence next door, south of the Acadian School where she taught her pupils of the neighbouring families figure-work in water-colours, both on paper and ivory; and also in pencil and chalk; landscape work in pencil, chalk or water-colours; and flower, fruit, birds and shell painting on paper, or on such pretty materials as velvet and satin, as prescribed by the custom of the day.

Doubtless as a natural outgrowth of her teaching, she began about this time to devote special attention to the painting of the wild flowers of her native land; a kind of work which had hitherto been neglected and for which, by talent and training, she was unusually well fitted. From a local botanist, Titus Smith of the Dutch Village, she received much practical assistance. For he it was who collected flowers for her, correctly determined them, labelled her drawings, and generally encouraged her in the undertaking. As a result of this union of enterprise, ninety-nine sheets (representing 146 species) of her flower paintings, natural size, on paper measuring 16 by 12 inches (water-marked 1834 and 1835, which approximately determined the time of their production), became the property of the Halifax Mechanics Institute, and are now among the treasures of the Provincial Museum at Halifax. This set incidentally is different from, and fewer in number, than the one retained by herself, and which later was to provide the originals for a series of published plates to appear early in 1840.

These plates were issued in parts through a London publisher (each number to contain three plates, quarto size), and altogether formed a most beautiful series of coloured full-size lithographs of her water-colour drawings, entitled *The Wild Flowers of Nova Scotia*, with descriptive text by Titus Smith, and under the patronage of Sir Colin Campbell. Part I contained plates of the Mayflower (floral emblem of Nova Scotia), the pigeon-berry and the white water-lily. Part II contained the Indian cup, the tree cranberry and the Indian hemp or milkweed. The price of each part was five shillings.

A second series, same size, with text by Dr. Alexander Forrester (Smith had died in January, 1850), was issued in 1853, presumably by Snow of London and MacKinlay of Halifax.

Part I of what may be considered as a third series, with the title of *Wild Flowers of British North America*, was published by Reeve and Co., colour-makers, London, in 1867, with information on the history, properties, etc., of the subjects, by Professor George Lawson, Ph.D., of Dalhousie College. The size of the work was 14¼ by 11¼ inches, and the first part contained six lithographic plates, hand-coloured, namely: the Mayflower, pigeon-berry, white water-lily, cranberry-tree, Indian cup and common milkweed. These were the same plates which had appeared in parts one and two of the first issue of 1840. It is not known definitely how many of these parts appeared. However, their sumptuous style was far ahead of the time—for Canada, that is—and since apparently only a few parts were published, they have become exceedingly scarce. Unfortunately for its projectors, the venture financially was a failure, though successful enough in all other respects.

However that may be, these beautiful plates, and the much more lovely originals, are sufficient to place this artist in the very first rank of Canadian botanical painters. Some of her floral paintings, shown at the London Exhibition of 1862, were highly praised by the London press.

Probably the best topographical artist that Halifax ever had was William Eagar, who began as a landscape painter in oils and water-colours. With Robert Petley, who was stationed at Halifax from 1832 to 1836 as a lieutenant of the 1st Battalion of the Rifle Brigade, he shares the credit of having introduced lithography into Nova Scotia.

An Irishman, born about 1796, Eagar took up art as a mere accomplishment, but ended by using it as a means of livelihood. By whom he was instructed or where is not known, though it is thought that he may have studied in Italy for a time. In 1831 he went to St. John's, Newfoundland, where he made a drawing of the town and harbour from Signal Hill which later was engraved in stipple. A copy, an aquatint in colour, is to be seen in the John Ross Robertson Historical Collection at Toronto. Eagar, while at St. John's, also painted a portrait of the Honourable William Carson, a well-known Whig politician and Speaker of the Legislative Assembly of Newfoundland. In 1834 he left St. John's and settled in Halifax, where, because of his deficiency as a portrait painter and the successful competition of Valentine, he did little or nothing at portraiture, but devoted himself to the representation of Nova Scotian scenery for which he was better fitted and in which he attained a commendable degree of proficiency. Some of his drawings, notably one of the two of Halifax from Fort Needham, evince excellent pictorial composition and a nice sense of arrangement. In December, 1837, Eagar announced through the *Nova-scotian* the proposed publication of a series of landscape illustrations of British North America, to be issued in two parts and ultimately to form two volumes (the first devoted to Nova Scotia, the second to New Brunswick), and to consist of lithography by himself, J. Gellatly, A. Ferguson and others, done after his own sketches. This undertaking, had it been completed, would doubtless have been a worthy work, but death took him before it was finished. The title of the work as published was *Nova Scotia Scenery*. It was issued in wrappers by Moore and Thayer, lithographers of Boston, the size of the page being 17 by 11¾ inches. A vignette view of the Prince's Lodge at Bedford Basin was used as a title-page decoration.

The first number, undated, appeared apparently in June, 1839. Only five or six plates of three plates each were published. Among the plates issued, now quite rare, were the following: (1) HALIFAX FROM MCNAB'S ISLAND; (2) HALIFAX FROM THE EASTERN PASSAGE; (3) ENTRANCE TO HALIFAX HARBOUR FROM REEVE'S HILL, DARTMOUTH (drawn on stone by Eagar himself); (4) HALIFAX FROM THE RED MILL, DARTMOUTH; (5) HALIFAX FROM FORT NEEDHAM; (6) HALIFAX FROM FORT NEEDHAM (a different view, lithographed by Allan Ferguson, Glasgow); (7) VIEW ON THE NORTH-WEST ARM; (8) VIEW ON BEDFORD BASIN (looking toward the Narrows); (9) RUINS OF THE DUKE OF KENT'S LODGE (Bedford Basin); (10) WINDSOR, N.S., FROM FORT HILL; (11) VIEW FROM HORTON MOUNTAIN (looking over the Grand Pré, with Blomidon in the distance; (12) VIEW FROM RETRENT FARM (Windsor, N.S., Major Thomas King's); (13) CORNWALLIS, GRAND PRIARE (Pré) AND BASIN OF MINAS (from North Mountain); (14) PICTOU FROM MORTIMAR'S POINT; (15) PICTOU FROM THE ROAD TO HALIFAX; (16) PICTOU FROM FORT HILL. Many of these plates were drawn directly on stone by Eagar himself. He also left a lithographic print of the Province Building, Halifax, from the corner of George and Hollis Streets, which he sketched directly on stone, and likewise a print showing the Tandem Club meeting on the Parade near St. Paul's Church, Halifax.

Besides these prints Eagar made a collection of water-colour drawings of various points of interest in the city, such as churches, streets and public buildings, of which a number are to be seen in the John Ross Robertson Historical Collection, Toronto. On returning from England, whither he had gone on business connected with the engraving of his plates, he was exposed to wet in crossing the St. John River, N.B., from the effects of which he died in Halifax, November, 1839, aged forty-four. His grave in the St. Paul's burying-ground remains unmarked. The publication of his work was never completed. No authentic portrait of him is known to exist.

Robert Petley, previously mentioned, drew from nature and on stone a VIEW OF YORK REDOUBT from Sleepy Cove near Halifax. Printed by the noted lithographer, C. Hullmandel, the drawing was tinted with colours and published about 1837, by J. Dickinson, of New Bond Street, London. A copy of this lithograph, which is not without merit, is in the Provincial Museum, Halifax. Petley also made sketches of the ROCKING STONE NEAR HALIFAX and of BEDFORD BASIN FROM NEAR THE THREE MILE HOUSE, which are now in the John Ross Robertson Collection at Toronto. To Lieutenant Petley or William Eagar, as has been said, is to be credited the introduction of lithography into Nova Scotia; each drew to some extent on stone. Since Petley was in Halifax from 1832 to 1836, and Eagar from 1834 to 1839, it is probably fair to assume, in the absence of more precise information, that the former was the first Nova Scotian to work on stone. The introduction of lithography into England had taken place about 1817, about twenty years after its discovery by Alois Senefelder, and about sixteen years before the production of Petley's drawings.

A miniature painter, who seems to have done good work, was J. Clow, who practised in Halifax between 1831 and 1837, and again in 1840. His studio was in the Exchange Coffee House, where he painted small-sized portraits in oils as well as miniatures in ivory. One of his subjects was a rectangular miniature of the Honourable Richard John Uniacke, who died at Mount Uniacke, N.S., in 1830, representing him three-quarter length, with short hair, seated, with books beside him; it was painted in 1830. There is some doubt, however, as to its originality, since it was done after Uniacke's death. It depicts him as a comparatively young man, without the long hair which characterized Uniacke in later life, and is likely a copy by Clow of Field's oil portrait of the attorney-general previously referred to. A miniature of Temple Stanyan Piers, long resident in Halifax, is more likely from Clow's brush.

Albert Gallatin Hoit, of Boston, was another artist of skill who visited Halifax in 1840, when he painted a fine full-length of Chief Justice Sir Brenton Haliburton, which hangs in the Province House. Hoit also, it is said, did a portrait of William Nyan Silver of Halifax; but it is not known whether he painted other subjects, unless the portrait of the Honourable William Stairs is by him. Hoit was born in Sandwich, New Hampshire, in 1809, worked for a while in St. John, N.B., prior to 1839, painted President Harrison of the United States in 1840, and died in 1856.

Born in Crewkerne, Somerset, September, 1810, George Smithers came to Halifax, in 1828, when about eighteen years of age and, in the following year, founded the firm of house painters and decorators long known in the town. When the opening of the Halifax Theatre was announced (in January, 1832), it was stated that the decorations of the house were by Smithers. As an artist he was self-taught. Among his earlier commissions were the painting of the banners of the St. George's, the St. Andrew's and the St. Patrick's societies of Halifax. He also painted in oils some *genre* subjects of moderate merit. Occasionally, too, he indulged a taste for heraldic design, which probably found expression in coats-of-arms for coach doors and tavern signs. Influenced possibly by the work of Morland, he produced canvases with such descriptive titles as THE SMUGGLERS, SHAVING, TAKING SNUFF and TAKING A NIGHT-CAP, as well as scenes suggested by Burns' poems. It was the day of the story picture. Smithers also lectured on drawing before the Halifax Mechanics Institute in 1840. He died at Halifax in March, 1868.

Major-General Anthony Crease, R.E., who as a lieutenant in the Engineers was believed to have been stationed at Halifax, is remembered for some water-colour drawings of the town, two of which are in the John Ross Robertson Historical Collection at Toronto, namely: HALIFAX, LOOKING UP THE HARBOUR FROM THE

CITADEL, 1849, and HALIFAX, LOOKING DOWN THE HARBOUR FROM
THE CITADEL, SEPTEMBER, 1849. Crease, who made several pictures of different places in Canada, was born in April, 1827, and
died presumably about 1892, as his name then drops from the
Army List.

One of the best of Nova Scotia's early marine painters, and
certainly the first of his kind in that Province, was John O'Brien,
who came to Halifax from Ireland about 1832. Unfortunately, in
order to find a market for his pictures, he was forced to spend much
of his time in making rather trivial and exaggerated representations
of ships under "a fine spread of canvas," with everything "drawing" to gratify the demands of vain ship-owners who knew much
about boats but little about art. The inevitable result of this
forced lowering of his standard of craftsmanship was to minimize
the amount of high-class marine work he did. Probably the best
example of these "pot-boilers" is his oil study of Strachan's famous
clipper barque *Stag*, painted about 1855, which represents her
under sail off Mauger Beach lighthouse. The *Stag* was lost off
Bermuda in 1859 or 1860.

A much finer canvas, done at this time, is O'Brien's portrait of
a 26-gun frigate, shortening sail in a squall, painted in quiet greys,
and indicative of the painter's power of expression when freed from
the artificial restraints of an over-insistent clientele. He also did
three compositions of H.M.S. *Galatea*, a fine 26-gun frigate, which
was on the Halifax station from about 1864 to 1867. These
represent the frigate in three positions, each of which is signed and
dated 1888. Evidently, apart from the drawing of the boat itself,
the paintings were almost wholly imaginative, which probably
explains why the sea, especially in the third picture, depicting a
cyclone in the Indian Ocean, was poorly handled. One of O'Brien's
faults was his tendency to accentuate details, thus sacrificing
atmospheric quality for an effect of reality, which no doubt was
largely a deliberate concession to the uninformed taste of the day.

Many of O'Brien's pictures may still be met with about
Halifax, and doubtless will prove to be of widely different merit.
One portrait at least he painted, that of the Honourable J. W.
Johnstone, which was the gift of the painter to his patron. With
the assistance of Halifax admirers and friends, O'Brien was sent to
study in England, France and, probably, Italy, after which he

returned to Halifax and devoted himself to painting sea-scapes, but was forced later to do less artistic brush-work in order to make a living. Even at that, he was the most skilful marine painter the Province ever had and, under more fortunate circumstances, might well have fulfilled the promise of his early years. After a lingering illness, he died unmarried at Halifax, in September, 1891, aged fifty-nine, and was buried in Holy Cross Cemetery.

11

"Of the hurried visitors to our shores," observes J. W. L. Forster, O.S.A., in his paper on "The Early Artists of Ontario," "Gush has left behind him more and better work than any other." This opinion, by a painter himself not unknown by reputation, is nevertheless open to question. In the first place, the works of Gush in Canada are seemingly not numerous; the only known portrait by him in Ontario is that of Egerton Ryerson, owned by Mr. Arthur Maybee of Toronto, a reproduction of which forms the frontispiece of Professor Sissons' "Life"; and, secondly, other painters, notably Robert Field, have excelled him in skill and quality of workmanship. Even so, if we are to judge by his full-length portrait of General Sir Fenwick Williams, which hangs in the Legislative Council Chamber of the Province Building at Halifax, Gush was an artist of undeniable ability. This canvas, commissioned by the provincial government, was completed in 1860 and forms a companion painting to a second full-length portrait for the Province, done two or three years later, that of another gallant Nova Scotian, Major-General Sir John Inglis, which hangs beside the Williams' portrait. On the back of this canvas is the inscription: *The late Sir John Inglis, Bart., K.C.B., by Mr. Gush, 15 Stratford Place* (London, England), which would seem to indicate that the painting was not completed until after Inglis' death in 1862. In composition, in colouring, in tonality and in general treatment the Williams' portrait is the better of the two, which is hardly astonishing when we reflect that the Inglis painting was most likely painted from a photograph, the Williams' canvas from life. When he painted direct from the sitter, Gush was capable of

Arthur Maybee, Esq., Toronto.

EGERTON RYERSON

WILLIAM GUSH

first-rate work, as is shown by his fine bust portrait of Lady Daly, as well as portraits of her parents, Sir Edward and Lady Kenny, and possibly others. He also, it seems, painted in Halifax a three-quarter length of the Reverend George McCawley, D.D., President of King's College from 1836 to 1875, which formerly hung in the Convocation Hall at Windsor, N.S. This painting is such a poor production compared with the Williams and Daly portraits as to suggest the possibility of its being an indifferent copy of an original. Colour is lent to this theory by the presence of the signature in unnecessarily large letters, whereas his other canvases are unsigned. That he was scarcely the artist to have appended his name to an obviously inferior example of his skill may be safely assumed. As a point of minor interest it may be mentioned that Gush's name seems to have been pronounced *Goosh*, which had led to the name being variously spelt; all authentic sources, however, give it correctly as Gush.

Campbell Hardy, soldier and sportsman-naturalist, while stationed at Halifax as a captain of artillery from 1852 to 1867, made some excellent water-colour drawings of Nova Scotia scenery. Two of his pictures were engraved in colours—a camping scene in the woods in summer, and a woodroad in winter. These were issued at London, in 1863, by Day and Son, lithographers. Others of his drawings appear in *Forest Life in Acadia* of which he was the author.

One of the most notable of Nova Scotian artists of the sixties and seventies was Forshaw Day, whose landscapes in oils and water-colours were well known to Canadians of an earlier generation. Born in London, England, in 1837, he was educated to the profession of architecture in Dublin and South Kensington. In 1862 he came to Halifax, and for many years was draughtsman in H.M. Naval Yard. At the same time he painted many views of local scenery and taught art. In 1879 Day was appointed to the position of professor of drawing and painting at the Royal Military College, Kingston, Ontario, and in 1880 became one of the founders of the Royal Canadian Academy of Arts—the only Nova Scotian artist on the original roll. After eighteen years at Kingston, he retired because of ill-health. Day returned to Halifax for a while, but finally went back to Kingston and died there in June, 1903. He is represented in the National Gallery, Ottawa, by ON THE NOUVELLE RIVER, BAY DES CHALEURS.

Two of Forshaw Day's more memorable works are GRAND PRÉ and LOUISBOURG, both Nova Scotian subjects, which gained favourable notice when exhibited in Paris. His work, however, varies a good deal in merit. Some of his canvases, pot-boilers no doubt, are faulty in composition and tonality and are often forced in colour. He had an evident partiality for the vivid tints of Autumn, which like those of gorgeous sunsets have often played sad havoc with the reputation of many an artist not extremely gifted. Perhaps the painter was not altogether to blame for this; his patrons may have been, and probably were, culpable in part.

Of the more recent artists who worked in Nova Scotia, one might mention: Robert Harris, sometime President of the Royal Canadian Academy, who when a young man in Halifax, in 1873, painted a portrait of the Honourable William Garvie, which hangs in the Provincial Museum; George Harvey, landscapist and art teacher, who was at Halifax from about 1822 till 1895, and who became the first headmaster of the Victoria School of Art and Design from 1887 to 1894; Henry M. Rosenberg, landscapist, figure painter and etcher, who was also principal of the Art School from 1898 to 1910 (a number of his *genre* paintings are on view in the Provincial Museum, Halifax); Lewis E. Smith, landscape painter, designer and etcher, a native of Halifax and principal of the Art School from 1910 till 1912; George Chauvignaud, landscapist, a native of France, who later lived and worked in Ontario (Meadowvale and Toronto), was principal of the Art School from 1912 till 1916; Arthur Lismer, A.R.C.A., landscapist and member of the Group of Seven, from 1916 to 1919; and Elizabeth Styring Nutt, A.R.C.A., who was appointed principal of the Art School in 1919, and still continues in that position.

F. Lee Hunter, who was in Halifax in 1888, produced a number of etchings of picturesque scenes along the city's waterfront. These now form part of the John Ross Robertson Collection at Toronto. Among them are listed: FISHING WHARVES, FALKLAND, N.S.; HALIFAX, N.S.—OLD WHARF; and OLD STREET SCENE, HALIFAX, N.S., all of which give the artist's address as Ossining, N.Y. Another artist, Arthur T. B. Barrett, born at Gaspereau, N.S., in 1852, studied for a time in Halifax and later lived until his death in 1939 at Roxbury, Mass. His chief contribution to the art of his native Province consists of several portraits painted in Halifax and at Acadia University, Wolfville, N.S. Better known to Canadians is Gyrth Russell, who takes for subjects the sea and the dockside. Born in Dartmouth, N.S., he went as a young man to Halifax, where he studied under H. M. Rosenberg of the Victoria School of Art; in Boston under Eric Pape, and in Paris at the Academie Julien. Besides being an accomplished painter, he is an etcher of international renown. His drawing of OLD PROVINCE HOUSE, HALIFAX, displays fine feeling, sound structure and sensitive perception.

A painter well known to Maritime Canada is Mabel Killam Day, a native of Yarmouth, who has spent most of her life in Nova Scotia and New Brunswick, where she has found subject material in their fog-shrouded harbours. In 1905 and later Mabel Day had the good fortune to be one of a group of painters, of whom Marion Long, R.C.A., of Toronto, was one, working under the direction of Robert Henri. It was a time of great enthusiasm in painting; Henri, Sloan, Glackens, Shinn and Prendergast were upsetting old conventions of art and were encouraging students to experiment, to look about themselves at actuality, and to paint American life and the American scene. On one occasion when she had sent some of her pictures to an exhibition in New York, Henri saw them. "We are glad [he wrote] to see your excellent pictures . . . anyone who can make such a fresh, frank, big transcript from nature can be a great artist and a true one. It has qualities one likes best in the great Constable." In Pittsburg, where Mrs. Day spent ten years of her life painting its yellow rivers, its bridges and steel mills, she became one of the directors of the Associated Artists of that city, whose annual exhibitions in the Carnegie Art Gallery were major events. In 1913 she was awarded first honour for her winter picture, THE ST. JOHN RIVER AT FREDERICTON. In 1922 she won the prize awarded by the Pittsburgh School of Design for the best picture painted by a woman. In 1929 she gained the second award and a prize of $100 for her painting, THE WHITE VILLAGE, depicting a scene in Sandy Cove, Nova Scotia. Unfortunately this picture, along with WOOD'S RUN, depicting a slum area in Pittsburg, was destroyed by fire in Halifax, together with a number of other canvases.

Reference must also be made to Ernest Lawson, N.A., a landscape painter of much reputation who was born in 1873 at Halifax, the son of Dr. Archibald Lawson. He first studied in Kansas City and in the city of Mexico, where his father was in practice, and then at the Art Students League in New York and later in Paris. He was awarded a silver medal at the Louisiana Purchase Exhibition, St. Louis, 1904; the Seman medal for landscape at the University of Pennsylvania; the Hallgarten Prize at the National Academy of Design, New York; and a gold medal at the Panama Pacific Exhibition, San Francisco, in 1915. He is represented in the National Gallery of Art at Washington, the Metropolitan Museum, New York, and many other public galleries. His SNOWBOUND BOATS is in the National Gallery, Ottawa. Shortly after its inception, Lawson became a member of the Canadian Art Club, and during its lifetime was one of its constant and most prominent exhibitors. "His work is of an unusually high order, being notable for its exquisite colour values, its tone and vibrating quality." Critics have acclaimed him one of the greatest of living American painters. However, since he received his art education in the United States and France, and none of his pictures were produced here, his only connection with Halifax is his birth and his boyhood days there. Whether he would have progressed so far as an artist had he remained in Canada opens up an inviting field of speculation. It sometimes happens, as with Lawson, that faraway fields have virtues other than their seeming verdancy to recommend them.

Throughout the Maritime Provinces there are artists of ability who, for one reason or another, have chosen to seek, and sometimes to find, the bubble Reputation abroad, thereby losing meanwhile their identity with their native land. One such is Muriel C. W. Boulton, who was born at Charlottetown, P.E.I. She studied under Sir Hubert Von Herkomer, R.A., at Bushey, England, and in Paris at the Academy Calarossi, under Renard and Krolig. In 1908 and 1910 she exhibited at the Paris Salon. Her *genre* painting, THE CHESS PROBLEM, was bought by the National Gallery, Ottawa, in 1907. Marjorie Earle Gass, born at Saint John, N.B., studied at the Montreal Art Association School under William Brymner, R.C.A., and Maurice Cullen, R.C.A.; but beyond these bare biographical details nothing is known of her after career. The same is true of Jean M. Maclean, who was born at Pictou, Nova Scotia, and for a time was a student at the Heatherly School of Art in London.

But of all the expatriate painters from the Maritimes, the name of Gilbert Stuart Newton, R.A., stands easily first. A native of

Halifax, N.S., where he was born in 1795, he was the son of the Honourable Henry Newton, Collector of Customs, and his wife Anne, elder sister of Gilbert Stuart, the famous American painter. It is likely that young Newton was taught the rudiments of art by Robert Field, by whom doubtless he was encouraged to continue his studies. He went to England where later, after a visit to Italy about 1818, he returned to become a student at the Royal Academy School in London. He soon rose to eminence, being elected an academician in 1832. Three years later he died. Apart possibly from Ernest Lawson, he was indubitably the greatest native artist Nova Scotia, if not the Maritime Provinces, has ever produced.

From the early days of the nineteenth century, exhibitions of the fine arts have been held in Nova Scotia. The first exhibition of pictures at Halifax was held in Dalhousie College in May, 1830, through the united efforts, it is said, of William Valentine, the artist, and W. H. Jones, a local instructor in painting, who had previously organized similar shows in Boston and Baltimore.

Among the pictures shown were some which had been captured in the War of 1812, loaned by Chief Justice Sampson Blowers, some of Sir Peregrine Maitland's own drawings, with others in his possession, as well as about fifty examples in oils of the work of Jones' pupils, many of them original. Unfortunately, many of the fine old paintings, which Valentine had borrowed from local sources for that exhibition, have long since left our shores.

The next exhibition of art in Halifax was held in September, 1848, again at Dalhousie College, under the supervision of the Halifax Mechanics Institute, a society which had done much to develop and foster local interest in art since its formation in 1831. This exhibition contained a number of good pictures. Of these, fortunately, we have a full critical account, presumably written by Dr. T. B. Akins, as a series of consecutive reviews for the *British Colonist* newspaper, October 3, 5 and 7, 1848, reviews which the historian is sure to value as they often fix the attribution of many of the paintings in the Province which might otherwise be doubtful.

It is interesting to note that the Royal Canadian Academy of Arts, which had been founded in 1879, held its second annual exhibition in the Province House in July, 1881, thus bringing together the most noteworthy collection of paintings ever assembled in Nova Scotia. The printed catalogue listed no less than 380 items, including paintings, drawings, architectural designs and so on. Financially the exhibition was not so successful.

In June, 1887, a loan exhibition, so-called, was likewise held in the Province House, in aid of the newly organized Victoria (now the Nova Scotia) School of Art and Design, at which were shown paintings, antique furniture, china, coins, textiles, fabrics, bric-a-brac, etc., thus antedating by some fifty-four years the exhibition— "From Jacques Cartier to Confederation"—held (1941) at the Art Gallery of Toronto. For this Halifax show the catalogue listed 810 entries, of which 213 were paintings and engravings. Another loan exhibition was held in 1894, at which 213 items were catalogued, all of them paintings, many of them old. Again, in 1904, a loan collection of fifty-odd pictures was shown at the Victoria School of Art. Finally, in 1906, there was inaugurated a series of annual art exhibitions in connection with the Provincial fair which indicated the increasing attention paid the fine arts by the people of the Maritime Provinces.

As with the art of Nova Scotia, so it was with the art of New Brunswick. The history of the one will be found upon examination to parallel closely that of the other. As a matter of fact, the early artists of Halifax very often proceeded to explore the environs of Saint John, Fredericton, Bathurst and the adjacent countryside in search of subject matter for their pictures whether drawings or paintings. It was so with Petley and Parkyns. It was so with Bartlett and Eagar, with Crease and with Hickman—all topographic artists and all recorders—stilted and in a sense archaic though their style may be—of the contemporary scene. Others whose work is valuable from the historic, if not the aesthetic point of view, are: W. P. Kay, P. Harry, M. G. Hall and William G. R. Hind. In Newfoundland there was the Reverend William Grey of Portugal Cove, whose lithographic impressions, coloured by hand, form interesting memorials of the early days of that colony. Birds of passage mostly, they did the day's work and went their way. Often ill-requited for their efforts with pencil, brush or lithographic crayon, they took their slender wages, content with that and the admiration and patronage of friends, without whose stimulating encouragement and appreciation they might have accomplished much less than they did, greatly, even irreparably, to our loss. Thus we have much to thank them for, even though their work may fail to elicit at this date the uncritical approval with which it was once greeted. Theirs was the role, though they knew it not, and none the less valuable because unconscious, to record in line and colour, on canvas and on stone, their day and generation. Indeed, the face of the Maritimes in the early and formative years would still be a *terra incognita* had it not been for the persisting and fruitful efforts of these little-known artists, delineating as they did its manifold character and beauty.

In his paper on art in Nova Scotia, read before the Nova Scotia Historical Society of 1914, Harry Piers expressed the belief that art was at a most lamentably low ebb in Nova Scotia (and by implication in New Brunswick and Prince Edward Island), with none of the vitality that had characterized it in the past.

> Our houses [he said] are filled with poor pictures, and we are frankly told by the Royal Canadian Academy that it will not exhibit here, because its members would not be able to sell their productions. The present roll of the Academy does not, I think, bear the name of a single Nova Scotia painter. It behooves us in some way to at least see that we keep up with the bright promise of the earlier days.

Happily the admonition thus conveyed has been heeded. Of late years, at any rate, there has been a re-awakening of interest, and not only of interest, but of active development in the art of the Maritimes, that continues to be a source of pride and inspiration to their fellow-Canadians throughout the Dominion. This renewed interest has been signalized by the formation of the Maritime Art Association, in 1940, under the direction of Professor Walter H. Abell of Acadia University, and of the president, John N. Meagher, of Halifax. The Association publishes, from October to June of each year, *Maritime Art*, a journal devoted to the discussion of the arts, not only of the Eastern Provinces, but throughout Canada. At present the Association lists among its members the Acadia University Fine Arts Club, the Art Society of Prince Edward Island, Dalhousie University, the Fredericton Art Club, the Moncton School of Art, the Nova Scotia College of Art, the New Glasgow Arts and Letters Club, the Nova Scotia Museum of Fine Arts, the Nova Scotia Society of Artists, the Provincial Normal School of Fredericton, the Sackville Art Association, the St. Andrew's Art Club, the Saint John Art Club, and the Saint John Vocational School. Truly an impressive showing, and one in which the people of the Atlantic seaboard may take a just pride In no other part of the Dominion, to my knowledge, is there an organization of the kind comparable to it. It constitutes a challenge to Canadians in all parts of the country, but more especially in the Provinces of Ontario and Quebec where similar opportunities are more manifest, and thickly populated centres with their cultural aids more general. Thus the cultural stimulus to which reference has been made would seem to have been revived; may it live and flourish and continue to benefit those who, in a large measure, a very complete measure, have been responsible for that revival.

Mention has already been made of the formal recognition of Maritime art by the Royal Canadian Academy of Arts, through the election to membership in that body of Stanley Royle of Sackville and Elizabeth Styring Nutt of Halifax. Others have been Maurice Cullen and John Hammond; but since these painters spent much of their active lives in Quebec, such official recognition fails to carry quite the same significance. At any rate, the condition which was once considered a reproach, if not a byword, no longer exists. So the art of Maritime Canada, one hopes, has set out on a new and invigorating path of progress. And not the least encouraging features of this new revival is the part played in it by the younger artists, such as Miller Brittain, Saint John; Donald Cameron MacKay, Halifax; Jack Humphrey, Saint John (two of whose paintings were recently acquired by the Art Gallery of Toronto), Charles Payzant, and the sculptor in wood, John Bradford, president of the Atlantic Woodcarvers' Guild of Wolfville, Nova Scotia.

Stanley Royle, R.B.A., A.R.W.A., R.C.A., is director of art at Mount Allison University, Sackville, New Brunswick Born in Lancashire, England, he studied at the Sheffield College of Art, where he won the King's Prize and the silver medal. While still a student he had three pictures accepted by the Royal Academy, London. He painted for some years outside Leeds, made many sketching trips, and became known for his snow scenes and paintings of old English villages. In 1920 he was elected a member of the Royal Society of British Artists, and in 1926 became an associate of the Royal West of England Academy. In 1936, he was elected an associate of the Royal Society of Arts, London, and in the same year an associate of the Royal Canadian Academy.

Royle came to Canada in 1930 as a teacher of painting at the Nova Scotia School of Art, Halifax, but returned to England in

1933. The year following he was appointed director of the Owens Art Museum and College of Art, and subsequently professor of drawing and painting and lecturer in art at Mount Allison University, a position he now holds.

His paintings are in the permanent collections of the galleries of Bristol, Blackpool, Oldham, Derby, Newcastle and Sheffield.

EVENING LIGHT: NOVA SCOTIA

STANLEY ROYLE

He is also represented in the Nova Scotia Museum of Fine Arts. A painting, PEGGY'S COVE, N.S., was his contribution to the Century of Canada Art Exhibition held in the Tate Gallery, London, in the autumn of 1933. The Art Association of Montreal, in 1939, acquired his winter scene entitled LUMBER WHARF, HALIFAX, for its permanent collection. For twenty-five consecutive years his paintings have been exhibited in the Royal Academy, England, as well as in exhibitions in the principal cities of England and Canada, and at the National Academy of Design, New York. His work is widely known through its frequent reproduction in various art publications and elsewhere.

12

The fine arts in the Canadian north-west territories and in British Columbia may be said for the most part to have followed Confederation in 1870. Before that, it is true, we have seen how the Rockies were first visited by Paul Kane in the forties, and how with the material aid of the Honourable George William Allen, of Toronto, and later under the guidance of Sir George Simpson, governor of the Hudson's Bay Company, he had explored for pictorial subjects the hills and rivers and lakes lying in what was then the almost virgin domain of the great fur-trading companies, where nomadic tribes of Indians roamed at will, and buffalo and feathered game abounded.

But something like an interval of thirty years or so was to elapse before the pioneer Kane was to be followed by such painters as Lucius O'Brien, William G. R. Hind, William Armstrong, C.E., John Fleming, Professor Henry Youle Hind, T. Mower Martin and F. M. Bell-Smith, all artists of the seventies and eighties; or who, like the surveyors of the group, followed art as an avocation or as an adjunct of their profession. Their work, much of it now represented in the John Ross Robertson Collection, remains as tangible evidence of their aesthetic skill as well as contemporary records of the western scene of an earlier and primitive day.

Of the group, Professor Hind was an Englishman who came to Canada in 1846 at the age of twenty-three. While a professor of chemistry and geography at Trinity University, Toronto, to which he had been appointed soon after its opening, the government of the time named him geographist to the first Red River Expedition in 1857, and the following year placed him in command of the Assiniboine and Saskatchewan exploring expeditions. He also explored a part of Labrador, made a survey of New Brunswick, examined the gold districts of Nova Scotia, and the mineral field of the north-eastern part of Newfoundland. He wrote many books, probably the most important of which were his prize-winning essay on the prevention of wheat rust, published in 1857, and his report on the findings of the Red River Expedition. In recognition of his manifold services to his adopted country, the University of King's College, Windsor, N.S., conferred on him the degree of

D.C.L. However, all this is by the way; what really concerns us at the moment is the large and valuable collection of his drawings and water-colour pictures which have become a legacy of lasting importance. Not only did he portray in colour the physical characteristics of the country traversed by the expedition, as in RED RIVER FROM THE STONE FORT, but his ethnological observations, as in TYPICAL GROUP OF OJIBWAY INDIANS AT FORT FRANCES, 1857, possess a distinct scientific value as well as a pleasing pictorial quality.

His brother, William G. R. Hind, born at Nottingham, England, in 1833, was an artist who had been early schooled in London and on the Continent. At the age of nineteen he came to Toronto, where he held classes in drawing for two years. He returned to England, but in 1861 again chose to join his brother, Henry Youle Hind, as artist on the Canadian Government Expedition to Labrador, for the purpose of making sketches and water-colour drawings of scenery and Indian life. In 1863-1864, and also early in the seventies, he was in Manitoba and British Columbia. During the latter part of his life he lived and worked in various parts of New Brunswick. Many of the early Canadian scenes in the John Ross Robertson Collection, the Indian drawings particularly, were made by him. Typical of his numerous sketches are SEAL HUNTING IN THE GULF OF ST. LAWRENCE, A MONTAGNAIS INDIAN TAKING HIS SQUAW TO BURIAL and SCENE FROM OJIA-PI-SI-TAGAN, OR TOP OF THE RIDGE PORTAGE, done on the Labrador Peninsula in 1861. His later water-colour sketches included BUFFALO HERD ON THE WESTERN PRAIRIES and BRITISH COLUMBIA MINER, 1864, done with fine vigour, ease and decision. He died in Sussex, N.B., in 1884.

In addition to his work as a civil engineer, William Armstrong was also an artist of some ability. A native of Dublin, he came to Canada, in 1851, as a young man of about thirty, when he was employed with the first Grand Trunk Railway. In 1870, as chief engineer with the Wolseley expedition to the North-West, he made his early Canadian sketches, many of which are still extant. His more important studies are to be seen in the collection of the Canadian National Railways, the John Ross Robertson Collection, and in public institutions and private homes. Specimens of his work occasionally come to light in old bookshops and auction rooms, and when they do the professional skill to which they bear evidence seldom fails to attract the attention of the knowing eye. His pictures, however, like much of the early painting done in Canada, are valuable chiefly for their historical and topographical content; although they are by no means lacking in aesthetic values.

The work of Lucius O'Brien, Bell-Smith, Mower Martin and G. Harlow White, among the earlier painters in the West, is too well known to require detailed mention here. With the coming of the railroad and the flood-tide of settlers to the new land, when the whistle of the train broke the long silence of the plain and scattered the covered wagons, and the advent of the red-coated "Mountie" brought law and order as well as a note of colour to the landscape, the foundations of that art were laid for which the new Provinces of British Columbia and the North-West Territories were to supply the colour, the life and the drama.

A rich vein of poetic inspiration lay within native themes and surroundings. The writer, the painter and the musician were to discover treasures in the virgin field of unending vistas, so far untrodden. A few hardier spirits will always follow the lure of the unknown compared to the multitudes content with the burdened security of the beaten trail. And so it was with the West and with British Columbia. The more adventurous of the painters came first, to be followed years later by others who were fortunate enough perhaps to be born in a more comfortable age – the age of what is euphemistically known as the age of modern conveniences. Well, we need not suppose that the art of these men suffered any diminution of interest or skill on that account. Hardship, although it may strengthen character, has ruined many a creative worker, and as a kindler of fruitful inspiration the comfortable home is likely to be as productive as the traditional garret. However that may be, the North-West, the Rockies and British Columbia have continued to enthral generation after generation of artists since their first discovery as themes by the pioneer painter a hundred years ago.

Up to the present, at any rate, the scenery and life of Western Canada has been interpreted through the eyes of such Eastern painters as Paul Kane, Captain Henry Warre, L. R. O'Brien, F. M. Bell-Smith, G. Harlow White, John Hammond and somewhat later by Arthur Heming, Charles W. Jefferys, Edmund Morris, J. W. Beatty, Frank H. Johnston, John F. Clymer and Frank Panabaker. As late as the exhibition of Canadian art at Paris in 1927, we find

Lawren Harris, Jefferys and Johnston represented by canvases descriptive of the Western landscape with its lakes and hills and parks. In attempting thus to interpret Western themes on their own terms, these painters have sought to omit elaboration of detail for the sake of a simple and unified presentation of an expression of art, which of all things has least to do with the imitative realism

Art Gallery of Toronto.

THE FALLEN MONARCH

FRANK S. PANABAKER

commonly supposed to be its end. In so striving for simplicity of statement, it is evident they have taken no liberties with things dependent upon true sight and precision of drawing which establish the identity of the subject. Probably Lawren Harris in his execution will be found to carry his principle farther than many of his contemporaries; but all essay to achieve an individual vision and technique without departing too radically from traditional forms.

Other painters from the East who have recorded their impressions of the West, and especially that portion of it which lies beyond the Rockies, are Edwin Holgate, of Montreal, A. Y. Jackson, of Toronto, Pegi Nichol, of Saint John, N.B., Annie D. Savage, of Montreal, and also the sculptor Florence Wyle, of Toronto, whose plaster models of Indian heads and totem poles would be a conspicuous contribution to any exhibition of Canadian West Coast art. Not the least interesting feature of Marius Barbeau's book on our West Coast Indian lore, *The Downfall of Temlaham,* is the fine series of illustrations in colour by Jackson, Holgate, Emily Carr, Annie D. Savage and the American artist, W. Langdon Kihn, whose portrayal and interpretation of Indian subjects, highly individualistic in style, has stirred the admiration of the art world for its pure beauty, and of scientists for its truth. Some of Mr. Kihn's paintings of the Nootka (totem pole) Indians of Vancouver Island also form the illustrations of Dr. Barbeau's explorative *Indian Days in the Rockies.*

This vast territory of the West extending to the Pacific Coast, which little more than two generations ago was the home only of the fur trader and the pioneer, is advancing rapidly in aesthetic development. Winnipeg, Calgary, Saskatoon, Regina, Vancouver and Victoria all are centres of art activities, all have their art clubs and artists grouped in intimate association. In Winnipeg there is the nucleus of a public collection and a thriving art club, apart from the art tuition given in the city's technical schools. Already a Manitoba Society of Painters exists and promises well for the future of the Province.

The small but enterprising Edmonton Museum of Fine Arts is also making a real contribution toward educating the public to a true appreciation of national and international works of art. Free classes for children under fourteen are held every Saturday morning, and it is gratifying to learn that they are well attended. Exhibitions are held from time to time of the works of British Columbia and Southern Alberta artists, as well as collections from sources more remote, such, for example, as the travelling loan exhibitions from the National Gallery, Ottawa.

A native-born artist of Winnipeg, whose work has attracted considerable attention in Canada, is L. LeMoine Fitzgerald. Trained first in the Keszthelyi School of Art, Winnipeg, and later at the Art Students' League, New York, he returned to Winnipeg to teach in its art school.   In spite of his necessary preoccupation with teaching, he has steadily pursued his bent as a landscape painter and has occasionally been represented in the more important exhibitions of Winnipeg, Toronto and elsewhere.   At one time a graphic and realistic painter, he has of late years developed a method of painting in softly modulated tones of grey that have imparted an atmospheric and poetic quality to his work peculiar to himself and altogether distinctive.   There is, it is true, a certain sketchiness in many of his pictures.   They are vignettes, and to

YORK BOAT
WALTER J. PHILLIPS

some observers would inevitably seem somewhat vague and unfinished; but a fine simplicity and sincerity are there, and a very clear, if rather sublimated, vision of the Canadian landscape. Only a true artist could paint with such tender restraint and insight.

A Western artist of conspicuous and diversified talent is Walter J. Phillips, of Winnipeg, who not only paints water-colour subjects of tender grace and beauty, but is also a wood-block engraver in black-and-white and colour of international repute. His prints of Western and British Columbia scenes are prized possessions of galleries both in Canada and abroad. A writer also of charm and distinction, he is the author of the *Technique of the Colour Wood-cut* (1926), which has come to be regarded as the standard work on the subject, and is a frequent contributor to magazines and periodicals on art topics. Two collections of his wood-block prints at least have been issued by Thomas Nelson and Sons of Toronto, and are now out of print. Born in England and schooled there, he came to Canada in 1913 and settled in Winnipeg, where he has since lived. He is a member of the Society of Canadian Painter-Etchers, a member of the Society of Print-makers of Los Angeles, and is represented in the California State Library. He is also a member of the Society of Graver-Printers in Colour, in London. In 1921 Phillips was elected an associate member of the Royal Canadian Academy, and in 1933 he attained to full membership in the engravers division, of which at present he is the solitary representative. Public recognition has come to him in the form of a medal from the Los Angeles International, 1924; the Arts and Crafts Medal from the Boston Art Club, 1932; and honourable mention at the Polish International Exhibition, 1933. He is represented also in the British Museum and the South Kensington Museum, London, in the New York Public Library, in the Los Angeles Museum, California, and in Tokio, Japan. In the field of publication, he has contributed illustrations to *Dreams of Fort Garry* and other works.

Another wood-block engraver is Hubert Valentine Fanshaw, who came to Canada in 1912 from Sheffield, England, and settled in Winnipeg. He is not only a landscape painter of merit, but is widely esteemed for his wood-block prints of Western subjects.

An artist of somewhat different reputation is A. C. Leighton, a water-colour painter of considerable ability, who has taken for subject material the prairies and the mountains, and has painted them with a fine feeling for colour, light and air. Born in England, he came to Canada first in 1925, and took up teaching a few years later at the Calgary Institute of Technology. In 1929 he was elected a member of the Royal Society of British Artists, London, and in 1931 became one of the founder-members and first president of the Alberta Society of Artists.

Although it is only in recent years that the public has come to know the work of Frederick G. Cross, of Brooks, Alberta, he has been sketching scenes of the prairies for many years. In 1925 three of his *tempera* paintings appeared in the exhibit of the Canadian Pacific Railway at the Wembley Exhibition. In the following year he won in open competition the award of the Engineering Institute of Canada for the best design submitted for a bronze memorial tablet. Then, so far as official art was concerned, he was in retirement until 1931, when he exhibited at the annual exhibition of the Royal Canadian Academy. Since that

FISHING BOATS: VICTORIA, B.C.

Frederick G. Cross

time he has produced a large number of water-colours. In 1932 his work appeared at all important exhibitions in Canada; two pictures of his were included in the Canadian collection of water-colours sent for exhibition to the Royal Scottish Academy's show at Edinburgh, Scotland. Coming to Canada from England in the old camp days on railway surveying and development work, Cross has contemplated its metamorphosis for thirty years from a point of view detached yet near at hand. His art, contrary to the usual custom, has not been concerned with the great pageantry of the West; rather it is a series of vignettes that, taken together, form a kind of social commentary, simple and direct, on the manifold, if minor, aspects of life on the range. Though he may be pleased to call his art "small," it has a character and sureness, a feeling for locality and a sensitivity of perception that make it of far greater value aesthetically and historically than is often found in more ambitious efforts. Mr. Cross is an artist who works almost entirely in the open air, and is especially noted for his paintings of skies. His interest in clouds and in the changing aspect of the heavens goes back many years to the time when he first settled in the West.

Four water-colour drawings by Cross may be taken as typical of his style. These are THE OPEN RANGE, DROUGHT, THE HORSE BARN and HEAD OF THE HERD, a study of the "boss" of the P/D Bar Ranch's herd at Duchess, Alberta, all of which are replete with detail, delightfully precise and graceful in handling. His subtle harmonies of tone and colour are exquisite in their general effect. A most interesting device of this painter is the way in which the sky—occupying, as it often does, two-thirds to three-quarters of the pictorial area—is made to convey an impression of boundless space and of vast aerial distances. This is the one thing that gives to his pictures a feeling of unity and individuality.

People who do not understand the West, who have not visited it and therefore know it only by remote intelligence, often appear to believe that it lacks, or almost entirely lacks, scenery; that is, there is nothing to be seen but the flatness of a limitless prairie. Yet, here, under the vast dome of the sky, the conflict of the elements in the heavens takes on its old commanding importance. To suggest this, without weakening the main theme of the composition, is one of the difficulties confronting the artist in the West. Here the clouds of a passing thunder-storm play an essential and a dramatic part in a picture. Again, as in Cross's picture DROUGHT, the very paleness of the skies adds a note of aloofness, almost of callosity, to the brooding sense of desolation which pervades the arid scene, as if nature herself secretly rejoiced over man's discomfiture and tragedy. Or dawn comes and brings with it the dewy freshness of the early morning air. But over all, the sky in the West plays a predominant part in a composition as it does nowhere else in Canada, save probably in the great Northland.

Evidence of the growing interest in Canadian art in the West is the collection of Canadian paintings in the Nutana Collegiate Institute, Saskatoon. Established as a memorial to the students of the school who lost their lives in the War of 1914-1918, this collection has grown in number and consequence, until it now contains representative canvases of many of our contemporary painters. This unusual but most inspiring memorial should have a fine cultural influence on the pupils of the school, and in time should exert its beneficient influence upon the whole community. The importance of this memorial collection, however, is the example it sets to larger and more pretentious places throughout the country.

Throughout the West are artists better known probably to their own kind than to the general public, but who by word and by example have contributed to the building up of what is now a considerable art body in the three Western Provinces. Of these the name of Henry J. DeForest comes first to mind. A landscape painter and ardently Victorian, he was inclined at first to rather literal interpretation, but in later years has affected a more vigorous and broader style of brush work. Born in Rothesay, N.B., in 1860, he studied drawing and painting at the South Kensington School of Art, London, the Julian Academy, Paris, and also in Edinburgh. Following a sketching trip to various parts of the world, he went to Vancouver, in 1898, later removing to Banff, where he made many paintings of the mountains. He died in Calgary in 1924.

Among Western artists, mention should be made of Roland Gissing, son of the English novelist, who has been painting in the Alberta foothills with considerable skill and feeling. His approach to his theme is that of the traditional English school, but his manner is markedly individual and his recent pictures are clear and soft in their tones and lit by a calm, subdued radiance.

J. H. Lee Grayson, an Englishman, studied art in England, France and Holland before coming to Canada in 1906. The loss of an eye in the last war handicapped but did not deter him from painting, and a number of fine examples of Saskatchewan landscapes have come from his brush. Like Grayson, Augustus F. Kenderdine was English born. He studied in Manchester and Paris before moving to the Canadian West. He interprets the Western landscape more imaginatively than circumstances would seem to require, and a preference for softly modulated tones and colours in his compositions suggests the quiet solitude of the French paysage rather than the breeze-swept plains of the Canadian prairie. As pure decoration, however, they are essentially beautiful.

Another artist whose work is well and favourably known in the West is James Henderson, who for more than thirty years has been painting in the Qu'Appelle Valley, Saskatchewan. One of the pioneer painters of Western Canada, he has divided his attention between Indian subjects and the local terrain. His happiest efforts are those in which he paints a vivid landscape with incidents of rude frontier life. His AFTERNOON IN THE COULÉE, with its glow of late sunlight on the hill beyond the snow-covered woodland, is a true and well-handled piece of work. A native of Glasgow, Henderson studied in the schools of his native town and of London before settling in Fort Qu'Appelle about forty years ago. He is a capable and conservative executant who follows the traditional school of British painting.

One of the first and most important painters to settle on the Pacific Coast was Thomas W. Fripp. Born in London in 1864, Fripp migrated to British Columbia in 1893, where he cleared for himself a farm from the bush. Youngest son of George Arthur Fripp, member of the Royal Water-Colour Society, England, and a grandson of Nicholas Pocode, one of the founders of the Society, Fripp attended classes at the Royal Academy School and later studied under his father before going to Italy for further study. Like Fowler he had come to Canada to better his fortune. An injury to his hand, however, compelled him to abandon farming and return to painting. Thereafter for a period of thirty years, or until his death in 1931, Fripp continued to paint in water-colour producing many pictures of the Rocky Mountains and the Pacific Coast. A number of his drawings in black-and-white chalk are also extant. Fripp was a founder-member of the British Columbia Society of Fine Arts, organized in 1917, a member of the Island Arts and Crafts Society of Victoria, and also of British Columbia Art League. He is represented in the National Gallery, Ottawa; in the Lieutenant-Governor's Chambers, Legislative Buildings, Toronto; in the Government House, Victoria, B.C., and in the Vancouver Art Gallery. Said to have been the best water-colour painter of the West Coast — he rarely painted in oils — his landscapes bear witness to a singularly fine vision and an individual handling of colour. One of the very few portraits he did, a piece called GLADYS, owned by John Bruce Cowan of Vancouver, was awarded a gold medal in Winnipeg in 1905. A life-size bust of Thomas Fripp, paid for by public subscription, and presented to the Vancouver Art Gallery, testifies to the general esteem in which he was held.

Charles John Collings lived at Salmon Arm, B.C. A painter in water-colours, he is reputed to be in some respects the finest colorist who ever worked in Canada. His principal market was in Great Britain, where his genius was early recognized.

In John Innis, British Columbia art had, until recently, a singular and engaging personality. Prior to his death in Vancouver, in January, 1941, Innis had been by turns a cartoonist, a magazine and newspaper illustrator, a soldier, a some-time Alberta rancher and a painter of Western Canadian life. A native Canadian, he was born in London, Ontario, in March, 1863, the son of the Very Reverend Dean Innis, D.D., whose family name is intimately associated with the early history of that section following the American Revolution. Educated at Hellmuth College, London, Ontario, King's College, Sherbourne, Eng., and the Dufferin Military Academy, he later studied art in London, New York and Toronto. His introduction to the Canadian West Innis received on government survey work. The West was just being penetrated by the Canadian Pacific and, like others before him, he came under the spell of its romantic lure. It was to point the way to his future life as an interpreter of the pioneer scene and the early beauties of that part of the Dominion. It was about this time presumably that he became a rancher near High River, Alberta, and rode the plains as a cowboy; subsequently he did cartoons for the Calgary *Herald*. He also operated the first telephone exchange in Calgary, but later moved to Banff, where he became part owner of a paper called *Mountain Echoes*. Innis was well known in Ontario during the nineties and, at the beginning of the century, when he was cartoonist and writer for *The Mail and Empire* and the old Toronto *World*. His series of articles, "Redbarn Relates," written for *The Mail and Empire* and filled with bucolic humour, had a wide following and are still remembered, as are also his illustrations for the *Canadian Magazine* done at this time, though they were often poorly done.

Innis' EPIC OF THE WEST, comprising a series of thirty oil paintings of Western scenes, created an impression of Western Canada which was reflected everywhere they were shown. They soon became widely known and as widely popular. Thirty of his historical canvases are owned by the Hudson's Bay Company, London, England; ten historical scenes are in the David Spencer Limited, department store, Vancouver. His collection of historical paintings, EPIC OF THE WEST, first shown at Vancouver, was also exhibited at Montreal, Leipzig and London.

Almost thirty-five years ago he went to Vancouver, travelling through the Kootenays by pack train from Calgary, putting the scenes of Western Canada on canvas as he went. Although John Innis was not of the first-flight of Canadian painters, his work will always be considered important because of its historic value. In some respects his paintings, in subject matter especially, bear a resemblance to the canvases of the American artist and illustrator, Frederic Remington; but he lacked the latter's disciplined hand, his patience, his technical skill and resource, and in that sense he is not comparable. Probably future historians will be disposed to link him with Kane and Krieghoff as a truthful, observant and, within his limitations, exact recorder of the life of Western Canada's formative years. Besides being a painter in oils and water-colour, Innis also was an etcher and, as I have said, an illustrator in pen-and-ink. A series of eight of his historical paintings hangs in the halls of the University of British Columbia. He is also represented at Washington, D.C., by his portrait HARDING IN CANADA, depicting the first visit of a President of the United States to British soil. This was a gift to the American Government. His EPIC OF TRANSPORTATION, a later subject from his brush, remains in Vancouver.[1]

An artist who is doing much to promote a more general interest in art in British Columbia is Charles Hepburn Scott, director of the Vancouver School of Art and lecturer on art education in the University of British Columbia. With a steadily increasing enrolment of students which must result in a group of competent and progressive painters on the West Coast, he has built, and will likely continue to build, a healthy and vigorous school of art in a community which, until late years at any rate, has stood greatly in need of one. In the school's first years he was

[1]Three Western paintings by Innis are also included in the George Eastman Collection, Rochester, N.Y.

fortunate in having as capable assistants two such eminent painters as F. Horsman Varley and J. W. G. Macdonald. Varley has since left Vancouver, for Ottawa, but happily Macdonald remains to continue the work so well begun. Born in Scotland, November, 1886, Scott studied first at the Glasgow School of Art, and then in Belgium, France, Holland, Germany and Italy, where he visited the famous galleries of these countries and employed some time in making sketches of the people and the countryside. In due course he came to Canada where, after exhibiting for a while, he became a member of the Canadian Group of Painters, the British Columbia Society of Fine Arts, and the Canadian Society of Graphic Arts. He is represented in the Vancouver Art Gallery by WINTER, a pastel. He has also exhibited at the Canadian Wembley Exhibition, the Dominion Overseas Exhibition and the Canadian Coronation Exhibition. In recognition of his services to Canadian art, Charles Scott was recently elected an associate of the Royal Canadian Academy.

F. H. Varley is not only a skilful draughtsman, but one of the finest portrait painters Canada has had. Much of his early work done here was as a commercial artist in Toronto. However, after a time he forsook commercial art to go on his own as a landscapist and painter of portraits. In both fields he excelled. His impressive portrayal of MR. IRVING HEWARD CAMERON, M.B., LL.D., exhibited at the fiftieth annual exhibition of the Ontario Society of Artists, in 1922, is still remembered for its shrewd insight, its fine design, sound construction and expressive brushwork. His study of JOHN, a boy's head, now in the National Gallery, Ottawa, is notable for its happy interpretation of a roguish, freckle-faced lad who might be a prototype of all boys. Nor is his landscape painting in any sense inferior. In his GEORGIAN BAY, also in the National Gallery, the feeling of impetuous drive of wind in rolling waves and bending pines is expressed with vigour, truth and beauty. In colouring and pattern, in form and mood, there is a fine harmony, a directness of statement and sincerity of expression that disarm criticism. The sheer perfection of its beauty holds one silent; which undoubtedly is the highest form of tribute one can pay to a craftsman. In the last war Varley was engaged for a time in painting portraits and war scenes for the Canadian War Records. He is further represented by mural decorations in St. Anne's Church, Toronto, and in the

National Gallery by SQUALLY WEATHER and VERA, an oil portrait. In 1930 he won the Lord Willingdon prize for the best painting of the year. He is now an instructor in drawing and painting at the Art Association of Ottawa.

Besides being art teacher at the Vancouver Technical School for Boys and Girls, James W. G. Macdonald is a landscape painter

FRIENDLY COVE, B.C.

J. W. G. MacDONALD

of the so-called modern school, an adept if somewhat heavy-handed interpreter of the Western scene. His brushwork is broad, vigorous, colourful, and his subjects are composed in formal decorative fashion. Probably his previous training as a designer has something to do with this, for he served an apprentice-ship as an architectural draughtsman in Scotland, where he was born, and later engaged as textile designer with Morton Sundour Fabrics, in England. In the Lord Willingdon competition in 1933,

189

landscape division, he was awarded an honourable mention. He is represented in the National Gallery, Ottawa, by an oil painting of LYTTON CHURCH, BRITISH COLUMBIA, and in the Vancouver Art Gallery by INDIAN BURIAL. He is a member of the Canadian Group of Painters and, in 1942, the British Columbia Society of Fine Arts elected him to the presidency of that body.

Vancouver's Art Gallery, opened in October, 1931, is acquiring a valuable collection of pictures representative of the art of Canada, Great Britain, France and other countries. At a recent exhibition – the thirty-first – of the British Columbia Society of Fine Arts, a well-selected but comprehensive group of entries was shown consisting of oil paintings, water-colours, pastels, drawings and sculpture, so that it would seem as if Vancouver were destined to become, indeed already has become, an important· art centre of the Dominion. What is especially encouraging is the interest being shown in the activities of the gallery by the people of the locality; in 1941 no fewer than 72,268 persons were recorded as having attended the various exhibitions, which for the twelve-month period totalled sixty-one. The total number visiting the Gallery since it opened, until June, 1943, was 827,964; and over 500 special exhibitions have been shown in that time.

Of all the painters who labour in British Columbia, Miss Emily Carr of Victoria, both by right of birth, training and style, seems to be attached most firmly to the West Coast country. She seems also, for the same reason, to have a closer kinship with the Group of Seven or, as it is now, the Canadian Group of Painters, than those artists who claim British Columbia their home by adoption. In her painting she stresses two main principles, simplification of form, with an intensification of colour. Naturally enough, Miss Carr is not so much concerned with detailed representation as she is with interpreting form and volume, rhythm of line and simplified masses; and these attributes of her craft find their full expression in the totem poles and Indian villages which distinguish her more characteristic themes. As an artist of originality she has been, as is perhaps natural, more sympathetic toward the exponents of the so-called modern school than the conventions of the traditionalists. Despite, therefore, an obvious leaning toward the theories of the modern European painters, she had developed a definite personal technique of her own. Her best work will likely be taken for what it is—ardently Canadian. Her recent painting, however, is characterized by an eccentricity of design and a cloudiness of colour which stand in marked contrast to her earlier work. It is hard to explain this apparent falling off unless it be the result of failing vision, or a perverse desire to carry still further a technique that was once effective and sincere. Whatever the cause, her painting has indubitably suffered because of it.

Quite late in life Emily Carr turned author, producing her first book, *Klee Wyck*, a series of vivid sketches of life among the West Coast Indians. In its classical restraint it is as far removed

A STUDY IN MOVEMENT

EMILY CARR

from the exuberancy of her painting as is possible to conceive. Undoubtedly one of the finest things of its kind in Canadian letters, it has attracted wide attention, and an American edition has been issued. That it should have been awarded the Governor-General's Medal for the best book in the non-fiction class for 1941 was a fitting tribute. Her second book of reminiscences, *The Book of Small*, issued in 1942, has repeated in many ways the well deserved success of the first.

A painter of the West Coast, whose name and reputation have gone far beyond the confines of British Columbia, is W. P. Weston,

A.R.C.A., landscape painter and art master of the Provincial Normal School, Vancouver. A native of London, England, he acquired a knowledge of drawing and painting at the Putney Art School. Since he came to Canada, he has interested himself in teaching and in promoting the cause of the fine arts. He is a charter member of both the Canadian Group of Painters and the British Columbia Society of Fine Arts. Although much of his time is devoted to teaching, he has yet found opportunity for both painting in oils and drawing in pen and pencil, and is a frequent contributor to exhibitions in Canada, England and the United States. He has exerted a wholesome and stimulating effect upon the art of the Province, and of course in Vancouver where he lives. Two of his works, RAMPARTS OF THE WEST, a landscape in oil, and THE SUMMIT, a pen drawing, are in the National Gallery at Ottawa; an oil study of the Rockies, MT. CHEAM, is in the collection of Hart House, University of Toronto. On the whole his work is significant, decorative and, of late years, strongly contemporary in feeling.

Among the artists of British Columbia whose work entitles them to recognition is Harry Hood, a former president of the Society of Fine Arts, and a painter of ability in oil and water-colour. He does not confine himself to landscape subjects, but handles figure and still-life with skill and dexterity. His water-colours of still-life are remarkable for their competency. He is represented in the Vancouver City Museum by HOTEL VAN-COUVER FROM GEORGIA STREET, painted in oils.

President of the B.C. Society of Fine Arts, Gerald H. Tyler is noted for his marines and landscapes. Apart from painting, he has for years studied the chemistry of paint. As a result of scientific experiment his help to artists has been invaluable.

Mildred Valley Thornton of Vancouver is a recognized painter of Indian subjects. However, she has done landscape and portraiture, notably a portrait study of THE RIGHT HONOURABLE ARTHUR MEIGHEN for the Arthur Meighen Club of Regina. Ontario born, she received her early training in Toronto and Chicago, and at Oliver College, Michigan.

Allan Whitcomb Edwards is a young portraitist of promise. A pupil of John Russell, Toronto, he was awarded at the age of sixteen the prize for the most outstanding amateur portrait at the Canadian National Exhibition, in 1931.

Lilias Farley of Vancouver is an artist of exceptional talent.

A sculptor in wood, a designer for the theatre and a craftsman in puppetry, she was awarded and highly commended for textile designs at the British Empire Industrial Arts Exhibition, London, 1930; her murals adorn the new Vancouver Hotel. Then there are such fine British Columbia painters as: James H. O. Armess; Colin Cameron Ramsay, who studied in Scotland under Maurice Greiffenhagen; Arthur Henry Parker, widely represented in private collections; R. S. Alexander, "a young portrait and landscape painter of vigour and promise"; and among women artists Mabel Bain, whose landscapes, both oils and water-colour, evidence a fine decorative sense; Kate Smith Hoole, a talented painter in all mediums, with a fine feeling for animals; Bessie Fry Symons, who does pleasing work in water-colour; Maisie Robertson, painter as well as sculptor, who has won awards in both fields; and Nesta Bowen Horne, "whose portraits and flower studies are notably fresh and clean." Sculpture in British Columbia, as in other parts of Canada, has relatively few devotees, but at present it is not unworthily represented by P. V. Ustinow, Lilias Farley and Marjorie Robertson, all of whom, it may be noted, use pigment as well as clay as a medium of expression.

J. L. Shadbolt, instructor at the Vancouver School of Art, is a young and versatile artist who has done much to foster an interest in the fine arts. His views on the function of art are stated with refreshing clarity and succinctness, and since it is not unreasonable to suspect they are held, in substance at any rate, by the generality of the younger contemporary painters, we may take leave to quote:

The problem of art is to express adequately the problem that exists in the mind—the world of experience. It is the difference between trying to make a photograph of a tree and trying to create a form that shall express our feelings about that tree.

And as illustrative of a common-sense attitude toward art and the practice of art, the following quotation may be taken as further typical of his enlightened point of view:

Among all our people practising, there are necessarily few producing lasting art. But it is the process that matters, and intelligent public interest and discrimination will encourage finer expression. Seriously, with intelligence and sensitiveness and courage, there are artists giving voice to Western Canada. The greatest stimulus to these people is not adulation or flattery, but intelligent appreciation. They do not ask to be liked, but to be understood.

With the art of Western Canada in such hands, there should be little concern for the future. Such a platform is broad enough for all to stand upon in common unity and oneness of endeavour.

It is strange that Lawren Harris, one of the founders of the Group of Seven, who had probably most to do with shaping its policies, should have come to succeed Varley at Vancouver, another of the original Group. But so it is, and the efforts of Harris to establish a distinctively Canadian type of painting may be expected in due course to be as manifest in the West as formerly they were in the East. The outcome therefore may be awaited with interest.

13

For one reason or another sculpture in Canada has never evoked anything like the popular interest and enthusiasm which has rewarded the work of the painter. Indeed, it suffers from apathy that in almost any other form of aesthetic expression would have long since proved fatal. For this neglect there are probably two reasons: first, the primary appeal that colour makes to the ordinary man to the exclusion of other important considerations; and, secondly, the inability of the "man in the street" to understand and appreciate sculpture as he believes himself competent to appraise and comprehend painting, for instance. There may yet be a third reason: I am not sure, but if there is, it is likely the impression produced by the type of statue that graces, or defaces, as it sometimes does, our public parks and areas.

One has only to stroll through our public gardens, or in the vicinity of governmental buildings in our capital cities, to be convinced of this truth. On all sides are to be seen memorials, many of them relics of the eighties, nineties and even later, which because of their sheer vulgarity, poverty of ideas or lack of imagination reflect little if any credit upon the sculptor who modelled them. The statute of Robert Burns in the Allan Gardens, Toronto, is one example: an example which I dare say is duplicated in scores of gardens and public places throughout the world. There are others, among them stuffy, frockcoated legislators and similar men of eminence whose number is legion. These dull memorials,

GIRL WITH FISH
FRANCES LORING

stupidly placed, are constant reminders of the incapacity of our former sculptors to foresee that in years to come their sculptured presentments would remain hopelessly outdated and outmoded, to vitiate public taste and often make the very name of sculpture a byword and a derision among men. Now, oddly enough, sculpture is beginning to interest the ordinary man. The work of the sculptor, thanks to a more enlightened point of view and a recognition of a changed public taste, shows signs of a steady improvement in craftsmanship and design. As a result of this revived interest and sympathetic appreciation, more sculpture is being carved and more sculptors trained. And as interest grows, intelligent criticism increases. All of this is encouraging and stimulating for artists, as well as for the citizen who desires to see more beauty in his city. Criticism of sculpture leads to the definition of the principles that guide it, and so, perhaps, to the illumination of all concerned.

Of sculptors working in Canada in the eighties there were two: Napoleon Bourassa and Hamilton McCarthy. Bourassa's work covered a wide range – painting, occasional architecture, and sculpture (both busts and images, as well as decorations for churches). NOTRE DAME DE LOURDES, on which he was assisted for some years by young Philippe Hébert, is the best-known example of his ecclesiastical sculpture. Hébert in 1880 had just returned to Canada from his first years in Paris, and was at the beginning of a career that was both remarkable and prolific. In 1880 Hamilton McCarthy arrived in Canada, and for years the work of these two men may fairly be said to illustrate the history of monument and architectural sculpture in Canada. In background and training Hébert was of Paris; McCarthy of London. Approximately in the order of execution a few of their earlier works may be noted.

From Philippe Hébert we acquired between 1880 and 1900: the DE SALABERRY monument at Chambly; the CARTIER statue at Ottawa; the eight historical statues in the façade of the Legislative Buildings, Quebec; the Indian figures in front of the same building; SIR JOHN A. MACDONALD at Ottawa; the MAISONNEUVE monument in the Place d'Armes, Montreal; the MADELEINE DE VERCHÈRES memorial at Vercheres (one of his first examples); and the bust of BISHOP BOUGET at Montreal.

Hamilton McCarthy modelled during approximately the same

BORIS HAMBOURG
CLEEVE HORNE

period: the EGERTON RYERSON statue in the grounds of the Normal School, Toronto; and that of SIR JOHN A. MACDONALD, in Queen's Park, Toronto; the SIEUR DE MONTS memorial at Annapolis Royal, Nova Scotia; and that to CHAMPLAIN at Ottawa.

In the first decade of the new century Walter Allward and George W. Hill appear as sculptors. Allward is said to be largely self-taught; Hill was Paris trained. Among the early works by Allward was the SOUTH AFRICAN WAR MEMORIAL on University Avenue, Toronto, and the statue of GOVERNOR SIMCOE in Queen's Park, Toronto. Hill did the STRATHCONA and the SOUTH AFRICAN WAR MEMORIAL in Dominion Square, Montreal. Both designs unfortunately are conventional in treatment and display little invention or imagination. To this period belongs also the Hill memorial to H.M. QUEEN VICTORIA at Ottawa, in 1901, and again in Hamilton six years later.

Because of the War of 1914-1918, few sculpture commissions were available. To this period belong: P. Hébert's SIR LEONARD TILLEY memorial at Saint John; the SOUTH AFRICAN memorial at Calgary; and the KING EDWARD VII monument on Phillip's Square, Montreal; Walter S. Allward's ALEXANDER GRAHAM BELL memorial at Brantford; and the LAFONTAINE group at Ottawa; George W. Hill's GEORGE BROWN group at Ottawa, the THOMAS D'ARCY MCGEE memorial, and the GEORGES ÉTIENNE CARTIER monument on Fletcher's Field, Montreal; Alfred Laliberte's first monumental works are of this period. These comprise DOLLARD DES ORMEAUX in Lafontaine Park at Montreal; and the statues of LOUIS HÉBERT, MARQUETTE, BRÉBEUF, the INTENDANT TALON and LORD DORCHESTER in the legislative buildings at Quebec.

An increase of business prosperity, and the public desire to memorialize its great, united in the immediate post-war period to open unusual opportunities to our Canadian sculptors for the display of their abilities. In all candour it cannot be said that they profited greatly by them. The EDWARD HANLAN memorial in the Exhibition Park, at Toronto, the SIR ADAM BECK memorial in University Avenue, Toronto, and the memorial to DEAN GALBRAITH of the University of Toronto, all of them the work of Emanuel Hahn, are distinguished by nothing save a respectable competency. Nor can the designs of Henri Hébert, as represented by the EVANGELINE memorial at Grand Pré, the OUTREMONT WAR

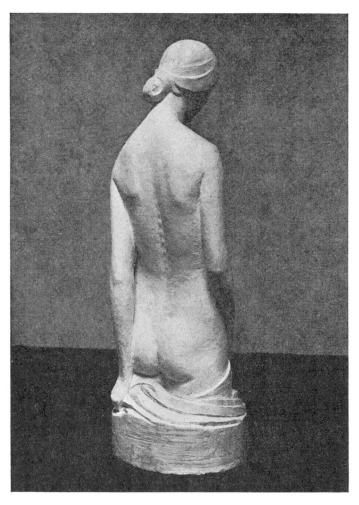

STUDY OF A GIRL
FLORENCE WYLE

MEMORIAL and the LAFONTAINE memorial at Montreal, be truth-fully said to surpass them in skill and invention.

At this time the women sculptors were granted the oppor-tunity, which had long been withheld from them, of exercising their talents on major works of sculpture. Hitherto their efforts were largely confined to portrait busts, memorial tablets, book ends, models for fountains and symbolistic studies. Now they were to try their hand on large-scale competitive modelling. From the manner in which they worked out their individual problems, it was evident that they had grasped the possibilities of simplicity that are latent in a reposeful and more significant composition. Especi-ally is this true of Frances Loring's war memorials at St. Stephen, N.B., Queen's University, Kingston, and Galt, Ontario, and also in her design of the VICTOR ROSS memorial at Pickering. In designing the EDITH CAVELL memorial at Toronto, Florence Wyle has invested the theme with the essential attributes of serenity, strength and dignity. It impresses one as something quite forceful and personal, and it is academic in the best sense of that term.

Of sculptors working in the twenties, we find Allward engaged from 1922 to 1936 on the great VIMY RIDGE CANADIAN WAR MEMORIAL in France, whose fate at the hands of the Germans during the present war is still undetermined. His portrait bust of William Lyon Mackenzie (1937) on the west side of the Legislative Buildings, Toronto, is as finely planned, as fresh and original in treatment, as anything of the kind yet done in Canada. We also find during this period George Hill working on war memorials in the city of Westmount, P.Q., the NURSE'S NATIONAL MEMORIAL in the Hall of Fame in the Parliament Buildings, Ottawa, and many others. Laliberté's LAURIER monument in the cemetery at Ottawa, and the CURÉ LABELLE, at St. Jerome, P.Q., are of this time.

To this post-war period, partly succeeding a career as the sculptor of youth, belongs Tait Mackenzie's new career as an internationally known sculptor of public memorials. Among his chief works in this *genre* may be recorded: the GENERAL WOLFE monument in Greenwich Park, Westerham, England; the SCOTTISH-AMERICAN WAR MEMORIAL at Edinburgh, Scotland; the DOMINION CONFEDERATION MEMORIAL in the Parliament Buildings at Ottawa; and the SPIRIT OF NURSING memorial in the Red Cross Gardens at Washington, D.C.

Not all of these monuments and memorials, to be sure, can be regarded as even reasonably successful in their ensemble of sculpture and supporting masonry. Some of them were atrocious as monuments, whatever may have been their sculptural merits. The masonry, perhaps, not because of the sculptor's fault, too often failed both of itself, and in relation to modelled sculpture,

Queen's Park, Toronto.

WILLIAM LYON MACKENZIE

WALTER S. ALLWARD

to rise above the quality level of very ordinary commercial tombstone work. But these defects, grave as they are, were anything but invariable. Some of our sculptors, Allward for one, have brilliantly demonstrated their skill in designing a harmonious whole. His MACKENZIE memorial, to which reference has been made, is an example. Others have worked in collaboration with able architects; this seems to have been the practice of Hébert's friend, Undenstock of Paris, France, who is said to have collaborated on the design of the MAISONNEUVE, BOURGET and KING EDWARD VII monuments, and perhaps some others. The Maxwells were collaborating architects on Hill's SOUTH AFRICAN and CARTIER monuments at Montreal.

Sculptors have at times protested, not entirely without reason, that commissions for architectural and decorative sculpture have been conspicuously rare events, and that the architects have so seldom left the beaten track of tradition that there remained but a limited scope for sculptors. Nevertheless, the Héberts, Allward, Sciortino, Scott Carter, and others have produced more than a little architectural sculpture — both ornament and figure. Panels in Moyse Hall, McGill University; McDougall and Cowans buildings on Notre Dame Street, Montreal; the new Stock Exchange Building on Bay Street, Toronto; and the heraldic plaques in colour for the doorways of the new wings of Trinity College, Toronto — these supply forceful illustration of change. Flattened, formalized, less insistent upon recognition for itself alone, work of this kind modestly retains its place as part of the new "flat" wall surfaces increasingly evident in current architecture. Not altogether beside the mark can be the thought that, at no distant day, sculpture and decorative painting may be called upon to take their place as successors to continuous architectural forms now passing out, and of which perhaps the Concourse Building on Adelaide Street, and the Clarendon Apartment dwellings on Avenue Road, Toronto, and more recently Trinity College, Toronto, are striking examples. Under the direction of Henry Falk, a man of courage and ideas, the former buildings have been decorated by Canadian artists — J. E. H. MacDonald and Thoreau MacDonald — who co-operated with the architects, Baldwin and Green; and Trinity College by A. Scott Carter working with the architects George and Moorhouse of Toronto.[1]

Not included in our present survey, but important, are the studio sculptors whose compositions are bringing them into favourable notice. Of these, probably Elizabeth Wyn Wood is the most notable. Her REEF AND RAINBOW of tin, and PASSING RAIN, a bas-relief in white plaster, are among the most highly imaginative and poetically conceived productions in the history of Canadian sculpture. Exhibited at the newly formed Sculptors' Society of

[1]The reredos of St. Thomas' Church, Toronto, done by Scott Carter and Edward Watson in collaboration, shows how well modern craftsmanship can recreate the design and feeling of the Middle Ages.

VILHJALMUR STEFANSSON
Emanuel Hahn

CAESAR FINN
Elizabeth Wyn Wood

Canada, in October, 1928, Passing Rain attracted general interest as possibly the most original conception in the show. This opinion was confirmed when, as an entry in the Willingdon Competition, it shared with the Bronze Head of Sylvia d'Aoust the Governor-General's award for sculpture. Her work has won high praise wherever it has been shown, and today in many quarters she is regarded as a Canadian sculptor whose art can successfully bear comparison with the most imaginative productions of the rest of the world. Her most important metal work is her war memorial at Welland, Ontario. On a lower plane, and yet capable of fine expressive efforts, are Cleeve Horne, whose bust portrait of Mark Hamburg is a revealing, sympathetic characterization handled with strength, discernment and vigour; and Frances Loring's study, Eskimo, which shows a respect for her material and a simplification of form, mass and detail that sets the theme apart from the commonplace or conventional. The subject may suffer from idealized treatment, but it is nevertheless a work of art, traditional in spirit, but in keeping with the movement toward the reduction of a subject to its simplest terms.

In Jacobine Jones we have, what is rare in Canada, a sculptor of animals. Born of English-Danish stock, she came to Canada from London in 1932. Her formal training in modelling she undertook under Harold Brownsword of the Regent Street Polytechnic, London, where her animal modelling won a gold medal. Subsequently she engaged in further study in Europe. Shortly after her arrival in Canada she was invited by the Ontario Agricultural College at Guelph to make studies of animal life. Her work soon came under the notice of Canadian architects who began to employ her on important commissions. For the Bank of Canada at Ottawa she designed a series of decorative figures in green bronze; for the doorway of Our Lady of Mercy Hospital, Sunnyside Avenue, Toronto, she modelled a group design, symbolical of the three generations of man. This sculpture she herself carved from Indiana limestone; and for the Gore Vale Fire Insurance building of Galt, Ontario she designed a decorative plaster panel in colour. Of these three buildings, Marani, Lawson and Morris of Toronto were the architects. Miss Jones was later commissioned by W. L. Somerville, R.C.A., to design nine panels in Queenston limestone for the St. Thomas Hospital of St. Thomas, Ontario, of which he was the principal architect.

BLACK CAVALRY

Jacobine Jones

Of pure sculpture alone there are many noteworthy examples, including a finely conceived and executed figure of ST. JOAN, handled with a simple austerity that comports well with the subject and is strongly imbued with a feeling for the mediæval. This piece, carved by the sculptor herself from Rouen stone, was first shown at the Royal Academy of London, and later, in 1930, at the Royal Scottish Academy, where it was bought by the Corporation of Glasgow, and is now in the Kelvin Museum, Glasgow. A boldly impressive piece of carving in black marble is BLACK CAVALRY, a portrait of a Nubian warrior mounted. The horse is modelled with a vigour that makes every line, plane and curve of the body alive, and instinct with bounding energy and strength. In conception and carving as well as in colour it forms a sharp and striking contrast to the more serene if not less firm and boldly handled study of St. Joan. These are among her more memorable subjects.

Her subjects range from a door knocker to a child's head. Studies of animals, however, represent the bulk of her work today. A number of these have taken the form of war memorials, including perhaps for the first time monuments to horses modelled in bronze or stone. A design for an Australian war memorial embodied the heroic figure of Sir John Monash, leader of the Anzac forces during the War of 1914-1918. Her *1914-1918*, another war memorial, graphically portrays artillery horses bringing up the guns. Occasionally she does portraits of dogs. RACING GREYHOUNDS, exhibited at her one-man show at Mellors Fine Art Galleries, Toronto, a few years ago, evidences how wholly such themes engage her skill and sympathy. In the belief that direct work by the sculptor is essential to the final sculpture, if the appearance of a copy from the clay model is to be avoided, Miss Jones carves her own work instead of delegating this task to another. She is probably the only sculptor in Canada who does so.

From the earliest times Quebec has been renowned for its sculpture. From the day of the wood carvers, Le Prevost and Le Blond de la Tour and their apprentices of the Cap Tourmente school (about 1695-1698), and of Leandre Parent and the Baillargé family of sculptors and wood carvers, down to the Herberts, Louis-Philippe and Henri, and Aurele de Foy Suzor-Côté a tradition of fine and faithful craftsmanship has been worthily maintained throughout the intervening years. Among the sculptors of later days, Alfred Laliberté is one of the most famous and original. A native of St. Elizabeth, Quebec, he studied in the École des Beaux-Arts in Paris under Injalbert. Soon after his student period, he was awarded an Honourable Mention in the Paris Salon. In 1912 he became an associate member of the Royal Canadian Academy, and seven years later attained full membership. When the Canadian Sculptors Society was formed in 1928, he became a founder member. Laliberté is represented in the National Gallery of Canada by three bronze pieces, JEUNES INDIENS CHASSANT, LOUVIGNY DE MONTIGNY, LE REPAS DU VEAU; and one marble figure, LA MUSE.

There are other workers in the plastic medium, whose performances indicate the possession of something more than mere manual dexterity. Sing Hoo, whose FADING and COMPANIONSHIP were exhibited at the O.S.A. (1941), elicited much favourable comment. Even more imaginative in conception are the compositions of John Sloan who, in A HEWER OF WOOD, A DRAWER OF WATER, and a sketch group for a memorial THERE IS NO TRUTH MORE TRUE THAN DEATH, shows definitely that our younger sculptors are gifted with invention and imagination as well as technical ability. In this category is included Lilias Farley of Vancouver, whose sculptured busts and carving in wood are exceptionally fine.

14

Etchings, prints and drawings, unless coloured wood-blocks or aquatints, received, until very recently at any rate, scant attention from the committees in charge of our art exhibitions. It may well be, as has been aptly remarked, that their unobtrusive dimensions have failed to command attention. However that may be, the visitor to the galleries usually found them set apart from the chief exhibits in a room often remote from the main gallery. This in itself was not entirely an unreasonable disposition, even if inconvenient, since in their very segregation they demanded and often received an attention and interest otherwise withheld. With the organization some years ago, however, of the Canadian

Society of Painter-Etchers, and the growth in size and importance of the Canadian Society of Graphic Art, black-and-white work, to use a generic term, has been promoted to a position in the arts to which its vitality, utility and common currency justly entitled it. This leads us to a consideration of the work of our etchers and illustrators.

Etching in Canada is virtually a new art: in age not more perhaps than half a century. As yet we have no Whistler, no

AN OLD ONTARIO VILLAGE

LEONARD HUTCHINSON

Seymour Haden, and to come to our own day, no Frank Brangwyn or Muirhead Bone. Yet the absence of such genius from the native group has not prevented Canadian etching from gaining wide recognition in Europe, England, Australia and the United States. Mention of Clarence Gagnon calls to mind that his first success as an artist was won as an etcher. Similarly his vivid impressions of the older purlieus of Montreal have given Herbert Raine a leading place among Canadian plate-makers. During the eighties and nineties and for some years after William J. Thompson depicted

209

Ontario scenes on copper to the enrichment of the art of his native Province and for the encouragement of those craftsmen who followed him. Contemporary with these men were W. W. Alexander, John Cotton, Ivan Neilson, F. S. Haines, Stanley Turner, Dorothy Stevens, Walter J. Phillips, and in more recent days, Harry Wallace, Nicholas Hornyansky, Jack Martin, and Eric Bergman. W. J. Phillips and Eric Bergman of Manitoba began etching, but left that medium for the subtleties of the wood-block, with which they have achieved world-wide fame, as has also Leonard Hutchinson of Hamilton.

The work of this group of etchers and engravers as a whole measures the development in this branch of the graphic arts in Canada. Long before he became famous as a painter Clarence Gagnon had achieved world-wide renown as an etcher. His prints, chiefly of scenes in France and Belgium, showed a marked under-standing of the etcher's craft which calls for precise drawing, the ability to translate values, and an exact knowledge of the action of acids—all this preliminary to the wiping of the plate and the printing operations which can make or mar an impression. In his CANAL MORET-SUR-LOING, for example, exhibited at the memorial exhibition of his work in Montreal and Toronto in 1942, Gagnon has well suggested a grey autumn day when the poplars edging the waterway are fast losing their leaves. The barges are well placed and the figures on the tow-paths add human interest to the composition which is imbued with delicacy, grace and tender feeling, heightened by a softness of line and clarity of tone which invariably distinguishes the work of this etcher. So, too, with his SAN AGOSTINO CANAL, VENICE: a print which reveals Gagnon's superb skill as a draftsman and his happy faculty of placing his shadows and salient points of interest most effectively. The rippling reflections, the glinting lights, and the shaded gondolas are set down with a light touch and yet with a certain firmness and precision. Equally felicitous is the treatment of the old brick wall exposed by broken plaster in the foreground. Here he displays a shrewd sense of colour and an apt recording of the corroding effect of time and weather. Taken with his other etchings, it is a plate that makes readily understandable the remarkable success which attended the exhibition of his prints in Europe, England and in Canada, and early placed him as a master of this medium.

One of the first in Canada to experiment with the etcher's tool,

Frederick S. Haines is remembered for his aquatints in colour of Ontario landscape and farm fields, which once common enough in the windows of the art shops of Toronto and elsewhere are in truth rare enough today. But reputation and the compensation of an appreciative public did not come easily. Haines' story is one of early struggles with the art, struggles which brought him at last, it is pleasant to record, fame abroad and an honorary membership in the Hungarian Society of Painter-Etchers, Budapest, to be

THE VILLAGE

FREDERICK S. HAINES

followed by recognition in England, Australia and the United States. Nowadays, since most of his time is devoted to teaching and administrative duties as Principal of the Ontario College of Art, Haines is able to devote but little of his time to painting and none at all, regrettably, to etching in which he made his first pronounced success.

Keen insight and creative imagination have given the etchings of John Cotton that quality which transports the observer from the literal present to the romantic past, in which artistic skill and a

211

sense of the dramatic are admirably combined. His plates are etched with an admirable feeling, a simple and effective handling of the bitten lines. From the architectural proportions of the University of Toronto and the Soldiers' Memorial Tower at Toronto, to the grim, gaunt mine shafts of northern Ontario, Cotton realizes the capacity of outlines in stone or brick or wood, attended by their circumstance of light and shadow, to impress the imagination, to stir the emotion. His work by its soberness and colour and firm simplicity wins us. In its own way, and in its own degree, it will always give pleasure.

Similarly significant are the dry points of Jack Martin, who shares with Haines the love of village and countryside. To his faithful and sympathetic and sensitive plates of rural byways and crossroads, he brings imaginative draftsmanship, an inborn love of people, humour, suffused with gentle feeling. In pieces which show these qualities at their best, Martin displays the ease and simplicity and directness in drawing derived from ripe knowledge and practised skill. In them, too, is seen the touch of the born etcher: one who works with swiftness, passion and confident sincerity; whose needle takes the impulse of his thought at white heat, who seldom if ever works with cool and calculated deliberation. Form and mass he indicates with lines which seem magically right and expressively complete. His selection of subject matter moreover is wide in range. Of his later prints perhaps St. Andrew's, Bendale, The Open Road, God's Acre and The Wayfarers are among his best because he has patently brought to his task all the varied and rich resources of his craft. In conception practically imaginative and in execution graceful, delicate and spirited, his plates in treatment always are concordant with the theme.

Of those etchers to whom architecture, whether in the noble and austere exteriors of French cathedral churches, or the open squares and modest house-fronts of the provincial towns was the chief preoccupation, Harry D. Wallace is among the best. He is also one among those who have painted. Master of a broad and vigorous style, which is not when necessity arises devoid of a fine precision, Wallace imparts to stone and wood a strong feeling of solidity, of massive strength, with an accurate sense of proportion, remote from any suggestion of the tracing board and T-square. His patient, careful and reverent treatment of Amiens

CATHEDRAL with its spacious and richly carved and ornamented porchway gives a fairly good idea of his work. And the marvel of it is that in spite of the wealth of detail, of images and carving and of profuse medieval decoration, he contrives to convey a certain spirit of largeness into his design. Though elaborate in detail, he seems always to have seen it steadily and seen it whole, his handling of it indeed far above a literal or minutely detailed description. It achieves in sum the drama of light on stone. In striking contrast to the robust yet thoughtful handling of this plate

MOTIF NO. 1: ROCKPORT, MASS.

CYRIL J. TRAVERS

is his sensitive realization of a rainy day in THE ROAD TO THE FERRY, notable for its limpid atmosphere and well-handled foreground suggested with that light touch and selection of detail which are among the first requisites of an etching. At times his style is rather reminiscent of Brangwyn, but the resemblance we may be sure is accidental, resulting more from the rugged technique and the daring treatment of his plates than from any conscious imitation of that master. Almost invariably his manner is distinctly fresh, virile and personal.

213

In his pictures of the sea John J. Barry uses needle and acid to produce a quite different effect. His etchings along the Eastern Atlantic seaboard are varying in mood, but of fair weather scenes, handled with a nicely calculated economy of line and lightness of touch so setting them apart from the brooding masses and ponderous weight characteristic of Wallace's intensely dramatic work. None the less, in certain of his prints, notably EARLY MORNING, Barry manages to achieve a quiet distinction of mood and manner. Outstanding by their fine craftsmanship and subtlety are the dry points of Woodruff Akroyd, whose plates of ancient buildings are rich in historic and romantic significance. His plate, THE WHITE HART, WITLEY, SURREY, is etched with admirable feeling, a simple and effective handling of the bitten lines, the scene is treated with the plainness and sincerity characteristic of him.

Other Canadian etchers whose work entitles them to mention are Stanley Turner for his individual treatment of street scenes in Toronto and Quebec; John Byrne for his figure studies done with finished artistry; Owen Staples for his finely recorded impressions of Toronto's streets, gardens and public buildings; Nicholas Hornyansky for his high pitched colour plates which so often sing in a major key; and W. W. Alexander for his unflagging enthusiasm, his intimate knowledge of the craft and his excellent book plates.

Printing in colour from two or more blocks was practised by the wood-engravers of Holland, Italy and Germany about the beginning of the sixteenth century. Its advent in Canada probably not more than three decades ago. Among its more prominent exponents have been Walter J. Phillips, Leonard Hutchinson, Mary Wrinch and Violet Depew. In his exquisite colour prints, HNAUSA, GIMILI NO. 2, LAKE LOUISE and THE DUCK HUNTER, Phillips' refined taste and virtuosity link him in accomplishment with the best of contemporary block-makers. He succeeds admirably in conveying an impression of light and air and atmospheric depth. Somewhat less dreamy and delicate in colour and treatment is the work of Mary Wrinch, whose FLASH OF SUNLIGHT and REFLECTIONS are coloured and lighted with extraordinary skill. The floral studies of Violet Depew, such as TIGER LILIES, in which the colours and the printing have well seconded the design. Hutchinson whether engaged on wood-block or colour-print— for he is adept at both—delights in depicting the rural life of Ontario, not only the rolling uplands, but those more intimate aspects of farm and

THE PRINCES' GATE: CANADIAN NATIONAL EXHIBITION
OWEN STAPLES

village as revealed in its scenery and buildings. Picturesque would be an apt definition; but underlying all is the insistent quest for beauty, implicit in sensitive line, in tinted sky at sunset, in grey smoke slowly rising from a farmhouse chimney, or in the interlacing branches of an ancient elm against the delicate opalescent hues of early dawn. So filled with simple loveliness that one

215

stands mute before them, absorbing with profound and sensuous delight their haunting beauty. In the black and white of wood engraving, a probing test of an engraver's skill, Hutchinson's GALLAGHER'S ACRES asserts his fine sense of colour and design. Clean lines, crisp and telling, balanced masses in harmonious arrangement, and over all the solemn hush that falls upon the scented fields at twilight. This is indeed art of a very high order, the kind one can enjoy and live with in perpetuity. It is obvious that both Phillips and Hutchinson have studied carefully the best work of the Japanese print-makers.

Among the makers of wood block prints none is more highly esteemed than Eric Bergman, who uses the graver with ease, intelligence and well-directed skill. His lines are beautifully clean, his arrangements well organized, and his style is markedly individual. All these qualities admirably expressed as they are in THE SNAKE FENCE, VINE AND WILLOW and FANTASY, have won for him high official honours abroad and wide recognition at home.

Already etching in Canada, no less than wood-block printing, is forcing its way into recognition with a beauty and vitality that promises well for its future development.

15

The miniature art of the bookplate, seldom exposed as are most works of art to public view, has few practitioners in Canada. There is something to be said, however, for an art which, in spite of "neglect, wilful or unconscious, continues not only in a traditional form, but gathers fresh momentum and finds new grounds for its existence."

A bookplate, of course, is a label pasted inside the cover of a book as a means of identifying its owner. Though useful in purpose, it may be and often is ornamental. In form, it may be printed, or, more frequently, designed by an artist who usually prints from the plate he etches. Now and then a collector will employ several plates of different design to conform to various classifications of volumes in his collection. But as a rule he is content with one or at most two plates; for a book label to be good requires not only thought and care in preparation, but a high degree of skill in execution, and not all book lovers are men of means.

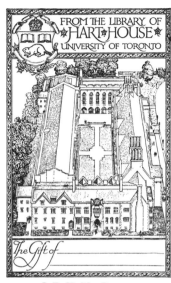

LESLIE VICTOR SMITH

J. E. H. MacDONALD

ALEXANDER SCOTT CARTER

WILLIAM W. ALEXANDER

BOOKPLATES BY CANADIAN DESIGNERS

Subjects selected for bookplate design are usually two—armorial and pictorial. The heraldic pattern, once so prevalent, is being superseded by the pictorial design, which expresses the artist's conception of his client's main interests, and reduces the bookplate to modern terms and common understanding.

The earliest European bookplate known is that of Hans Igler, dated 1450, which is the period of the introduction into Europe of printing from moveable types. For many years after, the majority of bookplates, if indeed not all, were heraldic in character. In truth a man's armorial bearings constituted his name, and no further identification was necessary. In Canada, the earliest bookplate known is that of John Bullock, who fought under Wolfe at the siege of Quebec. His plate shows the British and French armies engaged in battle on the Plains of Abraham. The arms of Bullock also form part of the design. One of the earliest engravers in Canada was C. W. Torbett, who worked in Halifax from about 1780 to 1825. Working in Quebec City about the same time were J. Jones and J. Smellie, Jr. Smellie engraved plates for, among others, Hoffman, McCallum, and Sir David William Smith, a member of Lieut.-Governor Simcoe's administration, 1793-1796, in Upper Canada. Jones is recorded as having made labels for the Honourable John Stewart and Samuel Wright, both in 1800. Following these men came F. Adams in Montreal, who engraved plates for a number of local bookmen, including John Caldwell Abbott, Charles W. Hagar, George C. Longley and G. H. Mathews.

An early plate is that of Louis Archambault Douglas, Comte de Montreal. He succeeded to the title in 1771, and went to live in France where his plate was probably made. In Quebec most of the bookplates were typeset labels; in Ontario nearly all were armorial or pictorial. Very little is known of bookplates used in Canada previous to the coming of the Loyalists in 1783. Bookplates began to appear in quantity about 1800. The designs were chiefly armorial in style — "die-sinkers" they were called — and were mostly engraved in England. With rare exceptions they were dull, uninteresting, and artistically pedestrian. Before 1890 engravers of bookplates in Canada were few in number and these of the older and more conventional school. Since many of their plates were unsigned, it is virtually impossible at this day to know who made them. However, many of these early makers of bookplates are mentioned by Phileas Gagnon in his *Essai de Biblio-graphie Canadienne* as artists and engravers of repute. Several pages are devoted to Ex-Libris and some 270 plates are listed.

The earliest *dated* bookplate of which we have record is that of Ann Watt, who lived in Quebec City. This plate, however, would be classed as a label; it bears the date, 1795. Then there is the "die-sinker" armorial plate of Richard John Uniacke of Halifax, Attorney-General for Nova Scotia and Member of His Majesty's Council. This plate is dated 1801. Another Halifax plate is that of Dr. A. N. Head, who lived about 1770. His label is of the then popular Chippendale design adapted from the mirror frames of the famous cabinet-maker.

In 1919 a new check-list compiled by Morley Ayearst and Stanley Harrod, and edited by Winward Prescott, was published in Boston. It is called *Canadian Bookplates*, and is well illustrated with reprints of the early plates.

It is only in recent years that artists in number have turned to the making of bookplates, and the talents of such designers as A. H. Howard, W. W. Alexander, Stanley Harrod, J. E. H. MacDonald, Leslie Victor Smith, Morley Ayearst, Owen Staples, A. Scott Carter, Toronto; Philip Kieran, Montreal; and Ida Hamilton of Hamilton, have been employed in devising plates for public institutions as well as private collectors. In this restricted field they have created not only artistic armorials, but some very fine original pictorials, quite fresh in theme and individual in treatment.

Although interest in the art of the bookplate in Canada grows, it has not yet reached the position of importance it enjoys in the United States and England, where bookplate societies issue impressive year-books and hold annual public exhibitions. That time may come, however, when the value of the bookplate as a work of art is more widely recognized and esteemed. In the meantime it is of interest to know that one Toronto collector[1] has more than 15,000 bookplates, of which about 3,000 are Canadian. The collection of another Torontonian,[2] gathered over the years, eventually went in part to the British Museum. It may or may not be significant that both collectors are themselves artists and designers of bookplates of wide repute.

[1]Leslie Victor Smith, Esq.
[2]Stanley Harrod, Esq.

16

The history of book, magazine and newspaper illustration in Canada over the years would seem to deserve a chapter by itself. Its importance in Canadian art may be roughly estimated by the manner in which it has engaged the abilities of some of our best known men. For some artists, even of academic distinction, illustration has been the chief life-work and means of livelihood. Only to frequenters of exhibitions are they thought of as painters.

In the eighties and nineties the name of Henry Sandham was familiar through his work in illustrated United States magazines such as *Scribner's*, *Harper's* and the *Century*, and in earlier Canadian periodicals as the *Dominion Illustrated* or *Belford's*, and still less often through the agency of the occasional book. One of the first, if not the first, woman illustrators in Canada, as she was also the first woman academician, was Charlotte Schreiber, who drew illustrations for the editors of Chaucer, Browning and other poets. L. R. O'Brien, with Henry Sandham, also drew many illustrations for *Picturesque Canada*. At a later date, William Cruikshank was an active magazine and newspaper illustrator. In this he excelled, for it was in black-and-white rather than colour that his exceptional ability as a draughtsman showed to advantage. As a colourist, he was not so good.

On the other hand, Henri Julien displayed versatility in both pen-and-ink and water-colour with often exceptionally happy results. His book illustrations for *Les Anciens Canadiens*, by Philippe-Aubert de Gaspé, for *Lé Legende d'un peuple* and *Originaux et Détraqués* by Louis Fréchette, were well done, though not perhaps so markedly as his more popular illustrations for the folk-tales *La Chasse-Gallerie* (The Ghost Canoe), *The Loup-Garou* (The Were-wolf), and *Joseph Violon*. With R. G. Mathews, Julien illustrated *A Bit of Atlantis*, by D. Erskine. And about this time also (1900) Arthur Heming was illustrating the works of W. A. Fraser, the Canadian novelist. Later in the century he was to illustrate his own, when he drew the pictures for his tales of the Canadian northland, *The Living Forest*, *The Drama of the Forests* and *Spirit Lake*.

Outside Canada the work of Canadian illustrators was to be found in periodicals of established reputation. Henri Julien contributed drawings to *Harper's* and the *Century* of New York, to *L'Illustration* of Paris, and to the *Graphic* of London; Robert E. Johnston, after studying under Dean Cornwell, drew illustrations for *Scribner's* and the *Saturday Evening Post*. Better known to the readers of the *Post* was William Arthur Brown, who for many years was one of its regular illustrators. Johnston died on the threshold of a career that seemed bright with promise. Norman Price and Arthur Crisp are other Canadian artists who have done well in the United States: Crisp as a muralist and Price as illustrator and designer. Besides the work of Julien, *L'Illustration* has reproduced in colours the illustrations of several Canadian artists, includng those of Clarence Gagnon.

The book illustrations of Frederick S. Coburn first appeared in the nineties with the publication of *The Habitant, Johnnie Courteau, Madeleine of Verchères,* and *The Great Fight,* French dialect poems, by Dr. William Henry Drummond; and in *Christmas in French Canada,* a romance by Louis Fréchette. At the end of this period appeared Ozias Leduc's illustrations for *Claude Paysan,* by Dr. Choquette; in 1907 Franchère's *Chansons Canadiens;* and, in 1906, J. S. Gordon's illustrations for the *Romance of Five Nations,* by Dr W. D. Lighthall. Within the next decade, Charles W. Jefferys illustrated *The Chronicles of Canada,* and, in 1922, a new edition of the Canadian classic, *The Golden Dog,* by William Kirby. It was during this period also that Suzor-Côté drew illustrations for Louis Hémon's classic of French Canada, *Maria Chapdelaine;* later illustrated, 1939, with pen-and-ink drawings by Thoreau MacDonald, in which episodes of French Canadian life were depicted with charming variety and tender sympathy.

In the twenties and thirties the number of books illustrated increased. Among them were Herbert Raine's finely executed etchings for *Old Montreal;* Dorothy Stevens' pen drawings for *Canadian Cities of Romance* and the companion volume, *Canadian Houses of Romance,* both of which suffer from having been handled in a manner much too casual; Franz Johnston's illustrations for *Canadian Folk Songs,* by J. Murray Gibbon; A. Y. Jackson's line drawings for *Chez Nous: Our Old Quebec Home,* by Adjutor Rivard. Then came Stanley Turner's illustrations in colour for *The First Canadian Christmas Carol,* and black-and-white drawings for

The House of Hate, by Austin Campbell. Further colour illustrations were done by Walter J. Phillips for *The Dream of Fort Garry*, and by Clarence Gagnon for the Mornay-Paris edition of *Le Grand Silence Blanc*, published in 1928; five years later he did the beautiful and memorable series of illustrations in colour for *Maria Chapdelaine*, also printed by Mornay of Paris. The excellence of these illustrations, or pictures as they more properly are called, is

MAIN STREET, GORE BAY

LEONARD BROOKS

indicated in a measure by the greatly enhanced prices which these books command today from collectors both in Canada and abroad. His latest effort was a series of paintings reproduced in colour for the new edition (1941) of W. H. Blake's classical essay on angling, *Brown Waters*.

Robert W. Pilot's charming illustrations for the guide-books of Blodwen Davies are too well known to require extended comment. They are among the best things of their kind that contemporary Canadian illustration has to show. His pen displays the felicity of his brush. A title which may be taken as typical of the series is *The Storied Streets of Quebec*. In text and format, as well as illustration, they are raised to a level high above the run-of-mill guide-book with its bald and uninspired presentation of facts and its often unimaginative and badly printed halftone cuts.

Eaton's College St. Fine Art Galleries.

THE CORNER STORE
Harold W. McCrae

In the same category may be put Charles Simpson's coloured drawings for another guide-book, *Here and There in Montreal*, by Charles W. Stokes, *The Lure of Quebec*, and Victor Morin's *Old Montreal, with Pen and Pencil*.

Other illustrators in Canada who have contributed to the magazines year after year are: in Great Britain—Charles de Belle, F. Horsman Varley and Elizabeth Styring Nutt; and in Canada—

223

Charles W. Jefferys, Stanley Turner, John F. Clymer, Thomas W. Mitchell, T. W. McLean, J. Ernest Sampson, Owen Staples, Evan Macdonald, Thoreau MacDonald, Rowley Murphy and Harold McCrae. All these artists have done illustrations for the book and periodical press with marked ability and a manner of treatment well adapted to its purpose.

National Gallery of Canada.

TRADING LAKE, NEAR DORSET

HERBERT S. PALMER

Happily, the opportunities for the illustrator, and not only for the illustrator but for the designer as well, are rapidly expanding, are becoming more numerous. New and improved reproductive processes, the urgent needs of publicity, modern god of commerce, the magazine pages, newspaper advertising, billboards, window-displays, booklets, folders, broadsides and all the munitions of industrial warfare, all call for the services of the illustrator, the designer and the painter. Certain it must be that commercial art, as it is invidiously called to distinguish it from easel art, reaching millions as it does through the medium of the printed page and the painted hoarding, possesses a dominating force of incalculable influence and worth to the agencies that employ it.

At its too infrequent best, it will be generally agreed, this work is stimulating and fine art of a high order: yet strangely enough one may not speak of commercial art as applied to the work of the landscape and portrait painter. With a certain snobbery that seems peculiar to all the arts, they prefer to be known as painters of easel pictures, and continue to produce for their pleasure, if not for their material profit, pictures of narrow appeal and restricted market. However, it may well be that in time to come the production of the easel painter will grow less and less as he continues to become more and more absorbed in the ranks of those employed in the utilitarian-aesthetic pursuit of bringing art to the service of Propaganda. The artist then will be better remunerated: whether he will be happier is another question. True it is that the artist cannot live by bread alone; equally certain is it that lacking bread he cannot live at all.

This survey, imperfect though it may be and necessarily restricted, denotes the distance travelled by the art of Canada— and here I use the word in its broadest sense—during the past hundred years or so. Owing partly to the now considerable body of writing on the subject, supplemented by much teaching and lecturing, which I suppose to be another form of instruction; partly to the increasing rejection of narrow or identical regulations as to form, the product is—at least when seen so close—a little chaotic. Thus it would be a proof of rashness rather than of foresight to undertake to say how far the promise of the past will be realized in the achievements of the future. But this much we can see and say: that the way has been stony, the ascent steep, and the wayfaring not bereft of toil and, at times, of high adventure.

We have witnessed the beginnings of art in Canada, crude and undeveloped as these first efforts were, from the time of the early settlements in the East to the formation much later of the Provinces in the West. And during this long procession of the years, and in widely separated places, we have traced the development of the arts in Canada from the work of the early surveyors and military officers who accompanied the British troops to Canada to the second decade of the present century when the "movement" of our younger Canadian painters to attempt an interpretation of the country (free, it was thought, of the European manner), became clearly apparent.

The truth is, as has been said, the history of Canadian art is a longer one than many persons imagine. For by the middle of the seventeenth century, or about 1650, a flourishing school of ecclesiastical craftsmanship had been established in the valley of

MILL ON THE MOIRA RIVER
Manly MacDonald

the St. Lawrence, which eventually brought to Canada artists from France to design and decorate with pictures and carvings the churches and seminaries of Old Quebec. From this foundation stems the succession of carvers and painters of religious subjects which have, until recent years at any rate, continued to follow in the footsteps of the first artists who settled in that Province. This craftsmanship in wood, in pigment and in metal, became a truly Canadian art. The germ of French culture, isolated in

Canada for so long, struck roots of its own, and now has its own tradition grounded upon, yet different from, those traditions of Old France from which it derived its early nurture. Similarly, the process is analogous in the origin and development of the arts in English Canada. In tradition and form they take their rise from the English Georgian.

17

During the nineteenth century, as we have seen, a more general or widely diffused expression of art gradually appeared, taking its form and direction partly from the European countries to which Canadian students had gone to supplement their training here, and partly from the teaching and technique of British and continental painters in Canada who had brought their own ideas and traditions with them. Before that event occurred, however, we were to witness a long period of comparative aesthetic aridity, in which the practitioners of art in Canada were content to stay well within the bounds of a traditional style and method, and in which the arts of painting and sculpture were largely, if not wholly, derivative. The period which gave us Kane, Krieghoff and Jacobi, contemporaries of the Hudson River school in the United States and the pre-Raphaelite Movement in England, could hardly be expected, considering their time, to give us, say, Thomson, Varley and Jackson. The truth is, it did not. But the period from 1830 to 1880 (the dates are approximate), did yield us a very respectable body of painting indeed, even though the advance of Canadian art during that period—if we exclude portraiture—was relatively superficial. However, travel, the study of painting in England and France particularly, and the rapid growth of public galleries and private collections at.home, were contributing to the creation of a new taste and the formation of a native tradition. Not the least influential of these fostering influences, as we have noted, were the foundation of the Ontario Society of Artists in 1872, and the Royal Canadian Academy of Arts in 1879; and subsequently, though localized, the Toronto Art Students League of the late eighties, to be followed by a number of lineal descendants.

The movement was to gain immeasurably in strength, impetus and breadth with the formation of provincial art societies and galleries in the first three decades of the new century, and from the opening of schools, and especially vocational schools, for instruction in the arts in the more thickly populated centres throughout the Dominion.

Oddly enough, in this forward movement, progress in the art of portraiture had not until very late years, at all events, kept pace

THE BREAK-UP

FRANKLIN ARBUCKLE

with the steady and continuous improvement in the technique of Canadian landscape painting. It may be that changes in the style of face painting arrive more slowly; anyhow, it would seem so. The technique, for example, of George Theodore Berthon is in general effect not much different from that of Kenneth Forbes fifty years later; although the discrepancy between a portrait by J. W. L. Forster, or even by Brymner, and a canvas by Lilias Torrance Newton, say, is so striking as to be startling. The explanation is, that the technique of Mrs. Newton stems from the late French school of "modernists," whereas both Forbes and Berthon are in the tradition of the English school of the nineteenth century—practitioners like Pickersgill, Lawrence and Martin Archer-Shee.

Portraiture in Canada in general, it may be affirmed, has its traditions and root-forces in the British; for it was England that,

THE BOAT WORKS

JACK MARTIN

during a period of less than half a century, produced such prodigies as Sir Joshua Reynolds, Gainsborough, Romney, Hoppner, Raeburn and Sir Thomas Lawrence, all of them primarily portraying the so-called courtly caste, the ladies of position, beauty and breeding, and doing it in such a manner as to establish an undisputed sway which lasted until the rise of the modern taste in art began seriously to challenge their supremacy, and the hegemony, incidentally, of such men as Whistler, Watts and Sargent who followed them.

229

THE CATCH

KENNETH K. FORBES

In Canada, unlike France or England, there is only beginning a pre-eminence in this style of painting, for the simple reason that, apart probably from Newton and Holgate who adhere consistently to the modern formula, our living portrait painters, including Grier, Williamson, Varley, Jongers, Barnes, Forbes and Barr, derive no part of their aesthetic impetus or content from Canada;

230

WILLIAM CRUIKSHANK, R.C.A.

CURTIS WILLIAMSON

all of it, or nearly all of it, is European or more specifically British in origin and chiefly absorbed from contemporary and past schools of English painting. If there is an exception to the rule it is probably Curtis Williamson, who has been influenced by the strong light and shade effects of the Dutch painters, as was also Wyatt Eaton, his predecessor.

DR. PELHAM EDGAR
ALLAN BARR

Meanwhile, in spite of the evident unwillingness of Canadian portraitists to experiment, to evolve and apply new ideas, new methods, a reluctance which in all fairness must be attributed in part to the innate conservatism, to call it nothing worse, of their clientele, much sound work has been produced, as witness Grier's PROVOST MACKLEM of Trinity; Williamson's WILLIAM CRUIK-SHANK; Jonger's RALPH; Barnes' MRS. SULLIVAN; Forbes' portrait of his daughter, June, in THE CATCH; Allan Barr's study of DR. PELHAM EDGAR; Varley's IRVING CAMERON; and I would add for its decision and strength Evan Macdonald's J. E. MCALLISTER.

There are, it is true, the surface or superficial painters—some of them extremely expert technicians—who wittingly or unwittingly throw in their lot with the producers of photographic resemblance. With a laborious infinitude of detail, an elaboration of accessories that recalls the work of the Dutch school, they can, and often do, carry a portrait to a high state of physical perfection, but they are not painters, in the true sense. They are, rather, highly expert technicians; they leave nothing to the imagination of the observer. They insist, to our discomfort, on dotting every "i" and crossing every "t". They are content to depict rather than suggest.

Then again we have such painters, to mention but a few, as Varley, Williamson and Jongers, and frequently Grier and Barr, who, combining superb manual dexterity with emotional intensity, create not merely a portrait but a vivid piece of characterization and a fine work of art. Canada at the moment, it must be admitted, is not overrich in portraitists of this type.

However, the early inclination of the portrait painter to be matter-of-fact is slowly yielding before the artist's desire to express his emotional response to the visual impression he may have absorbed. Temperament, in fact, and the personal element, national as well as individual, are entering more largely into the construction of the picture. Hence the main current of Canadian painting, in portraiture as in landscape work, is departing from exact representation, at the same time avoiding abstractions and the too sensational psychological adventures of modern art in Europe.

In the field of mural painting not a little good work has been done. The truth is the opportunities offered to our Canadian decorative painters have been regrettably few. Only occasion-

J. E. McALLISTER, ESQ.

EVAN MACDONALD

J. E. McAllister, Esq., Toronto.

A PORTRAIT OF A LADY
ARCHIBALD BARNES

ally have they been offered commissions at all, and many of these were awarded to foreign painters specializing in mural painting.

It is only fair to say, however, that on two occasions the Royal Canadian Academy has exercised initiative in an effort to stimulate interest and activity in this branch of the arts. The first was in 1923, when $1,000 was appropriated for prizes in a decorative painting competition. The subject chosen was the *Settlement of*

Trinity College, Toronto.

THE REV. DR. T. C. S. MACKLEM

PROVOST OF TRINITY COLLEGE, TORONTO: 1901-1921

SIR WYLY GRIER

Canada. From the preliminary contest six competitors were chosen for the final test, which called for full-size panels. These were shown at the Canadian National Exhibition, Toronto, in 1924. Two prizes were awarded, the first to J. E. H. MacDonald, and the second to F. Horsman Varley. Two years later another and similar competition was held. This time the project included painting on actual wall spaces in public buildings. After a preliminary competition, in which some sixty sketches were entered, six artists were chosen to cover the spaces selected: Earlscourt Public Library, Toronto, by George A. Reid; the Art Association building at Montreal, by Charles Simpson; the women's waiting-room in Windsor Station, Montreal, by H. Ross Perrigard; the Montreal High School, by Robert Pilot; the Strathearn School, Montreal, by Donald Hill; and the King Edward VIII School,

ALEXANDER CHUHALDIN
CHARLES COMFORT

Montreal, by H. Leslie Smith. All of which would seem to indicate either a disproportionate need of attention to the empty wall spaces of Montreal, or that other centres lacked successful contestants. However that may be, these decorations may be considered a contribution to the encouragement of mural painting, since they represent an effort by the artists out of all proportion to

QUEEN OF HEAVEN
Frederick S. Challener

the rather nominal total sum of $2,000 which the Academy had been able to set aside as compensation.

Canadian painters, none the less, have to their credit many successful and important works in public buildings, churches and private homes. Of these one might mention Charles Huot's in the churches and Legislative Buildings of Quebec cited elsewhere; the PIONEER panels in the city hall at Toronto, executed by George A. Reid in the nineties; the altar piece of the old Loretto Abbey, Toronto, by Grier in 1900; and in the earlier years the decoration of the chapel of Notre Dame de Lourdes at Montreal by Napoleon Bourassa, who may be accepted as our pioneer painter of religious subjects. In the first decade in the century F. S. Challener engaged in painting historical subjects for wall decoration, notably THE SETTLEMENT OF THE WEST for the Alexandra Hotel, Winnipeg, and the FRENCH AT FORT ROUILLÉ for the King Edward Hotel, Toronto. Following these he painted a number of large compositions for various theatres in Canada: the Royal Alexandra Theatre at Toronto; the Russell Theatre, Ottawa; and the Princess Theatre at Montreal. Other work of a much later period by Challener includes the Loblaw offices at Toronto; and the panels for "Parkwood," the home of R. S. McLaughlin at Oshawa, which are notable for the highly successful manner in which they conform to the strict requirements of mural decoration.

In the post-war period commissions were more frequently awarded, and it was during this interval that much of our best mural painting was done. We may note but a few of them: Scott Carter for the University Club, Montreal, and a series of coats-of-arms of the universities throughout the world for the main dining-hall of Hart House at the University of Toronto; Charles W. Jefferys' historic scenes for the Manoir Richelieu at Murray Bay, in 1929, the Chateau Laurier Hotel at Ottawa, in 1931, and the Royal Ontario Museum at Toronto in 1933. During these years also J. E. H. MacDonald decorated the Concourse Building at Toronto; G. A. Reid, the Jarvis Collegiate Institute, and recently the very fine series of decorations, depicting geological periods, in the Royal Ontario Museum, Toronto; Arthur Lismer, the Humberside Collegiate, Toronto; Robert Pilot, the châlet in Mount Royal Park, Montreal; F. H. Varley, St. Anne's Church, Toronto; Franz Johnston for the Bedford Theatre at Toronto;

John F. Clymer for the Eglinton Theatre, at Toronto; and Edwin Holgate for the Hotel Vancouver at Vancouver, B.C.

Had the government of Canada chosen, as it might easily have done during the depression years, as did the government of the United States under the W.P.A., to employ our Canadian painters and designers on the decoration of our public works, it would not only have relieved enormously the economic stress and strain on the artist, but created works of art to the benefit of the country— permanent memorials to its own wisdom and foresight. But governments in Canada are notoriously lax in matters of art, and choose to regard as unpractical the one thing that contributes most to a national culture and greatness. Blue-books may be the gauge of material wealth; but the gain in knowledge, in enjoyment, and in spiritual growth to be acquired from a well-selected body of art cannot be computed in tangible terms of dollars and cents. And so our government through a short-sighted, penny-pinching policy forfeited an opportunity in social enrichment which is not likely to return soon, if ever.

Regrettably, I think, in another field, little or nothing has been done by governments, universities or municipalities to encourage historical painting in Canada. The result is, that most of our public buildings are almost entirely devoid of pictures and mural paintings that serve to keep fresh in our minds events of our historic past. And, quite obviously as yet, national sentiment is not strong enough to initiate and support any move in that direction. Which is a pity.

Apart, however, from this lack of government initiative, there is doubtless another and very urgent economic reason why historical painting in Canada has hitherto failed to receive the practical encouragement which as a subject it merits, a reason which explains, in part at least, why many of our artists in Canada have been loath to undertake it: It demands on the part of the painter an amount of reading and research out of all proportion to the time required for the actual painting. There are also the exigencies of the subject often arising out of the period in which the scene is presented. For example, Edwin Abbey in the United States and later in England, in composing his great historical canvases would spend hours, if need be days, in public libraries and museums acquiring an exact knowledge of some detail of dress, a fashion or structural background. In Canada, where Charles W. Jefferys

240

THE
ICEBERG

AND OTHER POEMS *BY*
CHARLES G·D·ROBERTS

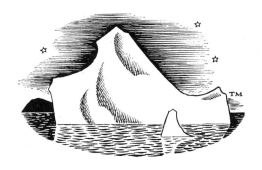

TORONTO The RYERSON PRESS 1934

TITLE PAGE
Thoreau MacDonald

and Frederick Challener are our chief historical painters, the same conscientious and highly commendable practice obtains.

With Jefferys, especially since among Canadian artists he has produced most of our historical painting and illustrations, every picture is a matter of careful, independent investigation of original sources, both printed and pictorial. In short, as one writer has pithily summarized it, the historical artist must have in addition to the persistency of a trained researcher, a vivid historic imagination, the skeptical mind of the scientist, the industry of a beaver, and the nose of a detective for clues. Small wonder, then, that few artists are prepared to enter such an exacting field—considering the lack of patronage, private and public, and the pitiful inadequacy of the reward. As was implied at the outset, they order these things better, if not in France, then certainly in the United States and England. Quite obviously we, as Canadians, might do worse than copy their example.

Just at this point it might be timely to suggest that if there is any one thing which the average Canadian mind needs it is an awakening of the artistic sense. Beauty of form and colour are not with us a daily necessity. As a people we are ingenious, fertile in resources and initiative; we are rapid in execution and quick witted to devise new conveniences to meet new conditions; but for some occult reason the artistic feeling, which is so evident in the Oriental, the European, the Indian tribes of our West Coast and in nearly all savage races, is a thing unknown to us as a nation. In proof of this, compare a garment made by a Czechoslovakian; a glass dish made in Sweden; or a bit of Chinese earthenware, costing but a few cents, with similar products made in Canada. The comparison is mortifying. The Chinese, the Scandinavian, or the Czechoslovakian has given a beauty, a finish, to everything he touches, no matter how insignificant its value, while our low-priced Canadian commodities in glassware and furniture, our package designs and book-jackets, our posters on the highways and our advertising in the press, our bookbinding, and, with a few honourable exceptions, our printed matter, our low-priced wallpapers and rugs, in short, every sort of commodity produced by the average mind and bought by the common average public, is too often vulgar to the last degree. Overloaded with meaningless ornament, or with no decoration at all, it conveys its message with

242

ill-bred emphasis, and is for the most part crude in colour and commonplace in conception.

It is difficult to understand this lack of taste, which is well nigh universal, not only among the working classes, so-called, but among many who have had superior opportunities, when a fine instinct for form and colour is discernible in many savage tribes and among the often illiterate peasantry of Europe. Even the West Coast tribes of British Columbia, in their carvings, their paintings and their textiles manifest an amazing sense of decorative fitness and beauty. Conceivably, such a ready and fertile source of native design might well be employed by our Canadian manufacturers, but so far it has not, and the thought inevitably occurs that the Canadian producer lacks either the imagination, the taste or the initiative to do so. An original and creative talent peculiarly Canadian is thus ignored or discarded in favour of a second or third-rate design, more often than not designed from the work of a similarly unimaginative producer. It may be argued that an absence of proper education has made this condition possible. However, it is to be doubted if education has anything to do with Canada's lack. Rather has it been the preponderance of our native genius, which is the natural result of an intelligent people meeting the stern requirements of pioneer life that has almost dried up the sources of music and poetry, as well as art, while trying to minister to pressing material needs. In our desire to express utility with economy, as was said once and may be said again, we have overlaid any aesthetic tendencies that survived puritanism.

True, it is hard to see how the artistic sense is to be awakened to such an extent that it will find a spontaneous, national expression; but with all our lack, we have, as a nation, a quick imitative spirit, a genuine desire for self-cultivation, an eagerness to appropriate that which appeals to us as best, and these qualities may, in time, help us to assimilate the art of older countries and give it a new and a fresh utterance.

Many influences obviously are working to this end: foreign travel, international expositions, an increase of art galleries, and art and vocational schools, instruction in the fine arts at the universities—notably at Queen's, at Toronto, at Acadia and at Mount Allison—and an increase of wealth and leisure, now sadly interrupted by war, which normally enable people to cultivate and enjoy the aesthetic side of life. And not a little is being done through the handicraft groups that are springing up on every side, but more particularly in the provinces of British Columbia, Quebec, New Brunswick and Nova Scotia. Some of these industries produce hand-loomed rugs, some ceramics, some wrought iron, and hand-woven textiles, some hand-lettered and hand-bound books, as is done for example under the direction of Franklin Carmichael, R.C.A., at the Ontario College of Art, and by Douglas Duncan of Toronto, working independently. Others again are at work on pottery, carved chests and everyday utilities, such as silver, clothing, and furniture. All sorts of commodities are represented, and the work generally is excellent in design and workmanship. Such efforts have revealed the fact though these enterprises were previously unknown to each other, they were prompted by the same impulse and are unified by a common aim.

One of the very few bookbinders in Canada who regard the binding of fine books as an art rather than merely a means of livelihood is Douglas Duncan of Toronto. Duncan learned his trade in Paris, where he attended a school conducted by Jules Domont, under whom he studied tooling. Later he joined a class taught by Henri Noulhag, a binder of superb technique and wide accomplishment, who followed, however, the rather conventional patterns in vogue before the War of 1914.

In 1928, having finished his course, he came back to Toronto, where he has since remained. His first important assignment, for a client in Buffalo, was the binding of a set of the works of Anatole France, printed in Paris. Other commissions have included wedding books, guest books, school prize books, both for private customers and public institutions. Although during this time he designed and bound many volumes of importance, he also has bound pieces of no value except for their sentimental interest to their owners.

For a period of about ten years, or until 1938, he worked alone. Later, however, his assistant, Madeline Glenn, does much of the binding while Duncan himself does tooling, a task for which he displays extraordinary aptitude and taste. Now and then he has worked with A. Scott Carter on bindings for illuminated addresses and memorial books, as well as coverings for the illuminated manuscripts of A. J. Casson and Thoreau MacDonald. Among his more important commissions was the designing and

244

WEST
by EAST
& OTHER POEMS BY
J·E·H·MACDONALD

Drawings by Thoreau MacDonald

binding of a guest book, illustrated and decorated by Thoreau MacDonald, for the Honourable Albert Matthews, Lieutenant-Governor of Ontario, in preparation for the visit of the King and Queen to Canada in 1939; the binding of *Parkwood Hunters*, limited to ten copies, for Colonel R. S. McLaughlin of Parkwood, Oshawa; and a presentation volume to Dr. Frederick P. Keppel of the Carnegie Corporation upon his retirement as president of the Foundation.   On this work he collaborated with Scott Carter, to whom was entrusted the decoration of the book.

The bindings of Douglas Duncan have become widely known through their appearance at the Paris Exposition in 1937; at the Royal Canadian Academy exhibition, Art and Industry, at Toronto, in 1938; at the Architecture and Allied Arts Exhibition held at the Art Gallery of Toronto; at the San Francisco World's Fair in 1939; at the Canadian Handicrafts Exhibition in Toronto in 1942, and at various handicraft exhibitions throughout the Dominion.   In all he does he reveals the trained hand, the patient skill and the artistic judgment of the true craftsman.

Let us consider for a moment this aspect of art as applied to large-scale production.   In these days when so many articles in common use are made by machinery, it is vital that design should be so simplified that daily demand can be brought within the reach of all.   At the same time they should be made pleasant to look at so that delight in them as well as demand for them may increase. A thing of beauty can be produced quite cheaply provided the form and decoration are right.   Regarded in this way, the artist who is a competent designer becomes an important factor in the essential process of simplification and reduction of cost, whilst at the same time enhancing the attractiveness of the product and so facilitating its sale.   It is necessary, however, that modern developments of design should be kept clear of the freakish.   Since excess in anything is bad, for the avoidance of this danger, a trained and cultured artistic judgment is necessary.

Now one of the chief obstacles to progress in the past has been the lack of contact and mutual sympathy and understanding between the artist and manufacturer.   The chemist, the accountant, the lawyer and the engineer have established themselves as essential partners in the great task of production.   The artist has not yet achieved an equivalent status.   We have an ample supply of talent, and it should be brought into productive use; for in this, as in other fields of technique, progress is essential to survival. We must move with the times and even anticipate future demands. To do this we need knowledge, foresight, courage and enterprise. With the advance of education, an appreciation of good and beautiful things has naturally grown and will continue to develop; but the measure of that development depends largely on making every effort to produce finer work, and to give the public opportunities of discriminating between good and bad.

Fortunately in Canada today exhibitions of the arts—applied art no less than easel art—are doing much to bring the general public into closer relation with the artist and his work, and even to something like an appreciation of the artist's place in the social and industrial plan. To the artist and the layman alike the educational value of such exhibitions—whether travelling or a local—can be hardly overestimated. The first requisite of course for a sympathetic appreciation of works of art is the opportunity for wide acquaintance with different styles and periods of artistic production. Only by seeing the work of men of our country in conjunction with that of the artists of countries older and richer in artistic achievement and tradition than our own, is it possible rightly to understand the aims of Canadian art and to perceive the direction in which it is going.

Meanwhile, there is an urgent need for the kindling and enrichment of the life of Canada by a wider and keener cultivation of the arts and crafts. Steam power, which began the industrial revolution, began also the elimination of the skilled handicraftsman; and the mass production of a machine age has carried the process much too far for the health of society. Happily a remedy is being provided in a gradual return to the handiwork of the past. Many of the crafts which have been handed down from generation to generation have been kept alive by the encouragement and support of a discerning few, who have valued their practical as well as artistic superiority when compared with the machine-made article of a later day. Much useful work in the way of educating the public to a just appreciation of our native arts and crafts is now undertaken by the Canadian Handicrafts Guild and kindred organizations.

At its exhibition held in Toronto in the spring of 1942, the first since 1933, an effort was made by a group of enlightened men and women to direct public attention to our immediate responsibilities and opportunities for developing the natural resources of Canada for use in our daily life, to encourage the acquisition and application of artistic skill and technical knowledge, and to promote the utilization of the artistic craftsmanship which immigrants and refugees from other countries have brought with them to Canada. This combined effort proved fruitful. Exhibits representative of the labours of literally hundreds of craftsmen, from the Maritimes to British Columbia, from Labrador to the lands within the Arctic Circle were shown. Visible evidence of the progress of the arts and crafts in Canada, this display demonstrated what individuals allying artistic skill to manual industry can accomplish with native materials. Silver fashioned to use and beauty by Canadian silversmiths; pottery made from Canadian clay by Canadian potters; clothes made from Canadian tweeds woven by Canadian weavers; and rugs, fabrics and furniture, the products of native skill, were so arranged as to offer immediate and convincing proof of our remarkable advance in the arts and crafts in less than a decade.

Visitors to the exhibition discovered with surprise what a varied wealth of artistic talent and original craftsmanship exists in this Dominion. These exhibitions of the Canadian Handicrafts Guilds aim to encourage and develop the crafts by uniting the artist and the craftsman in normal occupations from which they have long been excluded. Separating the artist and the craftsman from the domestic vocations of the community has shut out the average individual from the arts and led to a one-sided growth of human character. The exhibitions of the Canadian Handicrafts Guild illumine the possibilities of such a move for the purpose of utilizing our natural resources and providing a livelihood for many persons who are unfitted for agriculture, dislike office work, or do not wish to become automatic tenders of machines.

Already in New Brunswick what may well prove to be the first of a series of domestic enterprises is in operation. The home of the industry is the Dykelands Pottery and the operators are Kjeld and Erica Deichmann, formerly of Denmark, now of Kingston Peninsula. The pottery was opened in 1934 when the Deichmanns returned to Canada after a year of study in Denmark. For the first two years no Deichmann pottery was sold, for the potters were not satisfied with their work. Finally, after what seemed like endless experiments, the right kind of clay was discovered, and work began in earnest. The clay-mixture found most practicable was composed of one part Musquodoboit clay from Nova Scotia and two parts of clay from New Brunswick. It was thus that the years from 1935 to 1937 were spent discovering little by little new secrets, new mixtures, new formulas. By 1937 the pottery had passed from the experimental to the professional, and in that year the Deichmanns ventured to send some pieces to the Royal.Ontario Museum, Toronto. The quality of their work was considered so good that four pieces were sent from there to the Paris World Fair. In all, only thirty pieces of pottery were sent from Canada to Paris. In 1938 they exhibited at the Glasgow Exhibition; and, in 1939, three pieces were sent to the Canadian Pavilion at the New York World's Fair. Exhibits of the Deichmanns' pottery have been shown at the Women's Art Association, Toronto, yearly at the Canadian National Exhibition, and, in 1942, at the exhibition of the Canadian Handicrafts Guild held in Toronto. A permanent collection of their pottery—bowls, jugs, vases and dishes—is also exhibited in the Industrial Arts Section of the New Brunswick Museum.

The amateur and the self-taught form no small group among the artists of the country. They are to be found everywhere and in almost every occupation. Their leisure hours they devote to drawing or etching or sketching or to the more formidable task of putting their impressions of the countryside on canvas. Without thought of pecuniary gain or recompense other than their own pleasure, they are content, as someone wittily phrased it, "to paint for their own amazement." It is by no means an uncommon experience for the non-professional to have his work hung at exhibitions of the various established art societies beside the work of men of wide reputation. Indeed, nothing has contributed more to the development of a sound and just appreciation and taste in art throughout the Dominion than "the growth of that happy company: the unincorporated and undaunted," and usually unorganized, "society of amateurs."

Occasionally it happens that men and women who have taken up some form of art as a hobby, and not as a means of livelihood, have gathered themselves into a formal association for the holding of meetings, exhibitions and of course for study. Independent groups like the Teacher's Art Association of Toronto are invaluable. L. H. Kirby, a high school science master, has painted in Europe, and his canvases, BLUE ROCKS, N.S., and TRAFFIC, COPENHAGEN, have been hung at the Royal Canadian Academy shows. One of the better known of these groups is the Ontario Art Club of Toronto, which meets twice a week during the winter months for drawing and painting from the model. Organized under the direction of Captain Melville Millar, himself a painter and exhibitor of some standing, the Club has now a membership of about a hundred students who, engaged by day in commerce and industry, or professionally, in the evenings and at week-ends seek a welcome change of occupation by taking up foʳ a time the crayon, brush or etcher's needle. Amongst its members are listed Will Robins, D. I. McLeod, Fred Campbell, Mrs. Eola Sutherland, Stanley Wickens, Tom Low and Arthur Wickens. Periodically the members hold public as well as private exhibitions, when criticism of the work shown is invited. Much of the work displayed is often of a surprisingly good quality. Such canvases as AUTUMN EVENING by William Robins; GRAY HARBOUR DAY by D. I. McLeod; SPRINGTIME by Tom Low; WINTER IN THE WOODS by A. W. Campbell; and CLAM DIGGERS by Melville Millar would command respectful attention in almost any exhibition of practising painters. The floral studies of Mrs. Sutherland also are nicely composed, and for the most part painted with skill and taste.

Similarly, the landscape sketches and finished canvases of Judge Frank Denton of Toronto are notable for their faithful and discerning interpretation of nature.

Wakeford Dix, die-sinker, is another Toronto amateur, highly skilled both as modeller and water-colourist. He studied modelling under Emanuel Hahn, R.C.A., and painting under Peter Sheppard, A.R.C.A. His landscapes especially display a sensitive eye for colour and a nice sense of arrangement in design. As a lieutenant of engineers in the First Great War, he was cited in despatches by F.M. Sir Douglas Haig for conspicuous gallantry in action.

J. R. Tate, manufacturer of Toronto, has been an exhibitor for the past decade at the annual shows of the Royal Canadian Academy, the Art Association of Montreal, the Canadian National Exhibition and the Ontario Society of Artists. In both portraiture and landscape he has done such good work as to elicit the approval of the professional painter. His OLD BILL, a fine characterization of an Old Country labourer type, formed part of a travelling exhibition sponsored by the Academy. Other canvases of his have

IN MY STUDIO MIRROR

J. R. TATE

been included in travelling exhibits sent out by the Royal Canadian Academy. Tate is represented in the Historical Museum, St. John, N.B., in the Canadian collection at Queen's University, Kingston, and at the Trappist Monastery at Oka, Quebec. An inventor as well as painter, a valuable device perfected by him is now in use by the R.C.A.F.

An investment banker by vocation, D. I. McLeod took up outdoor sketching as a relief from the daily routine some twenty years ago. Since then he has sketched with A. Y. Jackson, Fred S. Haines, Manly Macdonald, Emile Gruppe, and the late J. W. Beatty. From time to time his canvases have been hung by the Royal Canadian Academy, the Ontario Society of Artists, the Montreal Art Association, and the Canadian National Exhibition. McLeod relates with amusement stories illustrative of the way the layman regards the initial efforts of the raw but ambitious amateur. One of these is said to have amused Sir Frederick Banting greatly. Shortly before Christmas one year, McLeod took a number of sketches to a local framer, a first-rate artisan incidentally, disposed to be rather outspoken in his views concerning Canadian art and artists. He was asked which, if any, of the dozen sketches were worthy of frames. For several minutes he surveyed them critically as he puffed his pipe. Then he said with grave deliberation: "You have no reason to be discouraged; when Doctor Banting first took up sketching, he came to me with some sketches to be framed, and some of them were even worse than these!"

And so it goes; only too often the amateur in water-colours and oils shares the fate of the fellow who spoke to the waiter in French. To survive he must be endowed with a sense of humour himself; and happily for himself, as well as for his friends, he not infrequently is.

A retrospective show of Sir Frederick Banting's work, of which there are numerous examples extant, was held in February, 1943, at Hart House, University of Toronto. A. Y. Jackson, O.S.A., LL.D., with whom he sketched in the Arctic, in Quebec and elsewhere, wrote the memoir and compiled the catalogue under the title *Banting as an Artist.*

In the sketch-room of Hart House are now and then to be seen exhibits of the professors of the various faculties of the University and graduate members of the House. The more prominent contributors to these shows have been Sir Frederick Banting, Dr.

Beecher Locke, Dr. Harvey Agnew, F. Erickson Brown, Professor C. H. C. Wright, Carlton McNaught, V. E. Henderson, Robert Finch, and Dr. E. M. Walker. Represented in the group are the professions of law, medicine, advertising, architecture and pharmacy. At one exhibition no less than seventy-five oils and water-colours, consisting chiefly of landscapes and still-life subjects, were on view. Such an event is significant mainly because of the

Courtesy of Hart House, University of Toronto.

STE. IRENÉE

Sir F. G. Banting

increasing desire it denotes on the part of those outside the strictly professional sphere of art to take up painting as an avocation. And from the ranks of amateurs in times past, as we know, has come more than one eminent professional. The name of Sir Seymour Haden comes readily to mind; many another might be mentioned. But the movement is general, is not confined to one place, nor to one class, and is bound in the long run to be beneficial in its results.

Designed to promote the arts in Canada, the Federation of Canadian Artists was formed in the Spring of 1942. The membership, as announced, consists of artists and related professional workers; but the direction of policy is in the hands of recognized artists. Just what is meant by "related professional workers" is not made clear, though one may suppose it to mean those men and women whose ordinary occupation or profession brings them into close and frequent contact with artists, and who may therefore be assumed to share their common aims and sympathies. Recognized artists are doubtless those who are established professionally and are regular contributors to important exhibitions. "The Federation," it is explained, "is an association of individuals. It is not a union of societies. Each member joins in his own right; not as a delegate from other societies. And so far as established art organizations are concerned, the Federation has no intention of duplicating their activities." So much for membership.

According to its constitution the Federation has for its primary objects:

(1) To unite all Canadian artists, critics, and related professional workers for fellowship, for mutual effort in promoting common aims, and for the expression of the artist's point of view as a creative factor in the national life of Canada. (2) To improve the economic status of the artist by promoting markets for his work, and by raising his professional status in any ways which may be open. (3) To encourage public support for the National Gallery of Canada and its extramural activities, and also for other galleries, civil and provincial, and such organizations and societies connected with art and art appreciation. (4) To promote research on problems affecting the development of Canadian culture, and to educate public opinion regarding such problems. (5) To issue a national magazine devoted to the interests of art in Canada. (6) To provide a national clearing house for the coordination and encouragement of efforts made by other groups or individuals along any of the above lines.

Divided into working sections, the Federation covers such artistic activities as:

(a) Painting and Graphic Arts; (b) Sculpture; (c) Industrial Arts and Crafts; (d) Architecture and Town Planning; (e) Education; (f) Exhibitions; (g) Public Relations.

Organized regional groups represent the Federation in the various Provinces. At present its enrolment consists of from one hundred and fifty to two hundred members. Its chief regional officers are: The Maritimes: Walter Abell; Quebec: Arthur Lismer; Ontario: A. Y. Jackson; the West: Ernest Lindner; and the West Coast: Lawren Harris. André Biéler and Elizabeth Harrison, of the Art

Department of Queen's University, Kingston, are members of the executive and assisted greatly in the formation of the new society. It is too early to predict what effect the Federation will have upon the expansion of the arts in Canada; but from the standing of its chief members and the programme outlined, one would be justified in anticipating some worthwhile advancement. More at this time one hesitates to venture.

Our art, like our population, is composite. As in early days of settlement, our people were drawn mainly from Britain and France, so the differences that distinguish our early art were, as one would suppose, principally those of the British and French schools of painting. Today the influences are as cosmopolitan as our immigration. But with every year the presence of our natural environment becomes stronger, the foreign element is more quickly assimilated, and the deciding factor that is evolving a national art seems to be the spell of Canada itself. Our earliest painters, wherever born or wherever trained, appear to have felt the fascination of the country, and so Canadian landscape art, based largely on British tradition, had its pioneers three generations ago. The landscape, it is true, still predominates in our exhibitions, but its point of view is more native, the painter seems more at home, and through many different temperaments and in many varieties of technical expression the peculiar northern poetry of our land is finding original interpretation.

18

Architecture in Canada, unlike painting and in a lesser degree our sculpture, has shown a decidedly tenacious adherence to traditional forms. Prevailing fashions, taste of client, or the passing mood of the architect, are among the causes for the appearance in our streets year after year of new buildings of entirely unrelated scale and style. Too often they were side by side, built in the same year, and almost never has mercy been shown to the sensitive eye or the rational mind. The appearance of our streets truly illustrates the chaos of our time. But very few of our buildings, apart possibly from the present-day domestic, no

OFFICE BUILDING

[Designed by Marani, Lawson and Morris, Architects, Toronto,
for the Provincial Paper Mills, Limited, Toronto]

matter. what the style or other pretension may be, can by any
stretch of the imagination be considered good architecture, or even
architecture at all.

The fact is, the long procession of revivals of the past one
hundred-odd years, succeeding the break with evolutionary

traditions, must have been architecture's greatest curse; for but rarely have architects become skilfully conversant with the peculiar limitations of the one before they were off with another. And yet from almost every period and every style there survive a few buildings showing lasting good form.[1]

Now it should be remembered, though the fact is too often overlooked, that these styles were generally developed under quite different conditions of construction and to meet quite different conditions of life in past ages. These current styles are admired not for aesthetic qualities or their ability to meet a functional need, but as symbols of that historic past for which we have appreciation and often excessive reverence, that for most of us these Gothic, Graeco-Roman, Byzantine, Renaissance and Georgian styles are souvenirs rather than works of art. Certain it is that they are, and may be so esteemed, an aesthetic anachronism in this day and age.

An impetus to aesthetic invention and adventure was given in Romanesque and early Gothic times by working out the problems of stone vault construction. Then every new invention was accepted eagerly and new forms invented to express and embody each structural advance, whereas now it seems that in modern architecture new constructional possibilities are accepted slowly and with a kind of grudging reluctance. Instead of inspiring the invention of new and appropriate plastic forms, the new methods seem to be slurred over and buried beneath the old stylistic conventions. Here and there one sees an attempt to accept the situation, but there is no concerted general effort. One senses, however, something of the enterprise, the experimental courage, the *élan* which the immense possibilities of modern building methods are beginning to inspire As with modern painting, it is just this atmosphere of fervour, of passionate research, of adventure, of inquiry and eager expectation which marks a period of aesthetic achievement.

How much greater that achievement would be if only there were a small group of architects ready to join in these voyages of discovery and to supply and receive mutual counsel and support. Rugged individualism may belong to business; it is the enemy of art. Urgent as the problem of style is, there are other problems

[1] For example, the buildings of the University of King's College, Halifax, N.S., designed by Andrew R. Cobb, and modelled on the old.

GARDEN ARRANGEMENT
Edwin Kay Limited, Toronto

equally pressing: Solution by architects of the problems of town planning, and the erection of modern homes of taste for the small wage-earner, emancipated from the domination of the jerry-builder, call for immediate attention. The harmonizing of the interior fitments of the houses he builds with their structural design will probably come with the gradual secession from the thraldom of a frankly derivative style and period to an architecture more in

TOWN RESIDENCE

[Designed by Forsey, Page and Steele, Architects, Toronto, for T. D. Mohan, Esq., Cobourg, Ontario]

keeping with the functional design of our day. An absolute break with tradition we cannot hope for; but it should be possible to evolve plastic forms to fulfil the needs of our time in a way not possible to alien styles of an age remote from our own.

To the Bank of Nova Scotia much credit is due for the part it has played in recent years in giving impetus to new motives in Canadian architecture. In 1929 John Lyle of Toronto saw the need of giving expression in architectural ornament to Canadian fauna and flora. The idea was first applied to the office of the Bank in Calgary where the primitive implements of the Indian, the cowboy with his stetson, the marsh marigold, the pitcher plant, and many other typical Canadian decorative forms have been conventionalized into a new Canadian "language of ornament." In its design and decorative features the building is so remarkable that a noted British sculptor is said to have esteemed it equal in design and construction to any similar building in the great centres of Europe.

Later, when the Bank erected its new head offices in Halifax a few years ago, further impetus was given the movement for the employment of native decoration when no less than eighty-six distinctive Canadian decorative forms were used. When the new executive office building of the Bank at the corner of Bay and King streets, Toronto, is erected, there will likely be further new and interesting developments of the kind.

As with architecture, so with painting. No country today in which landscape and the sciences of modern vision are not of absorbing interest to its painters can be said to have a living art; and it is a sure indication of the vitality of Canadian painting and a good sign for its future that so much of its attention is turned in this direction. Moreover, the increased attention given to the painting of out-of-door landscape has developed a keen sensitiveness on the part of the painter to the qualities of light, atmosphere and tone, which has affected the character of every other department of painting in Canada. Meanwhile, we are undergoing a period of transition and experiment. Of late years, as we have seen, there have been more and more evident departures from inherited forms. The baneful and stultifying influence of the dead hand in structure and decoration is visibly weakening, though the essential harmony of line, mass, colour and form has been retained. From this combination and new eclecticism emerges a novel and stimulating point of view in which the old is suffused with a strong contemporary feeling. Instead therefore of allowing itself to be overwhelmed by the influence of an inherited tradition, modern painting, sculpture and architecture in Canada have developed an

BANK BUILDING: DOORWAY TREATMENT

[Designed by John M. Lyle, Architect, Toronto,
  for the Bank of Nova Scotia, Halifax]

individuality and freshness of perception peculiar to our day. This spirit of innovation and improvement, though growing in strength as it is, demands and should receive our encouragement and support. There can be no alternative if the artist is to live and progress as he should. However, the painter, or the architect, or the sculptor, or the designer will only get the appreciation and material help that he requires and deserves when we as buyers in the marketplace turn our eyes from the past to the present and the future. Art belongs to the age that produces it. The more we support our living artists, the more alive will our national art become.

So early as the seventies this truth, which must be patent to all, was recognized. In a review of the first exhibition of the Ontario Society of Artists, the *Canadian Monthly* (Vol. III) 1873, affirmed:

Suffice it to say that this First Annual Exhibition of the Ontario Society of Artists has proved in all respects a most creditable success. It has shown that we have a body of artists in our midst who only require adequate remuneration to beget a native School of Canadian Art; and to contribute in many ways to the refinement of taste and the development of education in the highest developments of aesthetic culture.

As it was then, so even now.

CANADIAN, BRITISH, AMERICAN AND
FRENCH CONTEMPORARIES

This table shows which painters in the United States and abroad were living and working at the same time as the more prominent painters of the Canadian school.

Canadian

BEAUCOURT, FRANCOIS MALEPART DE (1735-1805?)
HERIOT, GEORGE (1766-1844)
FIELD, ROBERT (1770?-1819)
NEWTON, GILBERT STUART (1794-1835)
VALENTINE, WILLIAM (1798-1849)
HOWARD, JOHN G. (1803-1890)
PLAMONDON, ANTOINE (1804-1895)
COTE, JEAN BAPTISTE (1805-1870)
BERTHON, GEORGE THEODORE (1806-1892)
KANE, PAUL (1810-1871)
FOWLER, DANIEL (1810-1894)
KRIEGHOFF, CORNELIUS (1812-1872)
JACOBI, OTTO (1812-1901)
HAMEL, THEOPHILE (1817-1870)
CRESSWELL, WILLIAM NICHOL (1822-1888)
BOURASSA, NAPOLEON (1827-1916)
O'BRIEN, LUCIUS (1832-1899)
VERNER, FREDERICK ARTHUR (1836-1928)
FRASER, JOHN A. (1838-1898)
MARTIN, T. MOWER (1838-1934)
SANDHAM, HENRY (1842-1910)
JOBIN, LOUIS (1845-1928)
HAMEL, EUGENE (1845-1932)
BELL-SMITH, F. M. (1846-1923)
GAGEN, ROBERT FORD (1848-1926)
CRUIKSHANK, WILLIAM (1849-1922)
HARRIS, ROBERT (1849-1919)
COLLINGS, CHARLES JOHN (1849-1931)
HEBERT, LOUIS PHILIPPE (1850-1917)
DARLING, FRANK (1850-1923)
MANLY, C. MACDONALD (1855-1924)
HUOT, CHARLES (1855-1930)
BRYMNER, WILLIAM (1855-1925)
WATSON, HOMER RANSFORD (1855-1936)
BROWNELL, FRANKLIN (1857-   )
WALKER, HORATIO (1858-1938)
DYONNET, EDMOND (1859-   )
BRUCE, WILLIAM BLAIR (1859-1906)
KNOWLES, FARQUHAR MCGILLIVRAY (1859-1932)
REID, GEORGE AGNEW (1860-   )
PEEL, PAUL (1860-1892)
HOLMES, ROBERT (1861-1930)
RUSSELL, G. HORNE (1861-1933)
GRIER, SIR WYLY (1862-   )
HILL, GEORGE W. (1862-1934)

BROWNE, ARCHIBALD (1864-   )
MORRICE, JAMES WILSON (1865-1924)
CULLEN, MAURICE (1866-1934)
MCKENZIE, R. TAIT (1867-1938)
JEFFERYS, CHARLES WILLIAM (1869-   )
CHALLENER, FREDERICK S. (1869-   )
WILLIAMSON, CURTIS (1869-   )
COTÉ, M. A. SUZOR (1869-1937)
BEATTY, JOHN WILLIAM (1869-1941)
ALEXANDER, WILLIAM W. (1870-   )
HEMING, ARTHUR (1870-1940)
COBURN, FREDERICK SIMPSON (1871-   )
MORRIS, EDMUND (1871-1913)
BRIGDEN, FREDERICK H. (1872-   )
CARR, EMILY (1872-   )
JONGERS, ALPHONSE (1872-   )
MACDONALD, JAMES EDWARD HERVEY (1873-1932)
FOSBERY, ERNEST (1874-   )
NOBBS, PERCY E. (1875-   )
RAINE, HEBERT (1875-   )
ALLWARD, WALTER S. (1876-   )
THOMSON, TOM (1877-1917)
LALIBERTE, ALFRED (1878-   )
SIMPSON, CHARLES WALTER (1878-1942)
HAINES, FREDERICK S. (1879-   )
CARTER, ALEXANDER SCOTT (1881-   )
CROSS, FREDERICK G. (1881-1941)
GAGNON, CLARENCE (1881-1942)
HAHN, EMANUEL (1881-   )
PALMER, HERBERT S. (1881-   )
VARLEY, FREDERICK HORSMAN (1881-   )
JACKSON, ALEXANDER YOUNG (1882-   )
MILNE, DAVID (1882-   )
HEBERT, HENRI (1884-   )
PHILLIPS, WALTER J. (1884-   )
CORMIER, ERNEST (1885-   )
HARRIS, LAWREN (1885-   )
LISMER, ARTHUR (1885-   )
MCCREA, HAROLD (1887-   )
SAMPSON, J. ERNEST (1887-   )
JOHNSTON, FRANCIS HANS (1888-   )
ROYLE, STANLEY (1888-   )
MACDONALD, MANLY (1889-   )
CARMICHAEL, FRANK H. (1890-   )
HOLGATE, EDWIN (1892-   )
RUSSELL, GYRTH (1892-   )
HENNESSEY, FRANK (1893-1941)

FORBES, KENNETH K. (1894-   )
PANTON, LAWRENCE A. C. (1894-   )
NEWTON, LILIAS TORRANCE, (1896-   )
MACDONALD, JAMES W. G. (1897-   )
PILOT, ROBERT W. (1897-   )
CASSON, ALFRED JOSEPH (1898-   )
COMFORT, CHARLES FRASER (1900-   )
MACDONALD, THOREAU (1901-   )
WHEELER, ORSON (1902-   )
SCHAEFER, CARL F. (1903-   )
WOOD, ELIZABETH WYN (1903-   )

British

HIGHMORE, JOSEPH (1692-1780)
HOGARTH, WILLIAM (1697-1764)
HUDSON, THOMAS (1701-1779)
DEVIS, ARTHUR (1711-1787)
RAMSAY, ALLAN (1713-1784)
WILSON, RICHARD (1714-1782)
REYNOLDS, SIR JOSHUA (1723-1792)
COTES, FRANCIS (1725-1770)
STUBBS, GEORGE (1725-1806)
SANDBY, PAUL (1725-1809)
GAINSBOROUGH, THOMAS (1727-1788)
COZENS, JOHN ROBERT (1732-1799)
ZOFFANY, JOHN (1733-1810)
ROMNEY, GEORGE (1734-1802)
WEST, BENJAMIN (1738-1820)
RAEBURN, SIR HENRY (1756-1823)
BLAKE, WILLIAM (1757-1827)
HOPPNER, JOHN (1758-1810)
OPPIE, JOHN (1761-1807)
MORLAND, GEORGE (1763-1804)
CROME, JOHN (1768-1821)
LAWRENCE, SIR THOMAS (1769-1830)
GIRTIN, THOMAS (1773-1802)
TURNER, JOSEPH MALLORD WILLIAM (1775-1851)
CONSTABLE, JOHN (1776-1837)
COTMAN, JOHN SELL (1782-1842)
COX, DAVID (1783-1859)
WILKIE, SIR DAVID (1785-1841)
ETTY, WILLIAM (1787-1849)
BONINGTON, RICHARD PARKES (1802-1828)
LANDSEER, SIR EDWIN (1802-1873)
RICHMOND, GEORGE (1809-1896)
STEVENS, ALFRED (1817-1875)
WATTS, GEORGE FREDERICK (1817-1904)
FRITH, WILLIAM POWELL (1819-1909)
BROWN, FORD MADOX (1821-1893)
HUNT, WILLIAM HOLMAN (1827-1910)
ROSSETTI, DANTE GABRIEL (1828-1882)
MILLIAS, SIR JOHN EVERETT (1829-1896)
LEIGHTON, FREDERICK LORD (1830-1896)
BURNE-JONES, EDWARD (1833-1898)
WHISTLER, J. A. MCNEILL (1834-1903)
LEGROS, ALPHONSE (1837-1911)
MOORE, ALBERT (1841-1893)

CLAUSEN, SIR GEORGE (1852-   )
ABBEY, EDWIN A. (1852-1911)
SARGENT, JOHN SINGER (1856-1925)
SICKERT, WALTER RICHARD (1860-1942)
STEER, PHILIP WILSON (1860-1942)
HOLROYD, SIR CHARLES (1861-1917)
CAMERON, SIR DAVID YOUNG (1865-   )
BRANGWYN, SIR FRANK (1867-   )
NICHOLSON, SIR WILLIAM (1872-   )
BEARDSLEY, AUBREY VINCENT (1872-1898)
CONNARD, PHILIP (1875-   )
MUNNINGS, ALFRED JAMES (1878-   )
ORPEN, SIR WILLIAM (1878-1931)
JOHN, AUGUSTUS EDWYN (1879-   )
GRANT, DUNCAN (1885-   )
NASH, PAUL (1889-   )
NEVINSON, C. R. W. (1889-   )

United States

COPLEY, JOHN SINGLETON (1737-1815)
PRATT, MATTHEW (1738-1820)
WEST, BENJAMIN (1739-1820)
PINE, ROBERT EDGE (1742-1790)
STUART, GILBERT (1755-1828)
WRIGHT, JOSEPH (1756-1793)
TRUMBULL, JOHN (1756-1843)
VANDERLYN, JOHN (1776-1852)
MALBONE, EDWARD GREENE (1777-1807)
PEALE, REMBRANDT (1778-1860)
ALLSTON, WASHINGTON (1779-1843)
SULLY, THOMAS (1783-1872)
MORSE, SAMUEL F. B. (1791-1872)
HARDING, CHESTER (1792-1866)
DOUGHTY, THOMAS (1793-1856)
DURAND, ASHER B. (1796-1886)
COLE, THOMAS (1801-1848)
INMAN, HENRY (1803-1846)
POWERS, HIRAM (1805-1873)
ELLIOTT, CHARLES LORING (1812-1868)
KENSETT, JOHN FREDERICK (1818-1872)
HUNT, WILLIAM MORRIS (1824-1879)
JOHNSTON, EASTMAN (1824-1906)
INNESS, GEORGE (1825-1894)
CHURCH, FREDERICK EDWIN (1826-1900)
BROWN, HENRY KIRK (1831-1888)
LA FARGE, JOHN (1835-1910)
WYANT, ALEXANDER H. (1836-1892)
MARTIN, HOMER (1836-1896)
HOMER, WINSLOW (1836-1910)
EAKINS, THOMAS (1844-1916)
CASSATT, MARY (1845-1927)
RYDER, ALBERT PINKHAM (1847-1917)
*BLAKELOCK, RALPH ALBERT (1847-1919)
*SAINT-GAUDENS, AUGUSTUS (1848-1907)
DUVENECK, FRANK (1848-1917)
THAYER, ABBOTT HANDERSON (1849-1921)
ABBEY, EDWIN AUSTIN (1852-1911)
WEIR, J. ALDEN (1852-1919)

Contemporaries

TWACHTMAN, J. H. (1853-1902)
PYLE, HOWARD (1853-1924)
HASSAM, CHILDE (1859-1938)
MELCHERS, J. GARI (1860-1932)
REMINGTON, FREDERIC (1861-1909)
TARBELL, EDMUND C. (1862-   )
BENSON, FRANK WESTON (1862-   )
DAVIES, ARTHUR B. (1862-1928)
BEAUX, CECILIA (1863-   )
HENRI, ROBERT (1865-1929)
LUKS, GEORGE (1867-1933)
GLACKENS, WILLIAM (1870-   )
SLOAN, JOHN (1871-   )
ROBINSON, BOARDMAN (1876-   )
BELLOWS, GEORGE (1882-1925)
KENT, ROCKWELL (1882-   )
SPEICHER, EUGENE (1883-   )
MANSHIP, PAUL (1885-   )
BURCHFIELD, CHARLES (1893-   )

French

RIGAUD, HYACINTHE (1659-1743)
WATTEAU, ANTOINE (1683-1721)
NATTIER, JEAN MARC (1685-1766)
TOCQUE, LOUIS (1696-1772)
CHARDIN, JEAN BAPTISTE (1699-1779)
BOUCHER, FRANCOIS (1703-1770)
LE TOUR, MAURICE QUENTIN DE (1704-1788)
VERNET, CLAUDE JOSEPH (1714-1789)
COCHIN, CHARLES (1715-1790)
GREUZE, JEAN BAPTISTE (1725-1805)
FRAGONARD, JEAN HONORE (1732-1806)
ROBERT, HUBERT (1733-1806)
MOREAU THE ELDER (1739-1805)
PERRONNEAU, FRANCOIS HERBERT
*LOUTHERBOURG, PHILIP DE (1740-1813)
HOUDON, JEAN ANTOINE (1744-1826)
*GOYA, FRANCESCO (1746-1828)
DAVID, JACQUES LOUIS (1748-1825)
DEBUCOURT, PHILEBERT (1755-1832)

LEBRUN, MARIE-VIGEE (1755-1842)
PRUD'HON, PIERRE (1758-1823)
INGRES, JEAN DOMINIQUE AUGUSTIN (1780-1867)
GERICAULT, JEAN LOUIS ANDRÉ THÉODORE (1791-1824)
COROT, CAMILLE JEAN BAPTISTE (17-96 1875)
DELACROIX, EUGENE (1798-1869)
DAUMIER, HONORE (1808-1879)
MILLET, JEAN FRANCOIS (1814-1875)
COURBET, GUSTAVE (1819-1877)
CHAVANNES, PUVIS DE (1824-1898)
BOUDIN, LOUIS EUGENE (1824-1898)
PISSARRO, CAMILLE (1830-1903)
MANET, EDOUARD (1832-1883)
DEGAS, EDGAR HILAIRE (1834-1917)
LEGROS, ALPHONSE (1837-1911)
CEZANNE, PAUL (1839-1906)
*SISLEY, ALFRED (1840-1899)
MONET, CLAUDE (1840-1926)
REDON, ODILON (1841-1916)
RENOIR, PIERRE AUGUST (1841-1919)
ROUSSEAU, HENRI (1844-1910)
LEPAGE, JULES BASTIEN (1848-1884)
GAUGUIN, PAUL (1848-1903)
FORAIN, JEAN LOUIS (1852-1931)
VAN GOGH, VINCENT (1853-1890)
CASSATT, MARY (1855-1926)
SEURAT, GEORGES PIERRE (1859-1891)
LE SIDANER, H. E. (1862-   )
TOULOUSE-LAUTREC, HENRI DE (1864-1901)
VUILLARD, EDOUARD (1867-   )
MATISSE, HENRI (1869-   )
VLAMINCK, MAURICE DE (1876-   )
DERAIN, ANDRE (1880-   )
SIMON, LUCIEN (1881-   (
BRAQUE, GEORGES (1881-   )
UTRILLO, MAURICE (1883-   )
SEGONZAC, A. DE (1884-   )
LAURENCIN, MARIE (1885-   )
MODIGLIANI, AMEDEO (1885-1920)
KISLING, MOSES (1891-   )

BIBLIOGRAPHY

It is hoped that this list of books, pamphlets and papers will be found useful by students of Canadian art as a guide to source material; though it is hardly necessary to add that a number of the items contain comparatively little of local interest, but are mentioned to indicate that they have been consulted. The inclusion of others again, a very few, long out of print may be justified on the ground that they are still extant, though of course not always easy to come by. Collectively they present with some minor exceptions a true and adequate statement of the growth of the arts in Canada.

PRIMARY SOURCES

MANUSCRIPT MATERIAL

Robert F. Gagen: Early Ontario Artists.

Edmund Morris: Letter Books from 1899 to 1913.

Daniel Fowler: Autobiography.

James Mavor: Notes on G. T. Berthon and critical review of William Cruikshank, R.C.A.

T. A. Reed Collection: Photographs and records of the paintings in Hart House, University of Toronto.

The Irishman in Canada, by Nicholas Flood Davin. Includes material on the life and work of Paul Kane. 1877.

Charles Comfort: The Man and the Artist, by H. M. Jackson. Privately printed. Toronto: 1935.

Who Was Who in Canada, edited by Sir Charles G. D. Roberts and A. L. Tunnell, Trans-Canada Press: 1940.

The Beverley Papers: IV. *J. E. H. MacDonald: A Postscript* (1940); VI. *Thoreau MacDonald* (1942), by Lorne Pierce. The Ryerson Press, Toronto.

A Landmark of Canadian Art, by J. E. H. MacDonald. *The Rebel*, published by Members of the University of Toronto: November, 1917.

William Alexander: A Canadian Engraver, by Sidney H. Howard. Year Book of the American Bookplate Society. Washington, D.C.: 1940.

Alexander Scott Carter: Bookplate Designer, by Leslie Victor Smith. Ye ar Book of the American Bookplate Society. 1942.

Monographs on the work of Evan MacDonald, Leonard Brooks and Frank Panabaker, by William Colgate in *Bridle and Golfer*, Toronto. Vols. IX and X. Also of Kenneth Forbes and Franklin Arbuckle in *The Studio*, London. Vols. CVIII and CX.

The Fine Arts in Canada, by Newton MacTavish. Macmillan, Toronto: 1925.

Canadian Landscape Painters, by Albert H. Robson. Ryerson, Toronto: 1932.

Painting and Sculpture in Canada, by M. O. Hammond. Ryerson, Toronto: 1932.

Ateliers, A Study of Twenty-two Canadian Painters and Sculptors, by Jean Chauvin. Carrier, Montreal: 1928.

The Artists of Nova Scotia, by Harry Piers. From the Collections of the Nova Scotia Historical Society. Volume XVIII. Halifax: 1914.

History of the Royal Canadian Academy of Arts, by Hugh G. Jones, R.C.A., in collaboration with Edmund Dyonnet, R.C.A. Montreal: 1934.

Who's Who in Northwest Art, edited by Marion Brymner Appleton. Seattle: 1941.

George Theodore Berthon: A Canadian Painter of Eminent Victorians, by William Colgate. From the Papers and Records of the Ontario Historical Society: 1942.

Bibliography

Tom Thomson: Canadian Painter, by Dr. James M. MacCallum. *The Canadian Magazine*, Toronto: April, 1918.

Landmarks of Canada: A Guide to the J. Ross Robertson Historical Collection in the Public Reference Library, Toronto, Canada. Volumes I and II. Toronto: 1917 and 1921.

Municipal Handbook of Toronto: A History, by J. Edgar Middleton. Volume II: Toronto and New York.

Charles Huot: Sa Vie, sa carriere, ses œuvres, Par Hormisdas Magnan. Quebec: 1932.

Art in Canada: The Early Painters, by Edmund Morris, A.R.C.A. *Toronto Saturday Night*, January 21, 1911. Later privately printed by the artist.

Calendars, *Toronto Art Students' League:* 1893-1904.

Picturing Canada on Copper, by John McKenney Bingham. *Bridle and Golfer*, Toronto: November, 1933.

Maritime Art. Issues from October, 1940, to April, 1942.

Contemporary Art of Canada and Newfoundland. International Business Machines. Catalogue: 1940.

Art—Canada Hits Back, by Paul Oppé. *The London Mercury.* December: 1938.

"But Is It Education?" by E. A. Corbett. *Queen's Quarterly*, Kingston, Ontario, Canada. Winter Number 1941-1942.

Wanderings of an Artist, by Paul Kane. Originally published in 1859, by Longman's of London; reprinted by the Radisson Society of Canada. Toronto: 1925.

Charles DeBelle et Georges Delfosse, par Mgr. Olivier Maurault. A Critical Study. Les Editions Archonte, Montreal: 1940.

J. E. H. MacDonald Memorial Exhibition. A Critical Review. By William Colgate. *Bridle and Golfer*, May, 1934.

Toronto Art Students League, by Robert Holmes. *Canadian Magazine.* Vol. IV., 1894-1895.

A Canadian Art Movement, by F. B. Housser. Macmillan, Toronto: 1926.

William J. Thompson, Etcher: Monograph by W. W. Alexander, Toronto (1927).

Horatio Walker: A Study, by F. Newlin Price. Carrier, New York: 1928.

Artistes-peintres: les anciens: Biographies of Joseph Légaré, Antoine Plamondon, Théophile Hamel, Antoine Falardeau, Joseph A. Rho, and Napoléon Bourassa. 2 Volumes. Quebec: 1925 and 1926. Quebec: Librairie Garneau.

Art and War: Canadian War Memorials. London: 1919.

Articles on the Arts in Canada, by Goldwin Smith. *The Bystander.* Vols. 1883-1884.

Literature and the Fine Arts Since Confederation, by Sir Robert Falconer. The Cambridge History of the British Empire. Cambridge: 1930.

Records of the Founding of the Royal Canadian Academy, 1879-1880. The Globe Printing Company, Toronto: 1883.

Catalogue of the Annual Exhibition of the *Royal Canadian Academy of Arts* and the *Ontario Society of Artists*, held jointly in the Educational Museum, Toronto. T. Hill and Son, Caxton Press, Toronto: 1883.

Early Artists of Ontario, by J. W. L. Forster, O.S.A. *The Canadian Magazine*, December, 1895.

Cornelius Krieghoff. By Marius Barbeau. Macmillan. Toronto: 1934.

A People's Best. By O. J. Stevenson. Musson. Toronto: 1927.

Robert Field: His Life and Work: by Harry Piers. Frederick Fairchild Sherman: New York: 1928.

Clarence Gagnon, by Duncan Campbell Scott: *Maritime Art*, Vol. III, No. 2: Halifax, N.S.

James Wilson Morrice: Painter and Nomad, by Donald W. Buchanan. Ryerson Press, Toronto: 1936.

Architecture in Canada, by Percy E. Nobbs. Royal Institute of British Architects. London.

Bibliography

Une Maîtrise d'Art en Canada: (1800-1823), par Emile Vaillancourt. Montreal: G. Ducharme: 1920.

Un grand artisan: Louis Jobin, par Marius Barbeau. *La Presse*, Montreal. Août 26, 1933. A newspaper article.

Le sculpteur Levasseur et sa famille. Bulletin des Recherches Historiques (B.R.H.). Aug., 1931. Vol. XXXVII, No. 8.

Henri Julien, by Marius Barbeau. Canadian Artists Series. Ryerson, Toronto: 1941.

Thoreau MacDonald, by E. R. Hunter. Canadian Artists Series. Ryerson, Toronto: 1942.

Homer Watson: The Man of Doon, by Muriel Miller. Ryerson, Toronto: 1938.

SECONDARY SOURCES

Canadian Art and Artists, by E. F. B. Johnson. Publishers Association. Toronto: 1917.

Archibald Browne: An Appreciation, by R. C. Reade. Montreal: n.d.

Dictionnaire des Peintres, Sculpteurs, Graveurs, etc., by E. Benezit. Paris: 1924.

Bryan's *Dictionary of Painters, Engravers and Sculptors.* London: 1923.

American Miniatures: 1730 to 1850, by Harry B. Wehle. Contains a chapter on Robert Field with reproductions of his work. Doubleday, New York: 1927.

The Lamps. Arts and Letters Club. Toronto: 1919.

Pictures of Canadian History, by J. E. Wetherall and Charles W. Jefferys. Nelson, Toronto: 1927.

Contemporary Art of the Western Hemisphere. Permanent Collection of the International Business Machines Corporation. Toronto: 1941.

Catalogue: *Canadiana of the William H. Coverdale Collection* at the Manoir Richelieu, Murray Bay, P.Q., Canada. Ed. Percy F. Godenrath.

Catalogues of the National Gallery, Ottawa, Canada, from 1913 to 1940.

Catalogues of the Royal Canadian Academy and the Ontario Society of Artists, the Canadian Art Club, and those of similar Canadian societies having to do with the fine arts and handicrafts.

Toronto: Etchings by Stanley Turner. Rous and Mann, Toronto: 1921.

The Year Book of Canadian Art, compiled by the Arts and Letters Club of Toronto (1913). Dent, Toronto.

Yearbook of the Arts in Canada, ed. Bertram Brooker. Macmillan, Toronto: 1929.

McGill News Supplement; McGill University, Montreal, December, 1928. Articles by Lawren Harris and Percy Nobbs, dealing respectively with Canadian art and town planning.

Paddle and Palette. By Blodwen Davies. Ryerson Press, Toronto: 1930.

A Study of Tom Thomson. By Blodwen Davies. Ryerson Press, Toronto: 1935.

J. E. H. MacDonald: A Biography and Catalogue, by E. R. Hunter. Ryerson Press, Toronto: 1940.

Art and the Work of Archibald Browne, by E. F. B. Johnston. Canadian Magazine, Toronto: Vol. XXXI, No. 6.

Two Centuries of Woodcarving in French Canada, by Marius Barbeau. Royal Society of Canada, Ottawa: 1933.

French Canadian Art, by E. R. Adair. Can. Hist. Assoc. Report: 1929. Dept. of Public Archives, Ottawa.

Bibliography

Clarence A. Gagnon, by Albert H. Robson.   Ryerson, Toronto: 1938.

Paul Kane, by Albert H. Robson.   Ryerson, Toronto: 1938.

Cornelius Krieghoff, by Albert H. Robson.   Ryerson, Toronto: 1937.

A. Y. Jackson, by Albert H. Robson.   Ryerson, Toronto: 1938.

J E. H. MacDonald, by Albert H. Robson.   Ryerson, Toronto: 1937.

Tom Thomson, by Albert H. Robson.   Ryerson, Toronto: 1937.

BACKGROUND

Winter Studies and Summer Rambles, by Anna Jameson.   3 volumes.   London: 1838. Reprinted in 1923, by McClelland and Stewart, Toronto.

Small Houses of the Late Eighteenth and Early Nineteenth Centuries in Ontario, by Eric Arthur.   Published by the Department of Architecture in the University of Toronto: 1932.

The Early Buildings of Ontario, by Eric R. Arthur, Professor of Architectural Design, University of Toronto: With a foreword by John Alford, Professor of Fine Art, University of Toronto: 1938.

Picturesque Canada, edited by George Munro Grant.   Belford, Clark.   Toronto: 1882.

Canadian Scenery.   Text by N. P. Willis; illustrations by William Henry Bartlett. George Virtue.   London: 1842.

The Far North, by A. Y. Jackson; with an introduction by F. G. Banting.   Rous and Mann.   Toronto: 1927.   "A book of drawings, with descriptive notes by the artist."

Toronto of Old, by the Reverend Henry Scadding, D.D.   Adam, Stevenson and Co., Toronto: 1873.

The Evolution of French Canada, by Jean Charlemagne Bracq.   Macmillan, New York: 1924.

The Old Architecture of French Canada, by Ramsay Traquair.   McGill University Publications (Art and Architecture), Series XIII, No. 34.   Montreal: 1932.

Americanism in Painting, by Virgil Barker.   *The Yale Review,* New Haven: June, 1936.

Ars Longa, which includes a chapter on "Etching as a Fine Art," by Newton Mac-Tavish.   Ontario Publishing Co., Toronto: 1938.

The Old Silver of Quebec, by Ramsay Traquair.   Macmillan, Toronto: 1940.

Art of the British Empire Overseas.   The Studio, London: 1917.

The History of American Painting, by Samuel Isham, A.N.A., and Royal Cortissoz. Macmillan, New York: 1936.

The Dead Hand in Art, by William Colgate.   *The Canadian Forum,* November, 1938.

The Seven Years' War in Canada: A Pictorial History, by Sigmund Samuel.   Ryerson Press, Toronto: 1934.

Fifty Years of Brush and Pen.   A Historical Sketch of the Pen and Pencil Club of Montreal.   By Leo Cox.   *Queen's Quarterly:* Vol. XLVI.   No. 3.   1939.

Les lettres, les sciences et les arts au Canada sous le régime français.   Paris: Jouve et Cie: 1930.

Vieux manoirs, vieilles maisons, par P. G. Roy.   La commission des monuments historiques de la Province de Quebec.   Quebec: 1927.

Dramatic Episodes in Canada's Story, by C. W. Jefferys.   Ryerson, Toronto: 1930.

Canada's Past in Pictures, by C. W. Jefferys.   Ryerson, Toronto: 1934.

The Picture Gallery of Canadian History, by C. W. Jefferys, assisted by T. W. McLean. Ryerson, Toronto: 1942.

INDEX

271

Index

Index

273

Index

Index

New Brunswick, 142, 160-162, 169, 171, 175, 176, 184, 244, 248
New Brunswick Museum, 249, 250
New Brunswick Provincial Normal School, 173
Newfoundland, 175
New Glasgow Arts and Letters Club, 172
Newton, Gilbert Stuart, 144, 169
Newton, Lilias Torrance, 133, 228-230
Nice, Eugene, 20
Nichol, Pegi, 179
Notman & Fraser, 24
Notman, William, 20, 34, 156
Noulhag, Henri, 244
Nova Scotia, 142-144, 146, 160, 167, 170, 175, 176, 184, 244, 248, 249
Novascotian, 155, 156, 160
Nova Scotia Historical Society, 172
Nova Scotia Museum of Fine Arts, 172, 173
Nova Scotia Scenery, 160
Nova Scotia School of Art, 171-173
Nova Scotia Society of Artists, 172
Nutana Collegiate Institute, 184
Nutt, Elizabeth Styring, 142, 167, 173, 223

O

O'Brien, John, 163, 164
O'Brien, L. R., 23, 25, 28-35, 40, 175, 177, 220
Ogilvie, Will, 107
Ontario, 77-79, 81, 88, 94, 99, 173, 210
Ontario Agricultural College, 95, 205
Ontario Art Club, 250
Ontario School of Art, 25
Ontario College of Art, 36, 80, 81, 88, 99, 244
Ontario School of Art and Design, 25, 36, 45, 49, 68
Ontario Society of Artists, 6, 16, 18, 23, 25, 26-29, 35, 38, 66, 75, 80, 93, 94, 97, 99, 134, 140, 188, 208, 227, 250, 252, 262
Oppé, Paul, 101
Osgoode Hall, 14
Osler, Sir Edmund, 12, 74
Ottawa, 27, 30, 31, 36

P

Palmer, Herbert S., 37, 80
Panabaker, Frank, 177
Pan-American Exposition, 132
Panama Pacific Exhibition, 169
Panet, M., 111
Panton, L. A. C., 69
Papineau, Louis Joseph, 111, 115
Parkyns, J. G., 144, 171
Parker, Arthur Henry, 193
Parrish, S., 43

Patriot, Toronto, 10
Patterson, Dickson, 23
Payne, John, 25
Payzant, Charles, 173
Peale, Rembrandt, 148
Peel, Paul, 38, 77
Pen and Pencil Club, Montreal, 70
Pennell, Joseph, 46
Perré Henri, 29, 31
Perrigard, H. Ross, 237
Petley, Lieut. Robert, 144, 145, 159, 161, 171
Phillips, Walter, J., 107, 180, 210, 214, 216, 222
Picturesque Canada, 34, 39, 40, 220
Piers, Harry, 156, 172
Pilot, Robert W., 141, 142, 222, 237, 239
Plamondon, Antoine, 108-111
Pottlewell, John, 8
Prescott, Winward, 219
Prevost, Sir George, 149
Price, Norman, 47, 60, 61, 67, 68, 221
Prince Edward Island, 28
Proctor, Phimister, 75
Province House, Halifax, 155, 160, 162, 164, 170, 171
Provincial Museum, Halifax, 154, 158, 161, 167
Public Archives of Canada, 9, 11, 12, 145
Pyle, Howard, 46, 47

Q

Quebec, 27-29, 77, 88, 108, 109, 111, 112, 116-118, 120, 125, 130, 131, 134, 136-139, 142, 144, 145, 155, 173, 226, 252
Queen's University, 40, 95, 200, 243, 250, 255

R

Raine, Herbert, 209, 221
Ramsay, Colin Cameron, 193
Raphael, William, 29, 31, 130
Rebel, The, 99
Red River Expedition, 175
Regina, Sask., 179
Reid, George A., 26, 37, 38, 46, 107, 237
Remington, Frederic, 187
Renoir, Pierre Auguste, 47, 74
Revue Canadienne, 114
Rho, Joseph, Adolphe, 108, 115-117
Richey, Revd. Matthew, 156
Rivard, Adjutor, 221
Roberts Art Gallery, 42*n*
Roberts, Sir Charles G. D., 37, 38, 52, 76
Robertson, John Ross Historical Collection, 145, 159, 161, 162, 167, 175, 176
Robertson, Maisie, 193
Robertson, Marjorie, 193

Index

Robins, Will, 250
Robinson, Albert, 127
Robinson, Sir John Beverley, 9, 13, 14
Robson, Albert H., 67, 69, 71, 72
Romney, George, 222
Rosenberg, H. M., 167, 168
Ross, P. D., 100
Roughing it in the Bush, 4
Roy, Pierre Georges, 111
Royal Canadian Academy, 16-20, 22, 23, 26, 29, 30, opening; 31, 32, aims; 35, 36, 38, 66-69, 80, 99, 110, 115, 130, 131, 134, 140-142, 166, 167, 170-173, 181, 182, 188, 208, 227, 235, 239, 246, 250, 252
Royal Gazette, Nova Scotia, 152
Royal Military College, 166
Royal Ontario Museum, 1, 12, 73, 239, 249
Royal Scottish Academy, 182, 207
Royle, Stanley, 142, 173
Russell, G. Horne, 122
Russell, George W. (AE), 83, 83n
Russell, Gyrth, 168
Russell, John, 75, 192
Ryerson, Egerton, 164

S

Sackville, N.B., Art Association, 172
Salaberry, Colonel de, 112
St. Andrews, N.B., Art Club, 172
St. Catharines, Ontario, 31
St. George, Quetton, 25
St. James Church, Toronto, 5
St. John, New Brunswick, 143, 171
St. John Art Club, 172
St. John Vocational School, 172
St. Johns', Newfoundland, 159
Ste. Anne de Beaupré, 110
Sampson, J. E., 69, 107, 224
Samuel, Sigmund Historical Collection, 145
Sandham, Henry, 20, 22, 29, 31, 34, 35, 40, 50, 156, 220
Sangster, Charles, 52
Saskatoon, 179
Saturday Night, Toronto, 63, 67
Savage, Annie D., 179
Scadding, Dr. Henry, 5, 9, 14
Scandinavian Painters, 82
Schaefer, Carl, 71, 107
Schrieber, Charlotte, M. B., 29, 31, 220
Scott, Charles Hepburn, 71, 187
Scott, Duncan Campbell, 52, 76
Scott, T. S., 30
Sculptors Society of Canada, 202, 208
Sellon, Samuel, 156
Serres, Dominic, 145
Seven Years War in Canada, 145

Shadbolt, J. L., 193
Shepherd, Dr. Francis J., 36
Sheppard, Peter, 81, 250
Sherbrooke, Sir John Coape, 149
Shinn, Everett, 168
Short, Richard, 144, 145
Silhouettes, 145-147
Simcoe, Mrs. J. G., 2
Simpson, Charles W., 127, 130, 138, 223, 237
Simpson, Sir George, 11, 12, 175
Sing Hoo, 208
Sisley, Alfred, 47, 74
Sloan, Bert, 68
Sloan, John, 168, 208
Smith, Hon. David, 111
Smith, Goldwin, 25, 75
Smith, H. Leslie, 237
Smith, James, 30, 31
Smith, Leslie Victor, 219
Smith, Lorne K., 69
Smith, St. Thomas, 74
Smithers, George, 162
Société des Artisans Canadiens-francais, 113
Société des Artistes de Quebec, 130
Society of Artists and Amateurs, Toronto, 8
Society of Canadian Artists, 22, 23, 115
Society of Canadian Arts, Montreal, 109
Society of Canadian Painters-Etchers, 43, 45, 181
Somerville, W. L., 205
Southam, H. S., 36
Southam, Richard, 100
Spooner, James, 24, 25
Spurr, Gertrude, 42, 42n
Stairs, Hon. William, 162
Staples, Owen, 107, 214, 219, 224
Stevens, Dorothy, 210, 221
Storm, William George, 30, 31
Strachan, Revd. Dr. John, 14
Stuart, Gilbert, 48, 150, 153
Studio Building, Toronto, 92
Sutherland, Iola, 250
Suzor-Côté, W., 122, 123, 125, 126, 138, 207
Symons, Bessie Fry, 193

T

Tate Gallery, 86, 102, 137, 174
Tate, J. R., 250
Tazewell, S. O., 8
Teachers Art Association, Toronto, 249
Technique of the Wood-cut, 181
Telegram, Toronto, 69
Thomas, W. S., 31
Thompson, Sir John, 156
Thomson, D. F., 42, 50, 54, 56, 58, 61, 66, 69

277